D1496454

# THE OLYMPICS AND PHILOSOPHY

# THE OLYMPICS AND PHILOSOPHY

Edited by Heather L. Reid and Michael W. Austin

UNIVERSITY PRESS OF KENTUCKY

Copyright © 2012 by The University Press of Kentucky

Scholarly publisher for the Commonwealth,
serving Bellarmine University, Berea College, Centre
College of Kentucky, Eastern Kentucky University,
The Filson Historical Society, Georgetown College,
Kentucky Historical Society, Kentucky State University,
Morehead State University, Murray State University,
Northern Kentucky University, Transylvania University,
University of Kentucky, University of Louisville,
and Western Kentucky University.
All rights reserved.

*Editorial and Sales Offices:* The University Press of Kentucky
663 South Limestone Street, Lexington, Kentucky 40508-4008
www.kentuckypress.com

16  15  14  13  12          5  4  3  2  1

Library of Congress Cataloging-in-Publication Data

The Olympics and philosophy / edited by Heather L. Reid and Michael W. Austin.
    p. cm.
  Includes bibliographical references and index.
  ISBN 978-0-8131-3648-6 (hardcover : alk. paper) —
  ISBN 978-0-8131-3650-9 (pdf) — ISBN 978-0-8131-4071-1 (epub)
  1. Olympics—Philosophy. 2. Olympics—History. I. Reid, Heather Lynne,
1963– II. Austin, Michael W.
  GV721.6.O48 2012
  796.48—dc23
                                        2012013534

This book is printed on acid-free paper meeting
the requirements of the American National Standard
for Permanence in Paper for Printed Library Materials.

Manufactured in the United States of America.

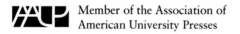

Member of the Association of
American University Presses

*To all the coaches and athletes
who realize that the Olympic ideal
is about more than sport*

# CONTENTS

## Part 3. Modern Ideals

## Part 4. Ethical Issues

## Part 5. Race and Gender Issues

# Part 6. Political Power

# INTRODUCTION

Philosophy and the Olympic Games not only share an origin in ancient Greece; the modern Olympics are the first and perhaps the only sports movement explicitly guided by a "philosophy of life." This philosophy of life is known as Olympism. The Fundamental Principles of Olympism, which are articulated in the Olympic Charter, guide the movement's values and aims, including its commitment to international cooperation and peace. The symbolism of the Olympic rings communicates the Olympic philosophy: each ring represents one of the five continents, and the colors represent all of the national flags of the world. The interlocking rings on a background of white symbolize the bringing together of these nations in peace. The Olympic rings are one of the world's most recognizable symbols, but even a passionate fan might be unaware of the philosophy they symbolize. It is the purpose of this book to explain and explore Olympic philosophy.

Each chapter in this book looks at the Olympic Games from a different philosophical perspective. What they have in common is a concern for understanding all of the elements of the Olympic Games: the history and heritage, the ideals, and the politics of the Games. Philosophical issues arise in all of these various aspects of the Olympics. This is true of many realms of life, not just sport. But what sets the Olympics apart is that at its heart, the Olympic movement is a philosophical movement. The contributors to this volume explore the philosophy of the Olympics as it relates to athletic excellence, moral development, issues of race and gender, nationalism, politics, and a host of other issues.

Part 1, "The Ideal Olympian," explores the concept of Olympic excellence as embodied in particular athletes. Michael Austin kicks off the section by asking what, for the Olympian, does it mean to be great? For many, the answer has simply to do with gold medals and Olympic or world record performances. Austin, however, instead employs some of Aristotle's ideas, arguing that true Olympic greatness includes moral excellence. He illustrates his thesis by examining the lives of three Olympians—Eugenio Monti, Wilma Rudolph, and Emil Zátopek—to uncover the links between moral and athletic excellence. In the second chapter, Raymond Angelo Belliotti considers the philosophy of Niccolò Machiavelli as it connects to the career of the Italian sprinter Pietro Mennea, a.k.a. "The Southern Arrow." Mennea's Machiavellian physical prowess and mental toughness may seem at odds with Olympic ideals such as international peace and brotherhood. But even if Machiavelli would reject those ideals, he would praise the international competition fostered by the Olympic Games and the athletic excellence on display during Mennea's twenty-year sprinting career. Finally, in "What's More than Gold," Scott F. Parker explores the case of Steve Prefontaine, one of the greatest American distance runners of all time, who failed in his career to win Olympic gold. Nevertheless, argues Parker, Pre embodied the essence of the Olympics and the overlapping ideals praised by the philosophers Friedrich Nietzsche and Ralph Waldo Emerson. The point of an Olympic race is not winning, but something else, and Pre embodied that "something else" as well as anyone.

Part 2, "Ancient Heritage," explores the ancient Greek roots of the Olympic Games and their philosophy. Paul Cantor and Peter Hufnagel begin by showing how the Olympic Games help us to better understand ancient Greek philosophy, and how that philosophy helps us to understand the Olympics. At the center of this understanding is the concept of *thumos,* the kind of spirited anger characteristic of Homer's Achilles, which can be fruitfully channeled through competitive activities like philosophy and athletics. In the next chapter, Jesús Ilundáin-Agurruza argues for an ancient Greek rethinking of the Olympic motto (Faster, Higher, Stronger) and its creed, which puts participation above winning. He proposes a model where we act out honor and duty toward the ancient Greek ideals of *aretē* (virtue), *andreia* (courage), and *kalon* (beauty). Finally, Heather Reid explores the concept of an Olympian soul by combining the philosophy of Plato and Aristotle with the enduring experience of competitive athletics. Reid argues that the ancient Greek concept of *aretē* (virtue) should be the real goal of Olympic sport, even in the modern world.

Modern Olympic ideals are the subject of Part 3. Douglas W. McLaughlin and Cesar R. Torres begin by interpreting the nineteenth-century philosophy of Olympism in terms of the contemporary philosophy of phenomenology, specifically the notion of intersubjectivity, which focuses on the communal aspect of human experience. The intersubjective approach not only enriches the modern Olympic movement's philosophical goals, including peace and education; it also resolves the apparent conflict between the Olympic motto and creed by noting that participation in a given sport's "testing family" is necessary and constitutive of striving for excellence. In his chapter, Milan Hosta continues to explore the paradoxical nature of Olympism in its individual, international, and transnational guises. He argues that Olympism begins and ends with individual athletes, whose personal striving and achievement inspire both their home nations and then humanity in general, thereby providing the common ground necessary for internationalism as well as the institutional focus characteristic of transnationalism. Jeffrey Fry concludes the section by considering whether the Olympic motto, *Citius, altius, fortius,* should be modified to include the term "Virtuous." He acknowledges that virtue is a key value in the Olympic Games, but he finds practical, political, and epistemological problems with the idea of instituting regular awards, such as medals, for athlete virtue. Fry concludes that infrequent "Fair Play" awards can express the value of virtue without threatening the thing they are trying to reward.

Part 4 takes on ethical issues in the Olympics, beginning with the problem of doping. Stephen Kershnar examines three arguments that are given for prohibiting performance-enhancing drugs, such as steroids. Kershnar shows that arguments based on risk, harm, and unfairness all fail. He concludes, therefore, that the International Olympic Committee (IOC) probably has no good moral reason to prohibit the use of performance-enhancing substances. Joseph Lewandowski picks up on the theme of overly strict regulations, this time in Olympic boxing. Fans of the "sweet science" who follow Olympic boxing likely know that the rules are a mess, having been periodically revised and tightened due to worries about fairness of judging, physical danger, and concerns about the Olympics having a "blood sport." Lewandowski argues that there are too many rules constraining the sport, and that those rules foster the wrong kind of constraints. He offers practical and precise suggestions with respect to how these problems could be rectified. In the last chapter of the section, Regan Reitsma asks whether Olympic gold should be the pinnacle of achievement in every sport. In that case, the Olympic men's football (soccer, for our American readers) tournament should be abolished, since the World Cup is the sport's real peak. Reitsma argues against abolishing the Olympic tournament, and claims that when it comes to men's football, the Olympics should settle for less than the best.

Race and gender issues are the subject of Part 5. Pellom McDaniels begins by locating the infamous 1968 medal-stand protest of Tommie Smith and John Carlos within the philosophies of Olympism and resistance to oppression, as well as a tradition of African American liberation that reaches back to slavery. The athletes' protest pointed out that the United States, like many other countries, depended for its international Olympic success on athletes who came from groups marginalized, discriminated against, and viewed as outsiders in their home country. The issue of gender comes next, with Kutte Jönsson's survey of the rise and fall of gender radicalism during the cold war era. In this period, the female athletes from East Germany and other Eastern bloc nations were controversial, in part because they challenged some of the gender norms surrounding what it meant to be female and an athlete. Many dismiss these athletes as dopers or cheaters, but Jönsson argues that they also made important contributions to the debates about gender and sport, especially in our modern context, in which sport seems to rest on masculine ideals and norms. Charlene Weaving concludes the section by exposing how the sexualization of women athletes today has resulted in their being distanced from the ideals of the Olympic movement. She argues that the uniform rule in beach volleyball is discriminatory. As such, it stands against the values which the Olympic movement celebrates, creating tension between being a woman and being an Olympian.

The final section looks at political power in the Olympics. Charles Taliaferro and Michel Le Gall begin by exploring the ethics of Olympic boycotts from the perspectives of both nations and individual athletes. Although boycotts may be justified for the protection of athletes, they conclude that political boycotts are at best ineffective and at worst harmful. They argue that Jesse Owens's performance at the 1936 Berlin Olympics had greater political benefits than any boycott could have had. In the next chapter, Alun R. Hardman and Hywel Iorwerth ask how much nationality matters in an international event like the Olympic Games by considering the phenomenon of nation-swapping athletes. Applying Coubertin's notion of sincere internationalism and the political notion of moderate patriotism, they argue that such transfers should represent real cultural attachments rather than the bald pursuit of money and glory. National attachments must have meaning for the benefits of internationalism to be gained at the Olympic Games. Matthew Sharpe concludes the section by asking if the Games are such big business, what exactly is it that they are selling? Drawing on the philosophy of art, he answers that question with an aesthetic account of the "Olympic Moment," emphasizing its political power to trade on a feeling of community consensus. The elaborate opening ceremonies at Beijing and Athens are great examples of Olympic spectacles, but Sharpe goes back to the Nazi Olympics of 1936 to explore the full political power of the Games' aesthetic.

According to the ancient author Philostratos, the origin of the Olympic Games was a footrace run at a religious gathering to determine who would light the sacrificial flame. Simple and distant as that eighth-century BCE event may seem, it contained all the seeds of the modern Olympic Games: the connection between athleticism and virtue, the philosophical attempt to discover unbiased truth, and the political need to unify and pacify rival groups. It is fitting that philosophy and the Olympics share their origin in ancient Greece, because in the end they seem inseparable—twin offspring of the common human desire to learn and know.

Part 1

# THE IDEAL OLYMPIAN

*Michael W. Austin*

# A GREATNESS OF OLYMPIC PROPORTIONS

What does it mean to be great? For the Olympic athlete, winning a gold medal seems like the most obvious answer. Or perhaps winning numerous gold medals, setting world records, and putting together a long and consistently excellent athletic career are what constitute true greatness. There is no doubt a form of greatness in such achievements, but I believe that a greatness of truly Olympic proportions includes more than mere athletic excellence. The truly great Olympians also display moral excellence. In this chapter I briefly consider Aristotle's views about moral excellence and then take a look at some examples of Olympic heroes who have done more than win medals—they've exhibited moral virtues, changed the world for the better, and inspired others to do the same.

## What Is Moral Excellence?

Like most questions in philosophy, there are a variety of answers that have been given to the question "What is moral excellence?" Some philosophers are skeptical about the notion of moral excellence; they argue that human beings should act in ways that serve their self-interest, which they define as the attainment of power, pleasure, and wealth. Many athletes, including Olympic athletes, appear to value these things more than they should. Other philosophers hold the view that moral excellence consists in obeying the moral law. Still others focus on the consequences of our actions.

Aristotle believed that *character* is the most fundamental thing in ethics, rather than the actions we perform or the consequences of those actions. He argued that we should make neither pleasure nor honor our ultimate aim in life. A life of pleasure is suitable for grazing animals, but not for human beings, who are *rational* animals. Honor is also not suitable as an ultimate aim in life, in part because we are rightly honored for virtue. Given this, honor is not the highest good in life. Having excellent character is conducive to the highest good in life, namely happiness, which Aristotle defines as human flourishing, fulfillment, and deep well-being, rather than merely getting what one wants or having pleasant mental states. For Aristotle, intellectual and moral virtues are conducive to human fulfillment, whereas intellectual and moral vices tend to prevent such fulfillment from being realized in our lives.

In his writings, Aristotle discusses several individual virtues, including prudence, courage, temperance, generosity, and friendliness. He also describes a different trait that is connected with these virtues—magnanimity.[1] Translators have interpreted this term in many ways. It literally means "great-souledness," but has also been translated as "pride," "superiority," "high-mindedness," and "dignity."[2] Aristotle describes the magnanimous person as someone who thinks that he is worthy of great things, and is in fact worthy of them.[3] Those who are magnanimous value themselves properly, according to their actual worth, rather than too much or too little. Magnanimity lies at the midpoint between the vices of pusillanimity (being weak or timid) and vanity. According to Aristotle, "Greatness of soul, then, seems to be a sort of adornment, as it were, of the excellences; for it augments them, and does not occur without them."[4] Magnanimity, this greatness of soul, not only requires the presence of all of the other virtues, but also enhances and strengthens those virtues. The magnanimous person *excels* at all of the virtues. As such, the magnanimous person is the morally excellent person.

Many Olympic athletes aspire to athletic excellence, but the athlete who achieves a greatness of Olympic proportions will also aspire to and exemplify moral excellence. She will be magnanimous, in the best sense of the term. In the remainder of this chapter, though Aristotle might not agree with everything I say about the lives and characters of the Olympians I discuss, I am inspired by his account of virtue and moral excellence.

Many Olympians have given us a glimpse of not only athletic excellence, but moral excellence as well. In this regard, many of my fellow Americans might think of Jesse Owens and his success in the 1936 Berlin

Games, or Tommie Smith and John Carlos raising their fists on the medal podium for the sake of justice in the 1968 Mexico City Games, or of the impact of Joan Benoit Samuelson's Olympic marathon victory in the Los Angeles Games of 1984 on women's running and women's sports in general. And of course people from other nations have their own Olympic heroes, such as Great Britain's Steve Redgrave, Finland's Paavo Nurmi, Hungary's Takács Károly, and many others from many other nations. From this group of athletes who have exhibited moral as well as athletic excellence, let's consider three Olympians who help us see what it is to be an excellent human being. While they have their flaws—which is to be expected of human beings, after all—they nevertheless display marks of moral excellence, of a greatness of character that is worth examining and emulating.

## The Flying Redhead

Italian downhill skier Eugenio Monti earned his nickname after winning the Italian slalom and giant slalom races as well as finishing third in the downhill in 1950. What seemed like a very promising future for Monti on the slopes ended with a serious knee injury that ended his skiing career. But Monti's athletic career was not over. The Flying Redhead would earn six medals over three different Olympic Games, including two golds in his final Olympic competition, not on a pair of skis, but at the helm of a bobsled.

Monti was born in 1928 in Dobbiaco, Italy, and would win silver medals in the two- and four-man bobsled thirty-two years later at the Cortina Games. He proceeded to win the bronze in both events at the Innsbruck Games of 1964, but his crowning achievement came in the 1968 Winter Games held in Grenoble, France. On a mountain made famous by the exploits of Fausto Coppi, Marco Pantini, and Lance Armstrong in the Tour de France—the Alpe d'Huez—Monti flew down the track to win gold in both the two-man and four-man events. It took patience, but at the age of forty, in what he knew would be his last chance to win Olympic gold, Eugenio Monti achieved his goal.[5]

But there is more to the story of this great athlete. Monti was the first recipient of the Pierre de Coubertin medal, which is given by the IOC to the athlete who demonstrates sportsmanship in the Olympic Games.

Monti won this medal due to his actions during the 1964 Games, where he won two bronze medals. A British bobsled pair in the 1964 Innsbruck Winter Games benefited from Monti's sportsmanship when he loaned them an axle for their sled to replace one that was broken. After Nash and Dixon went on to defeat him and win the gold, Monti told the press, "Nash didn't win because I gave him the bolt. He won because he had the fastest run."[6] Because of this unselfish and sportsmanlike act, Eugenio Monti is rightfully recognized on the official website of the Olympic movement not as "The Flying Redhead," but rather as "The Golden Sportsman." Not only did he win the gold; he also exemplified the virtue of sportsmanship and the rejection of a win-at-all-costs mentality befitting an Olympic athlete. Monti, like all genuine *athletes*—those who contend for the prize of victory that signifies their excellence—valued fair play and did not want to achieve victory because of his opponent's bad luck. Moreover, his actions also exemplify a commitment to truth. If the function of an athletic contest is in part to signify who is the best, then Monti also showed a commitment to truth by not allowing bad luck to play a deciding role in who won. Rather, he allowed the contest to fulfill its function of determining who was in fact the best, at least on that day.

The Golden Sportsman also displayed the virtue of perseverance, switching from skiing to bobsledding after his knee injury. He demonstrated the virtue of patience as he continued to pursue a gold medal, his patience being rewarded with success in his last try at the Olympics. Monti's sharing of equipment with a competitor who went on to defeat him in the 1964 bobsled race exemplifies his moral excellence, as well as a commitment to the common good, insofar as Monti was upholding some of the central values of the Olympic movement by his sportsmanship. He rejected a win-at-all-costs attitude, demonstrating that some things matter more than winning. This is not only consistent with the principles of the Olympic movement, it is also the right attitude to take toward victory in sport.

While many might be familiar with the slogan "Winning isn't everything, it's the only thing," widely attributed to American football coach Vince Lombardi (though not original to him), they might be less familiar with something Lombardi said at the end of his life.[7] Near the time of his death, Lombardi told a journalist, "I wished I'd never said the thing . . . I meant the effort. I meant having a goal. I sure didn't mean for people to crush human values and morality." There is something morally praise-worthy in what Monti did in sharing a bobsled bolt with his competitor, a respect for that opponent and a desire to win based on performance, not equipment failure. Winning matters, but it is not all that matters. Truth, and victory based on excellence, are higher values. And they are values that the morally excellent, or magnanimous, athlete will hold dear. We would need a fuller picture of Monti's life to determine whether or not he was truly magnanimous, but what we do know shows the kind of commitment to truth and morality that is characteristic of the morally excellent human being.

## The Tennessee Tornado

Wilma Rudolph was born in St. Bethlehem, Tennessee, on June 23, 1940, one of her father's twenty-two children from two marriages. Prematurely born, she weighed only 4.5 pounds, and she suffered from a variety of ailments as a child, including polio, pneumonia, and scarlet fever. Rudolph also had serious problems with her left leg, and at the age of six began using leg braces. Physicians prescribed massage therapy. Through her family administering this therapy, and through her own determination, after five years of treatment she shocked her doctors by removing her leg braces and walking. It wasn't long before she was demonstrating her incredible natural athletic talent. She once told the *Chicago Tribune*, "By the time I was twelve, I was challenging every boy in our neighborhood at running, jumping, everything."

Rudolph also played high school basketball and, of course, ran track. She successfully overcame her physical challenges and excelled at sports beyond the neighborhood and her school, qualifying for the 1956 Olympic team at the age of sixteen. We see in this part of her story a glimpse of the self-discipline, perseverance, and courage that are marks of moral excellence. She excelled at athletics as well, winning a bronze medal in the 4-by-100-meter relay event at the Melbourne Games. But this accomplishment was soon to be dwarfed by what she would do in the 1960 Games.

In Rome, Wilma Rudolph won three gold medals, more than any other American woman had ever won in a single Olympics. She triumphed in the 100-meter and the 200-meter races, and she anchored the 400-meter relay team by edging out her West German opponent at the finish line—all on a sprained ankle. Her achievements made her instantly famous worldwide. After the Olympics, fans in Greece, Holland, Germany, and England came to see her run. She then returned home to Clarksville, Tennessee, for a ceremony and parade held in her honor. It was there that Rudolph displayed further traits of the morally excellent person, a commitment to equality and the courage to take a stand against social injustice.

Growing up in the South in the 1950s, Wilma Rudolph was well acquainted with racism. Segregationist Tennessee governor Buford Ellington planned to be at the head of the celebration in honor of her return. However, Rudolph insisted that her homecoming parade and celebration be an integrated event. All such events in Clarksville were segregated, but the parade celebrating Wilma Rudolph's Olympic victories was not. It was the town's first racially integrated event. Subsequent to this, Rudolph was actively engaged in protests against the town's segregation laws until they were abolished.

As a female African American, Rudolph was risking a lot by taking a strong and public stand against segregation, but she did it anyway because it was the right thing to do for her and her community. This is a vital trait of the morally excellent person: the courage to stand up for important moral values even when doing so is unpopular or potentially dangerous.

According to Rudolph, her greatest achievement was not her Olympic triumph. Rather, it was the formation of the Wilma Rudolph Foundation, a nonprofit organization focused on community-based sports programs for young athletes. In reflecting on this program, Rudolph said, "I tell them [the young athletes] that the most important aspect is to be yourself and have confidence in yourself. I remind them the triumph can't be had without the struggle."[8] For her, this was no mere platitude; it was in fact the story of her life, both on and off the track. The demonstration of a variety of virtues in different contexts gives us good reason to think that Wilma Rudolph was a morally excellent person.

## The Human Locomotive

Emil Zátopek was born on September 19, 1922, in Koprivnice, a town in what is now Slovakia. He was renowned for his distinctive style of running, which led to his being nicknamed "The Bouncing Czech." However, his remarkable success as a runner and drive to excel are better described by his other moniker, "The Human Locomotive." Zátopek's intense training methods were and still are legendary. His hard interval training set the stage for an incredible string of victories and records, as well as one of the most amazing performances by a distance runner in the history of the Olympic Games.

Zátopek's racing style was unique. At times he would force the pace and race from the front so that others had to pursue him in order to win.[9] But he would also try to wear down his opponents with intermittent bursts of speed. This strategy is more challenging and difficult, but Zátopek was able to have great success with it, due to his strength of will and remarkably heavy training load. He was reported to have run 180 miles *in one week*. In 1954, he logged 4,901 miles, and this was late in his career.

The self-discipline and perseverance displayed by Zátopek are amazing. Early in his career, he would regularly run 20 by 200 meters or 20 by 400 meters. But this pales in comparison with what was to come. His training load became even more intense—he was known to do 60-by-400-meter training sessions on a regular basis. When he was accepted into the Army's officer training school, he was warned that his running career might be over because of the heavy demands of officer training. But he trained more consistently than before. After a day of fulfilling his military duties, Emil would run on the track that encircled the barracks or head out to train along the nearby river. Zátopek gave himself to this difficult training program because he believed that he had to in order to overcome his lack of natural ability.

But Zátopek was criticized for his intense training as well as for his running form: "The characteristic ungainly style, head rolling, face contorted in a grimace, arms pumping, legs pounding the track, was now a familiar sight in his homeland, though there were still plenty of critics only too ready to proclaim that his uneconomic gait and his punishing training sessions would soon put an end to him."[10]

But they were wrong. Over the course of his career, Zátopek set twenty world records at ten different distances, from distances of 5,000 up to 30,000 meters. He also won seven gold medals, one silver, and one bronze at the Olympic Games and European championships from 1946 to 1954, and placed sixth at the 1956 Olympic marathon in Melbourne.

Zátopek won *seventy-two consecutive races* at the 5,000- and 10,000-meter distances from 1948 to 1952. He was truly one of the greatest distance runners of all time. And yet he was humble, as evidenced after a performance in September 1951, in which he broke two world records in a single race. Emil obliterated the ten-mile world record by seventy seconds on his way to a record-setting 20,052 meters in one hour. Afterwards, Zátopek gave a speech on the radio and gave no indication that he'd just "belted the living daylight out of two tremendous World records" *in one run.* [11]

A particularly momentous accomplishment came at the 1952 Olympic Games in Helsinki. Early in the year, Emil had influenza and returned too early to his training schedule. Because of this, he was not the clear favorite in any of the three distance events for the Games. In the first of the distance events, Zátopek and French-Algerian runner Alain Mimoun pulled away from the rest of the 10,000-meter field, but with three laps to go Emil pulled away from his closest competitor, winning the race in Olympic record time. Two days later he competed in the 5,000-meter heats and made it through to the final. This race was a battle. Zátopek made his move in the final turn, winning by five yards. Three days later, he lined up with sixty-five other runners to compete in the Olympic marathon. He competed against a former Olympic marathon champion, a world record holder in the marathon, a European champion, and a winner of the Boston Marathon. This was Zátopek's first time to run the marathon, and in it he did not exhibit the rolling head and agonized expression present on the track: "He ran down the sunlit road, casually looking round as if to admire the suburban scenery and to acknowledge the plaudits of the bystanders, and he appeared to be running well within himself, not wanting to be too presumptuous and humiliate the worthy efforts of the seasoned marathoners trudging along behind him." [12] He broke the tape 2 minutes and 31.8 seconds before the silver medalist, whom Zátopek hurried to greet as he finished the race.

Emil returned home to a hero's welcome. One Czechoslovakian journalist had this to say: "The name Zátopek has become synonymous with the idea of speed, endurance, efficiency, reliability, fighting spirit and willpower. It would not surprise me if one day we should find his name in the dictionary as a common expression for all these terms. The delight in work, the conscientiousness, the courage, the feeling of responsibility of a Zátopek should run throughout our whole lives."[13] If this laudatory description is even approximately true, then we have in Emil Zátopek not only an amazing athletic competitor, but also an exemplary human being. And the manner in which he would face certain challenges later in life confirms this judgment.

One instance that displays Emil's courage off of the track occurred right before the Helsinki Games. A relay runner, Stanislav Jungwirth, was removed from the Olympic roster by the Communists because his father was a political prisoner. Zátopek refused to go to the Games unless Jungwirth was also allowed to go. Two days later, both men were on their way.

Zátopek's legendary status off the track was cemented by the strong stand he took in favor of political reform and against the Soviet and Warsaw Pact Armies' invasion of Prague in 1968.[14] In April of that year, the new Secretary of the Czech Communist Party, Alexander Dubcek, introduced liberal reforms to the country. Emil Zátopek and his wife, Dana, supported these reforms. However, this political liberalization was worrying to the Soviet Union and other Communist bloc countries, and in August of 1968 the tanks and soldiers arrived. As these forces invaded Czechoslovakia, Zátopek protested, demanding that the people of his nation be granted more freedom and better living conditions. This time, he paid a price for his stand. In 1969, he lost his rank as a colonel in the army and was forced to spend six years working in a uranium mine.

There are other examples of Zátopek's greatness of character. He cared about the common good and hoped that his athletic career was influential in bringing others to his sport, because he thought that wide participation in sports was good for people. His generosity and selflessness shine through in an episode involving Ron Clarke, an Australian runner who set many world records but never won a major championship. Clarke and Zátopek were in Prague, and after clearing customs at the airport Zátopek shook Clarke's hand to see him off. When he did so, Zátopek secretly put a small package in Clarke's hand. Clarke believed it was some message that Zátopek wanted to get to the outside world, but it was in fact his Olympic gold medal from the 10,000-meter race in the 1952 Helsinki Games. Clarke recalled Zátopek's words as he handed it over: "Because you deserved it."[15]

Emil Zátopek was known and praised for his character on the track as well as off of it. He was the kind of person who took pleasure in the successes of others and not merely his own. It was said by one columnist, "Win or lose, the famous Czech is always the same—a credit to his country and a credit to his sport."[16] He won many medals and awards, but remained modest. A lifelong friend of Emil and his wife said, "He never had any trophies at home. He gave them away to friends or to fans and some to random people."[17] And as we've just seen, he was willing to suffer for his moral and political convictions, giving further evidence that he was not only an excellent athlete, but also an excellent human being.

One journalist expressed his admiration for Zátopek in this way: "Zátopek was an exceptional athlete, agreed, but transcending that was his humanity. He was the personification of all that is worthy in sport, and in life. He was ambitious and successful but never lost his humility or sense of wonder. He had the capacity to enjoy himself and enrich the lives of others . . . His courage, on and off the track, was remarkable."[18] In Zátopek, we see the virtues of courage, generosity, and humility, among others. Giving away Olympic medals, avoiding a bloated sense of self-importance and pride, and taking joy in the success of others all show a strength of character we would do well to emulate. For these and many other reasons, years after his death in November 2000, Zátopek remains a legend both in his homeland and around the world.

## Moral Excellence and Modules of Virtue

While it is clear what the stories of Eugenio Monti, Wilma Rudolph, and Emil Zátopek have to do with the Olympics, it may not be so clear what they have to do with philosophy. One of the branches of philosophy, and the one which I focus on in my own work as a philosopher, is ethics. As an ethicist, my research focuses on how we ought to live and what sort of people we ought to be. Clearly, then, the stories of these three Olympians are very relevant to philosophy. Each of them shows us how we ought to live. We ought to strive to be courageous, humble, generous, and fair. We ought to strive for moral excellence. We can take away lessons about how to live from each of these great Olympians. But that's not all. We can also take away some more theoretical philosophical insights.

While there is much to admire in the lives of Monti, Rudolph, and Zátopek, any discussion of sports and character must confront a problem. For every Monti, Rudolph, and Zátopek, there is an athlete who seeks to win at all costs, avoids using their celebrity status to effect positive political change, and seeks vainly to exalt him- or herself above all others. Why is this so, if sports build character, as is so often claimed? I think the key to answering this question is found by gaining a deeper understanding of what it means to possess a virtue.

Contemporary philosopher Robert Adams argues that there are *modules of virtue*.[19] If Adams is right, this explains not only why some Olympic and other athletes excel at the moral life; it also explains why other excellent athletes are not also excellent human beings. Generally speaking, a module is an independent component part of some greater whole from which a more complex structure can be built. But what does it mean to say that there are modules of a virtue?

First, the modularity of virtue includes the claim that direct behavioral dispositions are often independent and specific to some particular domain of life. For example, one might be patient as a parent, but not as a coach. One might be honest as a businessperson, but behave dishonestly on the golf course. These domain-specific traits can be affected by other factors, such as emotions, intellectually challenging situations, and so on. I may have a domain-specific trait of courage as a soldier that is overridden in the midst of an incredibly intense battle, for example. This does not mean that there are no general moral virtues that are present in an individual's character across the many domains of that person's life. Rather, the point Adams makes is that some of these virtues are only present in some people as a module of virtue in a specific domain of life.

Second, the claim that there are modules of virtue also means that the particular modules can be added together for a more comprehensive trait. I may, for example, be patient on the soccer pitch, patient in traffic, patient with my children, and so on. I may have acquired these traits separately in each particular domain, but these modules of patience can be combined in my character to form the general virtue of patience, which I then display in many other contexts as well.

Now we can see why some athletes have such great self-control, courage, and patience in the context of their sport, but not in other areas of their lives. Take the trait of self-control. This virtue is essential for becoming an Olympian. The level of excellence that such athletes achieve requires self-control with respect to diet, sleep, consistent training, concentration, and many other areas as well. Why, then, do many such athletes not exhibit the same self-control with respect to their finances, relationships, or (if relevant) their academic lives? If Adams is right, the reason is that they have only developed *a module* of self-control and do not possess self-control as *a general and consistent character trait* across all of the domains of life. The claim that there are modules of virtue helps to explain what we observe about such athletes, and this is a piece of evidence supporting the concept.

An understanding of the modularity of virtue also helps us gain a deeper understanding of what it is to be magnanimous, or morally excellent. Recall that according to Aristotle, the magnanimous person excels at all of the virtues, and the other virtues are strengthened by magnanimity. The morally excellent person, then, not only has courage, self-control, and honesty across many domains of life. This person has all of the virtues across all of the domains of life. The life of the morally excellent person is deeply unified in this way. Understanding the modularity of the virtues can help us understand what it means to say that an individual is morally excellent, or magnanimous. She does not merely possess specific virtues in specific domains, but she possesses each virtue across all of the relevant domains of her life. Her character and her life are thus deeply unified, and we can explain this unity by attributing to such a person the virtue of magnanimity. We see at least a glimpse of this sort of unity in the lives of Monti, Rudolph, and Zátopek.

## Conclusion: Sports as Moral Practice

As the book in your hands makes clear, the Olympics is not merely a movement for sport, but also a *philosophical* movement whose ultimate goal is to build a peaceful and better world.[20] The Olympic Charter includes a commitment to Olympism as a philosophy of life, "based on the joy of effort, the educational value of good example and respect for universal fundamental ethical principles."[21]

Sports can build character and foster a commitment to fundamental ethical principles, but in order for it to do this, athletes and others involved must approach sports as a moral practice. There is great potential for moral development in sport because of the role of moral virtue in connection with the idea of fair play. As two sports philosophers write, "Such virtues as magnanimity, fairness, politeness, respect for rules, and cooperation are the qualities of character displayed and developed by those who play well. Often these virtues and their exhibition are the hardy perennials that have become embedded in and partly define the traditions of sport that are produced and reproduced by those who play."[22] Although there are obviously numerous instances of moral vices displayed in sports, at the end of the day sports are what we, their practitioners, make of them. If coaches, officials, athletes, and fans are committed to sports as a moral practice, putting virtues on display, developing virtues in the sporting domain, and expressing appreciation for these attitudes and actions, then sports will build character. The potential of sports as moral practice can only be realized as we make use of them to grow in virtue. It is up to us.

If athletes put the same methods of moral development to use in the other domains of their lives as they do in their sporting lives, then they have the potential to become not only excellent athletes, but also excellent human beings in the pattern of Monti, Rudolph, and Zátopek. And it is human moral excellence that is truly a greatness of Olympic proportions.

## Notes

1. Aristotle, *Nicomachean Ethics*, commentaries and translation by S. Broadie and C. Rowe (New York: Oxford University Press, 2002), 1123b–1125a15.

2. David Horner, "What It Takes to Be Great: Aristotle and Aquinas on Magnanimity," *Faith and Philosophy* 15, no. 4 (1998): 415–444.

3. Aristotle, *Nicomachean Ethics*, 1107b20, 1123a35–1125a35.

4. Ibid., 1124a1–5.

5. http://www.olympic.org/eugenio-monti (accessed March 15, 2011).

6. http://www.suite101.com/content/the-pierre-de-coubertin-medal-a62124 (accessed March 15, 2011).

7. Michael W. Austin, "Why Winning Matters," *Think* 9 (2010): 99–102.

8. http://espn.go.com/sportscentury/features/00016444.html (accessed March 10, 2011).

9. This and other information of Zátopek's life, unless otherwise noted, are drawn from Bob Phillips, *Zá-to-pek! Zá-to-pek! Zá-to-pek!* (rev. ed., Manchester: The Parrs Wood Press, 2004).

10. Ibid., 25.

11. Ibid., 60.

12. Ibid., 73.

13. Ibid., 79–80.

14. Ibid., 127; and Adam Ellick, "Emil Zatopek," *Running Times*, March 2001.

15. Phillips, *Zá-to-pek!*, 147.

16. Ibid., 113.

17. Ellick, "Emil Zatopek."

18. Phillips, *Zá-to-pek!*, 145.

19. Robert Adams, *A Theory of Virtue* (New York: Oxford University Press, 2006), 125–130.

20. http://www.olympic.org/olympism-in-action (accessed March 23, 2011).

21. http://www.olympic.org/Documents/olympic_charter_en.pdf (accessed March 23, 2011).

22. Carwyn Jones and Mike McNamee, "Moral Development and Sport: Character and Cognitive Developmentalism Contrasted," in *Sports Ethics: An Anthology,* ed. Jan Boxill (Malden, MA: Blackwell, 2003), 50.

*Raymond Angelo Belliotti*

# MACHIAVELLI, THE OLYMPIC IDEAL, AND THE SOUTHERN ARROW

What was he doing? Prior to a preliminary heat in the 200-meter dash competition at the 1972 Munich Olympics, a contestant appeared to be undressing in the middle of the track. Mercifully, he never reached full nudity. Stripped down to his athletic supporter, Pietro Mennea, known in Italy as *Freccia del Sud* ("The Southern Arrow"), needed to change his running shorts. A sprinter has to do what a sprinter has to do.

Mennea hailed from Barletta, in Southern Italy. This accident of birth accounted for half his nickname. The other half flowed from his speed and style. Lean and wiry, Mennea lacked the astonishing power of the muscular Bob Hayes and the majestic grace of the perfectly proportioned Carl Lewis. Instead, he appeared to float through the air at a dazzling velocity as if shot from an arrow. A notoriously slow starter, Mennea shifted gears in the straightaway and usually made up considerable ground even though he was competing against world class sprinters. As Mennea sped to the finish line, his feet were so nimble that they seemed not to touch ground as he flew through space. As he prepared for his preliminary heat in 1972, he was beginning a twenty-year commitment to the Olympic Ideal. He was also a glowing exemplar of physical prowess and mental toughness, character traits that political theorist and philosopher Niccolò Machiavelli defined as *virtù*.

## Machiavelli and *Virtù*

Few words in a political text have generated as much controversy as Niccolò Machiavelli's use of *virtù*. Typically, translators caution readers not to associate the term with moral virtue. That warning, though, is misleading because at times Machiavelli does speak of moral *virtù*. This, however, is not the primary way he uses the term. *Virtù* has been, more or less accurately, translated as efficiency, skill, strength, excellence, discipline, manliness, admirable qualities, ability, virtue, effectiveness, willpower, exceptional qualities, vigor, greatness, courage, intelligence, and a host of related attributes.

Consider the English word *good*. We are familiar with good people, good books, good knives, good cooks, good sex, good cars, good presentations, good times, good athletes, good singers, good teachers, and the like. "Good" sometimes, but not always, connotes "moral rectitude." At other times, "good" describes a person, event, or object that performs its function well. The word "excellent" does the same. In ordinary discourse we are rarely confused because context determines the meaning of such words. For example, we do not scratch our heads in puzzlement over how a car can manifest moral goodness. We understand, instead, that a good car is a vehicle that rarely breaks down, runs smoothly, and is easy to maintain.

For Machiavelli, *virtù* connotes an excellence relevant to a person's function. Human beings inhabit a world of scarce resources and keen competition that coalesces uncomfortably with our bottomless ambitions and passions. Worse, we are susceptible to the whims of *Fortuna*, which often conspire against our best-devised stratagems. Only people embodying *virtù* are able to cope with *Fortuna*, confront adversity with renewed purpose, imagine and pursue grand deeds, and maintain their resolve and passion in a relentlessly competitive world. In short, developing and exercising *virtù* requires challenging activity, confronting and overcoming resistance, turning adversity to practical advantage, and bravely facing worthy opponents.

Specifically, Machiavelli refers to military *virtù*, political *virtù*, civic *virtù*, moral *virtù*, and artistic *virtù* (P 7, 8, 12, 14, 15, 19, 21, 25, 26).[1] The qualities of excellence defining each type differ. Military commanders require discipline, bravery, single-mindedness, drive, skill, energy, military skill and knowledge, and the gumption to ignore conventional morality when necessary. Political leaders need many of the same qualities, but also a special shrewdness and prudence in dealing with foreign threats and internal plots. The attributes of the lion, in order to frighten wolves, and the fox, in order to evade traps, are crucial (P 18). Civic *virtù* is the hallmark of a sound republic. Citizens, initially motivated by self-interest and personal aggrandizement, are shaped by good laws, strong arms, and sound education into serving the common good of an expansionist state. By moral *virtù*, Machiavelli means exercising the values of conventional morality. Artistic *virtù* defines excellence in literature and the arts. The greatest men—those able to found, reform, preserve, and expand healthy political units—must exude military and political *virtù*. Such leaders must effectively size up the prevailing situation; reflect on the available choices, priorities, and probable consequences; and act decisively and successfully. Citizens in a healthy political unit must exhibit civic and moral *virtù* if the unit is to continue to flourish.

Clearly, for Machiavelli the most important forms of *virtù* are military and political. A sound political unit, grounded in good laws and strong arms, is a prerequisite for the rigorous education needed to promote civic and moral *virtù*. The opposite of *virtù* is corruption. Corruption, for Machiavelli, is weakness: *ozio* (sloth or idleness), civic and moral decay, lack of discipline, softness, timidity, muted will, resignation, inability to compete, hesitancy, indecisiveness, an *animo effeminate* (tepid spirit).

Much ink has been squirted discussing Machiavelli's description of the notorious Agathocles of Sicily, King of Syracuse. Within the space of a few sentences, Machiavelli seems to contradict his own words:

> One ought not, of course, to call it *virtù* to massacre one's fellow citizens, to betray one's friends, to break one's word, to be without mercy and without religion. By such means one can acquire power but not glory. If one considers the *virtù* Agathocles demonstrated in braving and facing down danger, and the strength of character he showed . . . then there seems to be no reason why he should be judged less admirable than any of the finest generals. But on the other hand, his inhuman cruelty and brutality . . . mean it would be wrong to praise him as one of the finest of men . . . one can attribute neither to fortune nor to *virtù* his accomplishments, which owed nothing to either (P 8).

At first blush, the paragraph is worthy of double-talk artists such as Casey Stengel or Doctor Irwin Corey. Did Agathocles embody and exercise *virtù* or not? I interpret the passage as attributing military *virtù* to Agathocles, in response to his undeniable courage and resolve in rising up the military ranks and seizing power. He lacked, however, political *virtù* because he misused power and meted out gratuitous cruelties. Also, he was without civic and moral *virtù*. We should not attribute his transient success to luck or to political *virtù* or to moral *virtù*. As an aside, Machiavelli claims that the "finest of men" are not inhumanely cruel and that acquiring power is not enough to merit glory. He preserves a distinction between tyrants and princes. A concern for enduring glory should inform a prince's deeds.

Harvey Mansfield argues that "Agathocles has *virtù* but cannot be said to have *virtù*. It is not enough to say that he uses the word in different 'senses'; he uses it in two contradictory senses as to whether it includes or excludes evil deeds. What could be more clear, more essential, and more inconsistent than that?"[2]

Mansfield's outrage misses the mark. Surely moral *virtù* excludes, almost always, evil deeds (although extreme cases include choices between degrees of evil). Just as surely, military and political *virtù* include "evil well-used" (P 8). At times, military and political leaders must transgress absolute moral principles in order to advance their highest goals: founding, reforming, preserving, and expanding a worthy state. That one form of *virtù* aspires to exclude evil deeds but other forms of *virtù* include evil well-used is no more a contradiction than saying a good knife cuts sharply while a good doctor heals cuts is a contradiction.

The keenest exemplar of Machiavelli's ideal prince exercising military and political *virtù* is sketched in his concise work, *Life of Castruccio Castracani*.[3] Written in 1520 as an audition for Machiavelli's *Florentine Histories,* this book glorifies the life and times of Castracani (1281–1328), a military leader from Lucca. Machiavelli regards the historical truth casually. Instead, he embellishes, distorts, and fabricates to suit his needs. Machiavelli's aspiration was apparently to romanticize the life of an actual person to illustrate the perfect prince.

In fact, Castracani was born to a wealthy Luccan family. Machiavelli, always appreciative of those who rose from humble origins, depicts Castracani as an abandoned baby discovered in a vineyard by the sister of a priest. As a youth, according to Machiavelli, Castruccio excelled athletically and enjoyed reading only books recording the deeds of military heroes. Yes, the priest under whose care he fell tried to indoctrinate the boy with literature pertaining to churchly matters, but by the age of fourteen Castruccio had outgrown such matters.

Readers absorb Machiavelli's suspicion of the Church and his esteem for the heroic ethic. Machiavelli also highlights the need for preparation: physical strength must be honed by study of the classics. Resoluteness, cunning, and power—the measures of the lion and the fox, the animals who best symbolize military and political *virtù*—blossom only from careful training.

Machiavelli lavishly celebrates warlike qualities nurtured by sports and taxing physical exercise. The virtues of sport—discipline, training, physical fitness, robust competitiveness—resound continually in all of Machiavelli's writings. Castruccio's youthful athletic prowess is what first draws the attention of adults and prefigures his military training. Machiavelli insists that a successful prince must be armed and must lead his own troops. He cannot lead an indolent life and retain respect. The quickest way to lose power and relinquish your state is to shy from learning and practicing the art of war. The unarmed man is compelled to obey the armed man. The prince must train himself for war by hunting. Hunting accustoms the body to hardships and forces the prince to confront nature's topography. While engaging in sport, the prince can study terrain and imagine military attacks and defenses (P 14).

Machiavelli perceives international affairs as an endless zero-sum game: benefit to my country flows from the defeat of your country. Machiavelli's message is as cold as steel tempered too hard. The world is a competitive battleground. A nation's choices—unless it is astonishingly insignificant—are to expand or to be subjugated. The bluff, guile, courage, knowledge, and panache of a political leader, the paradigm of military and political *virtù*, must be backed by strong arms. Conditions of scarcity, the basic nature of human beings, the rush for glory by those with *grandezza d'animo* (expansive spirit), and the relentless whims of *Fortuna* compel the need to triumph or to be destroyed. The call for enduring peace is a tinny hustle. A long-standing peace lures citizens into *ozio*—the indolent, soft, undisciplined, unworthy life—where leisure and the pursuit of luxury are paramount (D III 16). Whereas for Socrates the unexamined life is not worth living, for Machiavelli an unadventuresome, unheroic scramble for *la dolce vita* is no life at all. *Ozio*, the lack of heroic action, and a deficiency of *virtù* lead to political ruin (D II 30).

Machiavelli's unequivocal preference for the heroic life also gushes forth in his discussion of austerity. Physical comfort and material accumulations are unworthy consolations for those who are inadequate for higher military and political callings. He locates a robustly meaningful life in the public realm of international competition, not in private striving for more shining trinkets and baubles.

## The Olympic Ideal

To discuss "the Olympic Ideal" is misleading. Instead of a single, static aspiration, the Olympic Games have been animated by an evolving, mutually consistent plurality of guiding principles.

*The Truce.* Military hostilities should cease during the Games; a peaceful environment that ensures the safe transport and participation of athletes and spectators at the Games should prevail; and the youth of the world should be encouraged to mobilize their energies in the service of world peace.

*Fair Play and Sportsmanship.* In the search for excellence, all amateur athletes are equal. Victory should spring from ability, training, effort, and perseverance. Discrimination with regard to country or directed at an individual based on race, religion, ethnicity, politics, or gender is incompatible with the Olympic spirit. Use of prohibited performance-enhancing drugs mars the commitment to fair play. Competitors should strive to win with dignity or lose with grace. The links among amateurism, sportsmanship, political neutrality, and fair play are critical to Olympic competition.

*The Primacy of Process Values.* Quality of effort is more important than result. The founder of the modern Olympic Games, Baron Pierre de Coubertin of France, expressed that aim in 1908: "The most important thing in the Olympic Games is not to win but to take part, just as the most important thing in life is not the triumph, but the struggle. The essential thing is not to have conquered but to have fought well." This creed is flashed on the scoreboard at opening ceremonies at every Olympic Games.

*The Commitment to Excellence.* The Olympic motto is *Citius* (swifter), *Altius* (higher), *Fortius* (stronger). Part of the Olympic Ideal is to promote and accelerate human athletic performance and the discipline, effort, and talent that energize it.

*Promote Unity, Not Differences.* All competitors should be motivated by similar ends—competing to their fullest, performing at their best, participating fairly, and enjoying the competition for its own sake. The Olympic Games aspire to emphasize that which unites the world in a brotherhood and sisterhood, rather than that which divides it.

*The Integration of Mind and Body.* Maximum athletic performance requires enormous mental focus and toughness wedded to physical talent and development. The Olympic Games showcase those who have most closely integrated their minds and bodies, one of the aspirations of the ancient Greeks.

In sum, on the global level, Olympic Ideals promote international understanding among the peoples of the world through sport and culture in service of the harmonious development of the human race. On the individual level, Olympic Ideals underwrite the games that provide a forum for athletic excellence in terms of both the process and outcome values of sport. Olympic Ideals, then, aspire for nothing less than contributing to a better and more peaceful world. In practice, however, the lofty hopes of the Olympic Games have not always been realized. In particular, the Olympic notion of amateurism is less pure than advertised.[4] Moreover, the claim that the Olympic Games transcend politics invites ridicule.[5]

Machiavelli would scoff at many Olympic Ideals. For him, enduring world peace is a dangerous illusion that can lure *gabbiani* (gulls) into a complacent pacifism that promotes military defeat. The notion of an international brotherhood and sisterhood would earn Machiavelli's contempt. The hypocrisy that the Olympic Games transcend nationalism and politics would drive Machiavelli into paroxysms of laughter. Yet Machiavelli would relish international athletic competition at the highest level. He would appreciate the inexorable connections between athletic *virtù*, military *virtù*, and political success. Most important, Machiavelli cherished the glorious personal transformation accompanying the virtues of sport. Discipline, training, physical fitness, and robust competitiveness are the animating fuel of a salutary republic and the marks of a life lived well.

## Mennea, Olympic Ideals, and *Virtù*

Pietro Mennea's competitive résumé is impressive. He was the first runner to qualify for the finals in the same event in four straight Olympics; he set a world record in 1979 at the World Student Games in Mexico City of 19.72 in the 200-meter dash that stood for almost seventeen years; he won one Olympic gold and two bronze medals; he won gold medals in the 1974 and 1978 European championships; and he attained countless other victories in less heralded competitions.

Perhaps his greatest race was at the 1980 Moscow Olympics. Competing against Donald Quarrie of Jamaica, the reigning Olympic champion in the 200 meters, and Allan Wells, the greatest British sprinter in two decades, Mennea was seeking vindication. Quarrie had defeated him at the 1976 Montreal Olympics, and Wells had bested him at the 1979 European Cup in front of Mennea's national crowd at Turin. The latter event was especially galling. The Mennea family thereafter dubbed Wells "The Beast" for that *infamia*.

All three men were among the eight sprinters qualifying for the 200-meter final at the 1980 Moscow Olympics. Mennea drew the far outside lane, with The Beast beside him in lane seven. At the gun, The Beast characteristically spurted out of his stance and tore into the lead. Wells had made up the stagger after only fifty meters. Coming out of the turn, he enjoyed a comfortable two-meter lead over Silvio Leonard of Cuba, with Quarrie and Mennea lagging behind. Wells, a marine engineer from Edinburgh, had already become Great Britain's first 100-meter Olympic winner since Harold Abrahams, immortalized in *Chariots of Fire,* won at the 1924 Paris event. A double victory in the sprints seemed certain as Wells bolted into the final straightaway. But wait! Buzzing through the stretch with astonishing alacrity was The Southern Arrow. Seemingly shot not from an archer's bow but from a cannon, Mennea rushed past Wells with less than ten meters to the finish line. At the last instant, The Beast desperately flailed with his famous final dip, the maneuver that had earned him victory over Leonard in the 100-meter race. (Winners are determined by the first shoulder or torso across the finish line, not by the first set of arms or legs.) Not this trip! The Southern Arrow had pierced the heart of The Beast. Mennea won gold, Wells silver, Quarrie bronze.

Ironically, Pietro Mennea, who had earned a doctorate in political science two weeks prior to competing in the Olympics, almost did not participate in the event. He had been a candidate for local office for the Social Democratic Party, which supported a boycott of the Moscow Olympics as a protest of the Soviet invasion of Afghanistan. Mennea, motivated by almost fifteen years of training and his commitment to Olympic Ideals, finally decided to compete. He would continue to compete in the Olympic Games in 1984 and 1988. That Pietro Mennea embodied physical prowess and mental toughness, the predominant character traits of athletic *virtù*, is apparent from his success in the Olympics and his participation as a world class sprinter for over twenty years. Mennea, however, also turned social adversity into practical advantage, a hallmark of Machiavellian *virtù*.

Pietro Mennea faced and overcame significant prejudice in Europe because of his Southern Italian heritage.[6] From the standpoint of northerners, southerners were agrarian, backward, criminally inclined, and insular. From the standpoint of southerners, northerners had forever systematically betrayed, exploited, and demeaned them.[7] These intramural prejudices within Italy between northerners and southerners continue to echo beyond the peninsula and resonate throughout Europe. Mennea faced such bias during his career. The character he forged when faced with adversity—using it as motivation to excel instead of accepting it as an excuse to retreat—glistens with the philosophy of life embodied in the Olympic Charter. After he won his race in the 1980 Moscow Olympics, Mennea insisted, *"Io vinco le Olimpiadi perché sono meridionale"* ("I win the Olympics because I am a southerner"). The Southern Arrow was asserting the moral superiority of those who suffer unjustly and was identifying with the same historical rage as black Americans.[8]

Prior to entering the 1980 Olympics, Mennea faced an existential crisis. Torn between his allegiance to his political party, which supported a boycott of the Games, and his desire to compete, he consulted his conscience and examined his heart. He concluded that the values of the Olympic Ideals were paramount. Even though they are rarely, if ever, attained, the principles that guide Olympic competition speak to what is best in the human spirit. Mennea decided that allegiance to those principles was too precious to relinquish for transitory political purposes. He still believed that what unites human beings was more important than what sets them apart.

Mennea was also motivated by the need for one big score, a glorious conquest to silence once and forever those who had discriminated against him. He went, he won, he waved.

Pietro Mennea was elected in 1999 to a five-year term as a member of the European Parliament. Machiavelli would have nodded approvingly at the marriage of athletic and political *virtù*. Mennea lost a reelection bid in 2004 and now devotes considerable time to his campaign against the use of performance-enhancing drugs in athletics. Critics might snarl that Mennea is a deluded *gabbiano* (gull), but, for better or worse, The Southern Arrow, now a lawyer and professor of sports law, continues to venerate Olympic Ideals.

# Notes

As is common practice in Machiavelli scholarship, where I have cited from Machiavelli's writings the references in all cases have been given in the text and not in the endnotes. I use the following abbreviations:

P    *The Prince* in *Selected Political Writings*. Ed. and trans. David Wootton. Indianapolis, IN: Hackett Publishing Co., 1994.
D    *Discourses on the First Decade of Titus Livius ("The Discourses")* in *The Chief Works and Others*. Ed. and trans. Allan H. Gilbert. Durham, NC: Duke University Press, 1989.

All references are to chapters or sections. For example, P 18 refers to *The Prince*, Chapter 18; D I 55 refers to *The Discourses*, Book I, Chapter 55.

1. See, for example, Russell Price, "The Senses of *Virtù* in Machiavelli," *European Studies Review* 3 (1973): 315–345.
2. Harvey C. Mansfield, *Machiavelli's Virtue* (Chicago: University of Chicago Press, 1996), 6–7.
3. Niccolò Machiavelli, *Life of Castruccio Castracani* (1520), trans. Andrew Brown (London, UK: Hesperus Press, 2003).
4. The ancient Greek athletes, contrary to popular belief, were totally supported for almost a year prior to their Olympic Games. Although victors would receive only an olive wreath to commemorate their triumph, they earned fame and usually economic bounty upon their return home. The notion of amateurism developed in nineteenth-century England as a way to prevent athletes from poorer economic classes from competing with the wealthy. Only aristocrats could participate in sports at that

level without having to earn a living. Poorer athletes had only two choices: give up training in deference to making a living, or turn professional. Both options precluded competing in the Olympics. From earliest times onward, the code of amateurism has been fragile. For example, in the twentieth century, Communist countries insisted they had no professional athletes because they lacked professional sports. This position conflicted with their relentless, extensive sponsorship and support of potential Olympic participants.

5. To mention a few obvious transgressions: The 1916 Berlin Games were canceled due to World War I. The 1936 Berlin Games were used by Germany as an exercise in Nazi propaganda. The 1940 Tokyo Games were canceled when Japan invaded China. World War II prevented any games from occurring in 1944. The 1956 Melbourne Olympics were boycotted by Egypt, Iraq, and Lebanon in protest of the Israeli-led seizure of the Suez Canal, and by Holland, Spain, and Switzerland in protest of the Soviet invasion of Hungary. The 1972 Munich Games were devastated by the killings of eleven athletes, five Palestinian terrorists, and a policeman pursuant to the kidnapping of several Israeli athletes and the attempt to rescue them. The 1976 Montreal Olympics were marred by a boycott of African nations led by Tanzania. (The Africans demanded the expulsion of New Zealand from the games because a rugby team from New Zealand had made a tour of South Africa, a nation then ruled by apartheid.) The 1980 Moscow Olympics were boycotted by the United States and others in protest of the Soviet invasion of Afghanistan. The 1984 Los Angeles Olympics were boycotted by the Soviet Union and others in response to the 1980 boycott by the United States. The ideals of the Olympic Truce, the promotion of world unity, and the invigoration of global peace have often been violated. Rabid commercialism, extensive chicanery, and blatant nationalism—all anathema to Olympic Ideals—have also been injected into the games, by nations and individual contestants alike.

6. For background on the prejudices within Italy between northerners and southerners see Luigi Barzini, *The Italians* (New York: Atheneum Publishers, 1964), 246–247.

7. The exploitation of southerners by northerners within Italy was noticed throughout history by foreign observers. For example, Booker T. Washington, a man who knew slavery firsthand and fought against it, visited Italy in the nineteenth century and concluded: "The Negro is not the man farthest down. The condition of the colored farmer in the most backward parts of the Southern States in America, even where he has the least education and the least encouragement, is incomparably better than the condition and opportunities of the agricultural population in Sicily." Quoted in Jerre Mangione and Ben Morreale, *La Storia: Five Centuries of the Italian American Experience* (New York: HarperCollins Publishers, 1992), xv. Karl Marx once wrote in the *New York Tribune*, "In all human history no country or no people have suffered such terrible slavery, conquest and foreign oppression and no country and no people have struggled so strenuously for their emancipation as Sicily and the Sicilians." Karl Marx, *New York Tribune* (May 1860) quoted in Mangione and Morreale, *La Storia*, 58.

8. Alessandro Portelli, "The Problem of the Color Blind: Notes on the Discourse of Race in Italy," in *Race and Nation: Ethnic Systems in the Modern World,* ed. Paul Spickard (New York: Routledge Publishers, 2004), 358; Jeffrey Cole, *The New Racism in Europe: A Sicilian Ethnography* (New York: Cambridge University Press, 1997), 93.

*Scott F. Parker*

# WHAT'S MORE THAN GOLD

Egoism is the very essence of a noble soul.
—Friedrich Nietzsche

The power which resides in him is new in nature, and none but he knows what that is which he can do, nor does he know until he has tried.
—Ralph Waldo Emerson

A race is a work of art that people can look at and be affected by in as many ways as they're capable of understanding.
—Steve Prefontaine

## Prelude: Pre

Steve Prefontaine (Pre) qualified for the 1972 Munich Olympics in the 5K. At age twenty-one, Pre was young for that distance. The 5K, usually dominated by men in their late twenties and early thirties, is considered a thinking man's race, not a race for cocky and impetuous boys, qualities Pre had in spades. And if his age and disposition weren't disadvantage enough, his competitors had more international experience; Pre had run mostly against other collegiate athletes while winning several national titles at the University of Oregon. Additionally, his competitors were pampered in their countries. They were given cushy jobs so as to not interfere with their training. In Munich Pre and the other American athletes stayed in Spartan barracks and were only given a couple of dollars a day for food to protect their "amateur" status.[1] It seemed as if everything was against him in Munich—he also said he had one leg longer than the other —but that's the way Pre liked it. And that is why, despite all of the obstacles he faced, he liked his chances for gold.

This is not a chapter of suspense, and anyone who knows of Pre already knows where he finished, so here it is: not first, not second, and by a couple of stumbling steps not third. He finished fourth in Munich and never ran in another Olympics; he died in a car accident in 1975, a year before going to Montreal, where he would likely have been not just a contender for gold but the favorite. So why discuss Steve Prefontaine in relation to the Olympics? Judging by the record books, hundreds of Olympians have been more successful—hundreds of track and field athletes have been more successful. Twenty-one men have won Olympic gold at Pre's distance in the modern era,[2] not to mention silver and bronze. Why not a chapter on one of them? Because of philosophy, really—a particular bit of it anyway. I will attempt to show in this chapter that the Olympics shares its essence with certain writings of two philosophers: Friedrich Wilhelm Nietzsche (1844–1900) and Ralph Waldo Emerson (1803–1882)—and that Steve Prefontaine embodied that essence as well as any other Olympian.

## Citius, Altius, Fortius

To begin with, what is the essence of the Olympics? The following three defining statements articulate this essence, which can be summed up as an attitude of personal accomplishment grounded in an embrace of hard work.

First is the Olympic Charter, which asserts that Olympism is a philosophy of life, exalting and combining in a balanced whole the qualities of body, will, and mind. Blending sport with culture and education, Olympism seeks to create a way of life based on the joy found in effort, the educational value of good example, and respect for universal fundamental ethical principles.

Next, the Olympic Creed: The most important thing in the Olympic Games is not to win but to take part, just as the most important thing in life is not the triumph but the struggle. The essential thing is not to have conquered but to have fought well.

And then there is the Olympic Motto: *Citius, altius, fortius* (Faster, higher, stronger).

None of these three precepts mentions winning as being a fundamental aspect of what the Olympics are about. The Charter indicates a relationship between sports and ethics. The Creed stresses full participation. The Motto, lacking a predicate, suggests that *faster, higher,* and *stronger* are relative standards.[3] Taking the three precepts together, we see that the essence of the Olympics is simply doing one's best.[4]

Our own viewing of the Olympics reinforces this attitude. We watch the opening ceremonies and are as happy for and proud of the men and women representing smaller countries who have no realistic hope of winning a medal in their events but will assuredly give their best efforts as we are for the parade of dominating Americans. We don't mock the losers, either, the way we might when watching games in the NBA (the Los Angeles Clippers) or the MLB (sadly, my Chicago Cubs). What's the difference? Are we agreeing, as the original Olympians intended, to put down our fire and join arms to celebrate our common humanity? Maybe that's part of it,[5] but there's something else at work too. When the Cubs lose year after year we think it's pathetic because they are on the same playing field, so to speak, as other teams who are not perennial losers. Therefore, they must be doing something wrong. When the USA Dream Team beat Angola 116–48 in the Barcelona Olympics, we didn't mock Angola, we acknowledged that they were in hopelessly over their heads, and we respected them because, despite that, they did their best—all they could do. They were successful, though not victorious. In this case, success is defined differently by the participants: it's defined *by them.*

## Two Men

The nineteenth-century German philosopher Friedrich Nietzsche shared this directive toward self-accomplishment. In a theme that he developed throughout his work, Nietzsche distinguished between two kinds of men —the higher and the last—each having distinct attributes. The higher man expresses the Nietzschean virtues of creativity, strength, boldness, vigor, and exuberance. These are virtues for Nietzsche because it is through them that one can reach the highest goal: the affirmation of life. Life, for Nietzsche, requires affirmation because, in and of itself, it is meaningless. God is dead, and there is no external source to provide meaning. For life to become meaningful, meaning (or value) must be created. This is no small task. To create value requires the virtues just named (creativity, strength, boldness, vigor, exuberance)—virtues that, Nietzsche claims, only the highest among us are capable of sustaining.

Sports, particularly in the mold of the Olympic essence, as we'll see below, offer a good opportunity for a person to affirm life by doing his or her best and constantly overcoming what he or she is, constructing a new self by going beyond old limits. Nietzsche's own self-overcoming was largely exhibited in his writing, but he valued exercise greatly. He was known for taking long, invigorating walks in the mountains. He even said, "Give no credence to any thought that was not born outdoors while one moved about freely—in which the muscles are not celebrating a feast."[6]

In contrast to the higher man is Nietzsche's last man. The last man lacks the value-creating and life-affirming ethos of the higher man. Instead, he trembles before meaninglessness and flounders in nihilism, grasping onto the lesser values of survival and easy pleasure. This grasping onto survival is the source of the term *last man*. Because this person values survival, he will outlive the higher man, who values living. The devotion to pleasure—another virtue of the last man—is a weakness to Nietzsche. To seek pleasure is to avoid struggle, which is a renunciation of the essence of life in its self-overcoming nature. The higher man renounces this renunciation and creates new values in his own image. And because he must create his own values the higher man must have his own standards. He is like the ideal Olympian: he does his best and through his hard work affirms life.

A nice illustration of the higher man comes from Nietzsche's *Twilight of the Idols*:

> The genius, in work and deed, is necessarily a squanderer: that he squanders himself, that is his greatness. The instinct of self-preservation is suspended, as it were; the overpowering pressure of outflowing forces forbids him any such care or caution. People call this "self-sacrifice" and praise his "heroism," his indifference to his own well-being, his devotion to an idea, a great cause, a fatherland: without exception, misunderstandings. He flows out, he overflows, he uses himself up, he does not spare himself—and this is a calamitous, involuntary fatality, no less than a river's flooding the land.[7]

## Self-Reliance

Another philosopher, American transcendentalist Ralph Waldo Emerson, who was a near contemporary of Nietzsche's, developed similar themes. Unlike Nietzsche, Emerson was religious, believing in a transcendent reality that is more real than the everyday physical world. What Emerson's transcendentalism has in common with Nietzsche is the mechanism through which Emerson thought the transcendent could be experienced: namely, personal intuition. Emerson considered traditional doctrinal religion to be cold and stifling to the individual. The problem of evil troubled him, too: How could an omnipotent, omniscient, benevolent God allow evil in the world? To answer this question Emerson recommended turning inward and examining one's own experiences. What could be discovered to be true firsthand was true for all. "To believe your own thought, to believe that what is true for you in your private heart, is true for all men,—this is genius."[8]

This commonality that Emerson describes is dependent upon his idea of the transcendent unity, what he calls the "Over-soul." Without that connection our individual experiences might be isolated and we might become solipsistic. The conclusions of Emerson's individualism are less radical than are Nietzsche's, but the processes are similar. For Emerson, anything short of self-reliance is inadequate. Whether it be society, religion, books, or some other form of authority, there is no substitute for one's own thinking. "Whoso would be a man must be a nonconformist. He who would gather immortal palms must not be hindered by the name of goodness, but must explore if it be goodness. Nothing is at last sacred but the integrity of your own mind."[9]

This makes sense for a couple of reasons. First, if our values are received from authority, they are not really our values. To find value in something we must give it value through our own valuations based on our own understanding of *good*. Second, there is autonomy even in conformity. We have to trust ourselves in order to conform. If we really did not rely on ourselves we could not trust ourselves to properly conform. Conformity then is just a failed escape from our own freedom. Better to acknowledge this and rely on ourselves explicitly.

## Nietzsche, Emerson, and Prefontaine

The Olympic essence, Nietzsche's Higher Man, Emerson's self-reliance—all of these emphasize the value of valuing, that is, of creating your own values rather than either passively adopting the cultural values of your time and place and holding yourself to someone else's standards or having your values dictated to you. Value, according to the Olympics, Nietzsche, and Emerson, is what the valuer assigns him- or herself. But that does not mean that valuation is arbitrary. There are some objective standards. A runner cannot praise himself in good conscience without earning the right through the virtues of hard work, discipline, and effort. These virtues are universal: for the Olympics, because it is through them that one succeeds; for Nietzsche, because it is through them that one affirms life; for Emerson, because they are among the universal goods available to a person's intuition.

And if we apply these virtues to the Olympics, what do we find? Who is the personification of the ideal Olympian? I think we find someone like Steve Prefontaine. Pre exhibited all these virtues and, through them, relied on himself, did his best, and affirmed life. Rather than argue for this interpretation of Pre, in an effort to capture something of the Nietzschean and Emersonian spirit, I'm going to quote quickly and boldly in this section as it suits the points I want to make. In so doing I'm going to try to show that Nietzsche, Emerson, and Prefontaine articulated similar thematic beliefs about the kinds of virtues present in Pre's running. I defend this unorthodox method by pointing out that while both Nietzsche's and Emerson's diagnoses about the need for revaluating values and self-reliance were rational, their prescriptions for these processes were not limited to rationality, emphasizing in addition intuition and intoxication.

*Front Running.* One of the distinct features of Pre's running style was his front running. In front running the athlete runs as hard as he can, takes the early lead, and keeps it as long as he can. Front running is not considered a wise strategy in distance events. The front runner has to do more work than any of his competitors, who can stay behind him for the majority of the race, draft, save energy, and then outkick the leader at the finish. So why do it? Because when you are out in front you can rely only on yourself. Front running is an extreme form of testing yourself. Pre: "A lot of people run a race to see who is fastest. I run to see who has the most guts, who can punish himself into exhausting pace, and then at the end, punish himself even more." Emerson: "Do not go where the path may lead, go instead where there is no path and leave a trail."

*Effort.* The effort it takes to be a front runner is substantial. A front runner uses up a considerable amount of energy, a scare resource, breaking the wind. But Pre did it anyway, thinking it was more important to do his best than to try to win at all costs. Pre: "To give anything less than your best is to sacrifice the gift." Nietzsche would approve of Pre's effort: "That which does not kill us only makes us stronger."

*Confidence.* To run with sustained effort requires a great deal of confidence, something Pre was never short on. But his confidence wasn't only about winning. Winning depends on what other runners do, but running hard depends only on you. Nietzsche: "Of all that is written, I love only what a person has written with his own blood." Pre: "Somebody may beat me, but they are going to have to bleed to do it." Bold words that resonate in the context of the 1970 NCAA Championship three-mile race, which Pre won despite running on a severely cut foot, making one wonder if bleeding would have been enough for his competitors.

*Will.* Pre considered his running ability to be the product of his will, which was honed in his lifetime of overcoming obstacles: "How does a kid from Coos Bay, with one leg longer than the other, win races?" Pre again: "I'm going to work so that it's a pure guts race at the end, and if it is, I am the only one who can win it." Emerson: "Shallow men believe in luck. Strong men believe in cause and effect." Nietzsche: "I assess the power of a will by how much resistance, pain, torture it endures and knows how to turn to its advantage."

*Intoxication.* Nietzsche: "For art to exist, for any sort of aesthetic activity to exist, a certain physiological precondition is indispensable: intoxication." Emerson: "Nothing great was ever achieved without enthusiasm." A typical assessment of Pre: "In addition to his outstanding athletic performances, he was admired for his enthusiasm, determination, and charisma."[10]

*Art.* Nietzsche: "Art is the proper task of life." Emerson: "Love of beauty is taste. The creation of beauty is art." Pre: "Some people create with words or with music or a brush and paints. I like to make something beautiful when I run."

If all of these quotes and virtues seem to overlap, they should. They are all derivatives of the primary virtue: self-valuation. I'll give Pre the final word on this: "You have to wonder at times what you're doing out there. Over the years, I've given myself a thousand reasons to keep running, but it always comes back to where it started. It comes down to self-satisfaction and a sense of achievement."

## Pre's 5K Final: *Amor Fati*

Let's look now at Pre's sole Olympic Games and see how he embodies the Olympic essence he extolled like Nietzsche and Emerson before him. Munich 1972, 5K final. After an unusually slow first two miles, Prefontaine takes the lead with a mile to go and pushes the pace, separating the contenders from the rest of the field. Lasse Viren, Mohamed Gammoudi, Ian Stewart, and Emiel Puttemans chase after him. After two laps he falls back into that small pack before making another drive with 600 meters to go, retaking the lead. This time only Viren and Gammoudi can stay with him. Again Prefontaine can't distance himself. He falls back briefly before making a final surge for the lead with 200 meters to go. In the final 100 meters Viren goes out to a comfortable win, Gammoudi pulls ahead into second, and Pre stumbles to the finish, getting passed in the final 10 meters by Ian Stewart. For all his will, his confidence, his effort, and the beauty that he brought to the race, Pre walks away without even a medal to show for it.

The question now is: Was the race a success for Pre even though he didn't win? We can't answer that. By the standards established in this chapter, only Pre can assess his race, because only he can know if he did his best. But we can speculate that the sight of Pre stumbling down the home stretch indicates that he used every bit of his energy in his three strong drives for the lead, and that he could have been proud of his race.

And if he was proud, he might have been demonstrating what Nietzsche called *amor fati,* the love of fate. "My formula for greatness in a human being is amor fati: that one wants nothing to be different, not forward, not backward, not in all eternity. Not merely bear what is necessary, still less conceal it—all idealism is mendaciousness in the face of what is necessary—but love it."[11] This is as bold an idea as there could be. Not *accept*, he says—*love*. It is a logical outgrowth of Nietzsche's virtue of affirming life. To affirm life means to affirm all of it always, not just parts of it when it's convenient. Pre then, if he did his best, should have had no regrets and actually embraced his failure.[12] Failure and loss are part of life. A strong person, a higher man, embraces them when it is appropriate. Pity and regret would expose fear and renunciation of life, something a self-reliant, higher man would have no truck with. As fans, when we watch Pre's Munich race we can participate in that love of life if we are strong enough to affirm the tragedy of the race. We do so if we are able to affirm Pre's virtues and not pity his failure. We should be like Emerson in this, saying, "Our love goes out to him and embraces him, because he did not need it."[13]

Assuming that Pre was able to affirm his failure—and, through it, life—we must also consider the man who passed him at the finish. Can Ian Stewart affirm his third-place finish in the same way that Pre affirms his fourth? Watching the video of the race, two things are striking: how uninteresting the first eight laps are; and how enthralling the last four are because of how Pre runs them. Stewart is a nonfactor in the video, kind of hanging around until he steals third place at the last minute. From the viewing alone we cannot say for sure that Stewart ran this race like Nietzsche's last man. We can imagine that he was putting as much into the race as Pre was, but his equivalent effort doesn't come across as such on video. This quote of Stewart's, however, from the documentary *Fire on the Track* (1995), makes us think otherwise: "In fairness to Prefontaine, he ran better than I did that day. I probably didn't deserve to get a medal probably. Not the way I ran."

At issue in this discussion is the point of an Olympic race. As I have argued in this chapter, for Nietzsche, Emerson, Prefontaine, and the Olympics themselves, the point is to attain personal accomplishment through overcoming challenges and competing at one's highest level. Not winning. There is little doubt that in Munich and for the whole of his short running life, Prefontaine ran with such goals in mind.

But let's not admire him too much, warns Nietzsche: "Admiration for a quality or an art can be so great it can hinder us from striving to possess it."[14] Instead, we should learn from Prefontaine's example and apply it to our own lives, our own overcomings, doing our own bests. Ultimately, philosophers like Nietzsche and Emerson are not just to be understood intellectually. Similarly, the Olympic essence isn't to be admired from afar. The philosophers' wisdom and the Olympic essence are to be embodied as Pre embodied them. Pre's kind of life-affirming creativity is possible for us all.

In a chapter about self-reliance and originality I have quoted enough, some will think, to undermine my own argument. Anticipating this response, I quote again from Emerson:

> Our debt to tradition through reading and conversation is so massive, our protest so rare and insignificant—and this commonly on the ground of other reading and hearing—that in large sense, one would say there is no pure originality. All minds quote. Old and new make the warp and woof of every moment. There is no thread that is not a twist of these two strands. By necessity, by proclivity, and by delight, we all quote. It is as difficult to appropriate the thoughts of others as it is to invent.[15]

I come into a world already made. I create from what I find—some of it Nietzsche's, some of it Emerson's, some of it Prefontaine's. And some of it Montaigne's: "Let people see in what I borrow whether I have known how to choose what would enhance my theme. For I make others say what I cannot say so well, now through the weakness of my language, now through the weakness of my understanding."[16]

## Coda: Lauryn Williams

To end with a more recent example, one athlete who absolutely understood the essence of the Olympics was Lauryn Williams. At the 2008 Olympics in Beijing, the American women's 4-by-100 relay team was favored to medal; but in the semifinal race, as Torri Edwards was handing off to Williams to begin the anchor leg, they dropped the baton. Although the Americans were, by this misstep, disqualified, Williams ran backwards on the track to retrieve the baton and then sprinted to the finish line as fast as she could.

# Notes

1. Pre would be instrumental in the eventual overturning of the Amateur Athletic Union (AAU), track and field's governing body, which profited at their athletes' expenses: Pre famously lived off food stamps in a trailer park in Eugene, Oregon, after college, turning down a $200,000 professional contract so he could keep his eligibility for the Montreal Olympics in 1976.

2. Lasee Viren, gold medalist in 1972, defended in 1976; there were no Olympics in 1916, 1940, and 1944 due to World Wars I and II.

3. A point that Pre's coach, Bill Bowerman (played by Donald Sutherland), makes in the 1998 biopic, *Without Limits* (dir. Robert Towne).

4. Keep in mind that anyone with the opportunity to do their best at the Olympics is already exceptionally good at what they do compared to others around them. Those of us 5K runners who have not made the Olympics must practice our virtuous efforts in local road races—an ethically equivalent opportunity, if slightly less spectacular sight.

5. Though his own 1972 Olympics provides the saddest counterexample to this pollyannaism.

6. Friedrich Nietzsche, *"On the Genealogy of Morals" and "Ecce Homo,"* trans. Walter Kaufmann (New York: Vintage, 1989), 239–240.

7. Friedrich Nietzsche, *The Portable Nietzsche,* trans. Walter Kaufmann (New York: Penguin Books, 1982), 548.

8. Ralph Waldo Emerson, *Emerson's Prose and Poetry* (New York: W. W. Norton, 2001), 121.

9. Ibid., 122.

10. Oregon Blue Book. Notable Oregonians, http://bluebook.state.or.us/notable/notprefontaine.htm.

11. Nietzsche, *"On The Genealogy of Morals" and "Ecce Homo,"* 258.

12. Yes, being only the fourth fastest person in the world can be a kind of failure.

13. Emerson, *Emerson's Prose and Poetry,* 133.

14. Nietzsche, *Human, All Too Human,* trans. R. J. Hollingdale (Cambridge: Cambridge University Press, 1996), 294.

15. Emerson, *Emerson's Prose and Poetry,* 331. Compare this with his better known saying, "I hate quotations. Tell me what you know," which can probably only be reconciled with his most famous quote: "A foolish constancy is the hobgoblin of small minds."

16. Michel de Montaigne, "Of Books," from *The Art of the Personal Essay,* selected and with an introduction by Philip Lopate (New York: Anchor, 1997), 46.

.

Part 2

# ANCIENT HERITAGE

*Paul A. Cantor and Peter Hufnagel*

# THE OLYMPICS OF THE MIND
## Philosophy and Athletics in the Ancient Greek World

> Every talent must unfold itself in fighting: that is the command
> of Hellenic popular pedagogy. . . . And just as the youths were
> educated through contests, their educators were also engaged in
> contests with each other. The great musical masters, Pindar and
> Simonides, stood side by side, mistrustful and jealous; in the
> spirit of contest, the sophist . . . meets another sophist; even the
> . . . drama was meted out to the people only in the form of a
> tremendous wrestling among the great musical and dramatic
> artists. . . . "Even the artist hates the artist." . . . The Greek
> knows the artist *only as engaged in a personal fight*.
> —Friedrich Nietzsche, "Homer's Contest"

The ancient Greeks were the most competitive people in history. As a
profound student of the Hellenic world, the German philosopher
Friedrich Nietzsche—a classical scholar by profession—devotes his essay
"Homer's Contest" to detailing the many ways in which the ancient
Greeks, above all the Athenians, loved to engage in combat, both literal
and metaphorical. Even the art of drama in Athens took the form of civic
contests, in which tragedians like Aeschylus and Sophocles competed
against each other for prizes. It comes as no surprise, then, to learn that
the ancient Greeks invented athletic competition as we know it, and
indeed we take our words *athlete* and *athletics* from ancient Greek. One
of the many ways in which we moderns are the heirs of the ancient Greeks
is our revival and recreation of the supreme athletic competition they first
staged, the Olympic Games. As Nietzsche realized, no subject takes us

closer to the heart of the ancient Greek world than the competitive spirit of the Olympics.

Nietzsche perceived how this competitive spirit extended even into the rarefied world of philosophy itself. We think of philosophers as detached and disinterested thinkers, with their heads in the clouds, far removed from the hustle and bustle of everyday life. But as a philosopher himself, Nietzsche intuited how much a spirit of rivalry permeated ancient philosophical disputes, as well as those between philosophers and other claimants to wisdom, such as poets and rhetoricians. Today, Plato may be our model of the serene master of thought, but Nietzsche argues that a contentious spirit was at the root of the Athenian's art as a philosopher:

> What, for example, is of special artistic significance in Plato's dialogues is for the most part the result of a contest with the art of the orators, the sophists, and the dramatists of his time, invented for the purpose of enabling him to say in the end: "Look, I too can do what my great rivals can do; indeed, I can do it better than they. No Protagoras has invented myths as beautiful as mine; no dramatist such a vivid and captivating whole as my *Symposium;* no orator has written orations like those in my *Gorgias*—and now I repudiate all this entirely and condemn all imitative art. Only the contest made me a poet, a sophist, an orator."[1]

The philosopher as athlete of the mind—that is Nietzsche's great insight into the debates we see in Plato's dialogues between Socrates and all the pretenders to wisdom in Athens he interrogates, humiliates, and defeats in argument. Thus to understand ancient Greek philosophy, it helps to look at the Olympics, and to understand the Olympics, it helps to look at ancient Greek philosophy. Wherever we turn in the Hellenic world, we see Greek pitted against Greek in the kind of competition epitomized by the Olympics. The Greek dream is to be the best, to be the first, to be the last man standing. The same competitive spirit that manifests itself on the race course and in the boxing arena comes out in Plato's dialogues (Socrates is literally the last man standing at the end of the all-night drinking contest in the *Symposium*). Socrates using his mental strength and agility to triumph over his opponents is the distant descendant of the very physical heroes of Homer's *Iliad*—not just Achilles, but all the athletes in the funeral games of Book XXIII, who prefigure the Olympians of later days. In Nietzsche's understanding, Plato's dialogues are the Olympics of philosophy.

The ancient Greeks were so possessed by the spirit of competition that they had a special word for it: *thumos*.[2] The word appears as early as Homer's epics, but receives its definitive analysis, appropriately enough, in Plato's dialogue *The Republic*.[3] The term comes up in the course of Socrates' attempt to distinguish the parts of the soul. We easily recognize the first two he discusses: (1) *logismos*—a word that designates the rational or calculating part of the soul, the logical power that can govern the passions; (2) *epithumia*—a word that designates appetites like hunger and thirst, and all forms of desire, including sexual impulses. But Socrates insists that a third part of the soul exists, an irrational element that is nevertheless not a form of desire and can in fact become the ally of *logos* against *epithumia*. This is what Socrates calls *thumos*, a term that at first looks very strange to us.[4] It is even difficult to find a single word in English that corresponds to what the ancient Greeks mean by *thumos*. Perhaps the closest equivalent in English is "spirit" or "spiritedness." But we are all familiar with the aspect of human nature Socrates is talking about. In fact, our best access to the phenomenon today is precisely in the world of athletics.

When we watch a boxer get off the canvas to snatch victory from defeat, or a wrestler struggling through pain to pin his opponent, or a swimmer straining to out-touch his rival in the next lane, or a cyclist pushing herself beyond the limits of endurance, we are watching *thumos* in action. The modern Olympics, like its ancient counterpart, is a festival of *thumos*. *Thumos* is what makes human beings—men and women— competitive; it is the passion to be first, to excel in any form of endeavor. It is an irrational force that leads human beings to scorn the limitations of their bodies and continually break through existing boundaries of performance. It is the drive to the finish line. The Greeks think of *thumos* in very physical terms; Homer consistently pictures it as located in the chest.[5] In fact, we would not go too far wrong if we translated *thumos* as "heart" or "guts." It is exactly what we are talking about in such expressions as: "You gotta have heart" or "That took a lotta guts." *Thumos* is manifest in warfare as well as in athletics. Soldiers on the battlefield, struggling to conquer their enemies, are equally driven by *thumos*, and indeed it does take an irrational force to get human beings to risk their lives in combat. *Thumos* is thus closely linked to the warlike qualities of courage and aggressiveness, and often takes the form of anger, a disposition to take offense and seek revenge. *Thumos* is what makes human beings stake out and defend a turf. The characteristic thumotic gesture is to draw a line in the sand and challenge anyone to step across it. And then to beat one's chest.[6]

In ancient Greek literature, the classic portrait of the thumotic man is Achilles in Homer's *Iliad*. Achilles' spirited indignation over what he regards as a slight to his honor by the Greek leader Agamemnon leads him to withdraw in a huff from battle, with disastrous consequences for the Greek army. In Homer's portrait of Achilles, we see the archetypal ancient Greek hero, and he embodies the whole complex of passions associated with *thumos:* competitiveness, the compulsion to be first in everything, aggressiveness in battle, a quick temper, sensitivity in matters of honor, a capacity for noble indignation—all linked to the basic emotion of raw anger. The announced theme of the *Iliad* is, after all, the wrath of Achilles. In his tragic story, Homer reveals how truly problematic *thumos* can be. *Thumos* is the source of Achilles' glory; it is what drives him to be a hero, even at the risk of his life; it leads him to his ultimate triumph over his great antagonist Hector. And yet Achilles' petulant withdrawal from battle at the beginning of the *Iliad* eventually costs the life of his friend Patroclus and threatens to cause the Greeks to lose the war against Troy. *Thumos* is after all an irrational part of the soul, and can be a disruptive and destructive force in human life.

Thus the *Iliad* portrays the potential for tragedy in *thumos,* and explores how this dangerous force might be controlled (as we will see, Homer offers athletics as one possible solution). In particular, the *Iliad* reveals the tragic tension between the thumotic hero and the community that both needs and cannot live with his spiritedness, especially when it leads him into insubordination and rebellion. The hope of all communities is to turn spiritedness into public spiritedness, to channel this potentially divisive and dangerous force, with its obsession with private honor, into support for the public good. The trick to making *thumos* serve the community is to link the courage it inspires with patriotism, and thereby to get spirited individuals to fight for their homelands, not just for themselves. The *Iliad* is the first in a long line of martial epics that show just how difficult this task can be.

How to control *thumos* is also a central concern of Plato's *Republic*. In the overall scheme of the dialogue, Socrates correlates the three parts of the soul with the three classes of people in the best city he is constructing in speech. *Logismos* corresponds to the philosopher-kings who will rule the city; *epithumia* corresponds to all the citizens who will be devoted to serving the needs and desires of the body—the farmers, the artisans, the merchants. *Thumos* (or *thumoeides*) corresponds to the guardian class, the warriors who will protect the city from its enemies. That of course is why this class must be characterized by *thumos;* the warriors need to be aggressive in battle. But their warlike character creates a problem for the city. Who will guard the guardians? Precisely because of their proud and aggressive nature, they may want to rule the city themselves, and with all its arms in their hands, they will have the power to do so.

Thus much of the *Republic* is devoted to the question of the education of the warrior class, how they can be raised so that they will be fierce with the city's enemies but at the same time be willing to accept tamely a subordinate position within the city, and in particular to accept the rule of the philosopher-kings. The *thumos* of the warriors must be moderated by their education in gymnastics and music. Gymnastic exercises will toughen them up, but at the same time impose discipline on them.[7] We see the fundamental Greek impulse to use athletics to divert *thumos* into acceptable channels, where it cannot do harm to the community. By "music," the ancient Greeks meant something more comprehensive than we do by the term—anything having to do with the Muses and hence all the arts—and that included what we would call education in poetry. In Socrates' plan, the city's warriors will be educated by an expurgated version of Homer's epics, one that will omit the more passionate scenes, including those that seem to endorse unbridled expressions of *thumos.* The warriors in Socrates' city will not be allowed to grow up into copies of Achilles. Their *thumos* will be thoroughly socialized to eliminate the tragic possibility of its coming into conflict with the city's demands. Carefully tamed in their education, their *thumos* will be fully in the service of the city and its ruling philosopher-kings.

In the overall parallel between the soul and the city in the *Republic,* Socrates' plan is thus to enlist *thumos* on the side of reason against desire. That is why the dialogue offers such a positive evaluation of *thumos,* even while acknowledging that it is one of the two irrational parts of the soul. From the beginning of his analysis of *thumos,* Socrates offers it as a force that can help reason deal with the power of desire. The spirited man

is too proud—he has too much sense of his dignity as a rational creature—
to give in to the baseness of his bodily desires: "Notice that, when desires
force someone contrary to the calculating part [*logismos*], he reproaches
himself and his spirit is aroused against that in him which is doing the
forcing, and, just as though there were two parties at faction, such a
man's spirit becomes the ally of speech. . . . In the factions of the soul, it
sets its arms on the side of the calculating part."[8] As usual, Socrates sums
up his analysis in the form of a question, expecting (and receiving) a
"yes" from his interlocutor, Glaucon: "just as there were three classes in
the city that held it together, money-making, auxiliary, and deliberative,
is there in the soul too this third, the spirited, by nature an auxiliary to
the calculating part, if it's not corrupted by bad rearing?"[9] In sum,
Socrates acknowledges good and bad forms of *thumos,* one that can
serve the city and one that can tear it apart. The central purpose of
education in the *Republic* is to bring out the good side of the competitive
spirit of the guardians and make them fight in the service of the city and
on behalf of its ruling philosopher-kings.

Plato has Socrates go further in enlisting *thumos* on the side of
philosophy. Indeed, he presents philosophy as itself a thumotic activity,
since it involves warring on behalf of truth. To understand this point, we
must cease to treat the *Republic* as if it were a philosophical treatise, and
instead analyze it as the genuine drama of ideas that it is. The problem of
*thumos* is the key to the dramatic action of the *Republic.*[10] It explains
Socrates' interaction with his two principal interlocutors in the dialogue,
Glaucon and Adeimantus. Plato characterizes these two figures, especially
Glaucon, as the kind of spirited young men Socrates was always attracted
to, and whom he hoped to win away from their devotion to Athens over
to a life of philosophy (in this context, recall that Glaucon and Adeimantus
were Plato's brothers). The problem for Socrates is that it is precisely the
*thumos* of Glaucon and Adeimantus that attaches them to the city. The
way Athens has socialized their *thumos* gets in the way of his efforts to
open them up to the possibility of philosophy. Their pride and ambition
make them obsessed with being honored in the eyes of their fellow
Athenians, and hence they devote themselves to areas of life conventionally
regarded as glorious by the city, such as athletic competition and warfare.
Moreover, spirited young men have been taught by Athens to have
contempt for philosophers, who are not honored by the city and even

appear to be disreputable characters, engaged in unmanly pursuits that take the form of "all talk and no action." Under these circumstances, how is the philosopher to gain a foothold among the thumotic youth of the city?

The core of Socrates' strategy, as we have already seen Nietzsche suggest, is to assimilate philosophy to the city's conventional models of honorable activity—to turn philosophic argument into a kind of contest, a form of warfare or athletics, in which Socrates can prove himself superior to any man in Athens. Then he can win the respect and admiration of the spirited Glaucon and Adeimantus. In the *Republic,* as in most of Plato's dialogues, Socrates must use a form of intellectual combat to establish himself as the best of the Greeks. Thus the first book of the *Republic* shows Socrates taking on all comers in argument, and defeating them. Above all, he manages to tame the hostile rhetorician Thrasymachus by exposing the inner contradictions in his argument. Only by neutralizing the rhetorical power of Thrasymachus and his clever celebration of injustice can Socrates prepare Glaucon and Adeimantus to listen patiently to arguments on behalf of justice as the best way of life (and philosophy as the highest form of justice). In his rhetorical combat with Thrasymachus, Socrates exhibits all the characteristics of the warlike and athletic hero. A master of strategy and tactics, he must be tenacious and even dogged in argument, always going on the attack, never letting his opponents off the hook, pursuing the fallacies in their arguments until he corners them and delivers the philosophical equivalent of a knockout punch. It does not take long for Glaucon and Adeimantus to realize that Socrates is the strongest man in Athens when it comes to philosophic argument. Fascinated by Socrates' power, they become willing to engage in a remarkably long discussion of the nature of justice in the city and in the soul. The way Socrates engages these spirited young men in philosophic dialogue is the ultimate example in the *Republic* of how *thumos* can be enlisted in the service of reason, of how spiritedness can be diverted from its normal and often dangerous channels into higher, intellectual pursuits.[11]

The *Republic* represents a relatively late and certainly very philosophical attempt to deal with the problem of *thumos* among the ancient Greeks. But as we have seen, even at the beginning of Greek literature, in the *Iliad,* Homer already presents *thumos* as problematic, and it turns out that athletics is very much part of the picture when the epic poet tries to deal with the phenomenon. In particular, an analogy from athletics may help us understand one of the major cruxes in the interpretation of the *Iliad*. Commentators have long puzzled over and debated what appears to be Achilles' change of heart at the end of the poem. For much of the *Iliad*, Achilles appears as a fierce and fearsome warrior. In the grip of *thumos,* he boils over with anger and rage, and leaves death and destruction in his wake. Once he sets out to avenge his comrade Patroclus, he becomes an implacable killing machine. Nothing can stop him in the frenzy of his *thumos,* not even the intervention of a river god or Apollo. In his final confrontation with the noble Hector, Achilles shows no mercy. He hounds his opponent to his death and afterwards desecrates Hector's body by dragging it behind his chariot in his relentless effort to triumph over and humiliate the man who killed Patroclus. By carrying revenge to its limits and beyond, Achilles demonstrates how truly frightening *thumos* in action can be, and seems to be on the verge of losing his very humanity in Book XXII.

When King Priam longs to reclaim his son Hector's body from the enraged Achilles in order to give it proper burial, his wife, Hecuba, cautions him against even trying. She fears that Achilles will continue his campaign of vengeance by murdering the Trojan king if he can just get his hands on Priam. And yet when Priam comes to Achilles' tent as a suppliant, the thumotic warrior treats him hospitably, serving him dinner, preparing him a bed, and promising not to resume fighting for the twelve days the Trojans will need for the funeral of Hector. By talking of his son, Priam makes Achilles think of his own father, Peleus, and that creates a bond between the Greek and the Trojan. At one point Achilles even takes Priam by the hand and shares his grief with him. Since antiquity, many explanations have been offered for Achilles' seemingly abrupt change from an uncontrollable killer to a man willing to make a truce with his bitter enemy. On the surface, Achilles' reconciliation with Priam appears to be an act of piety; Zeus sends a message to Achilles cautioning him against carrying his vendetta too far and ordering him to return Hector's body. But why should Achilles choose to do the pious thing at this moment? Earlier in the poem he repeatedly defies the gods, even when Apollo directly confronts him. Something must have changed in Achilles. Thus some commentators want to read a moral out of Book XXIV; they view Achilles as having learned a lesson in human mortality by the end of the poem. In Patroclus' death, perhaps even more so in Hector's death, Achilles has seen a mirror of his own fate, and finally comes to accept his own mortality and hence his humanity. In the end he recognizes the common element of mortality that unites Greek and Trojan, and that allows him to experience a new form of fellow feeling with Priam. After all his thumotic efforts to outdo even the gods, Achilles becomes a human being at the end of the *Iliad,* and many interpreters welcome this transformation, this humanizing of the godlike hero.[12]

This reading makes the end of the *Iliad* very moving, and the structure of the poem as a whole—the contrast between the opening and closing books—does seem to comment on the need to moderate *thumos* and bring it under control. In Achilles' savage treatment of Hector's corpse, we see what happens when thumotic anger operates without restraint. The calm that descends upon Achilles in Book XXIV does appear to be some kind of restoration of balance in his soul. And yet: what brought it about at just this moment? Here, as elsewhere, in interpreting the ancient Greeks, we must beware of Christianizing a pagan phenomenon. As Nietzsche warns in "Homer's Contest" and other writings, our modern prejudices may get in the way of our understanding ancient phenomena such as Greek competitiveness. The language of learning a moral lesson may be anachronistic in analyzing the world of Homer. Are we saying that, by the end of the *Iliad,* Achilles has undergone a character transformation and truly become a man of peace? That he has learned his lesson and will never kill a fellow human being again? This reading seems more appropriate to a nineteenth-century novel than a pre-Christian epic. We know from what survives of the ancient Greek epic cycle beyond Homer that the events at the end of the *Iliad* did not bring Achilles' career as a superhuman warrior to a close.[13] His raging *thumos* was to flare up again in further battles; only his death could bring his warlike behavior truly to an end.

Here is where an analogy from the world of athletics may help us understand the *Iliad.* When athletes cool down after the heat of competition, the reason is not that they have learned a moral lesson about the dangers of overexerting themselves; the reason is that they have expended a tremendous amount of energy and are exhausted. This is the pattern of athletic competition: athletes must build up, mentally as well as physically, to their big events, and then they must give their all at the moment of competition. "I left it all in the pool," Michael Phelps kept saying in the interviews he gave after his Achilles-like triumphs at the Beijing Olympics in 2008. It is obvious that athletes are physically exhausted after their great victories, but anyone who really knows sports is aware that they are mentally exhausted as well. *Thumos* is the point where the mental and the physical intersect, and that is why it is the key to understanding athletics, to realizing that it involves the soul as well as the body. The ancient Greeks located *thumos* physically in the body—in the guts—but they also knew that it has what we would call a mental component. *Thumos* is one of the words Homer uses in places where we would say "mind." In building up to their big events, the great athletes are building up the *thumos* in their souls. That combination of competitiveness, pride, aggressiveness, and even anger is what fuels their best efforts. That explains why many athletes, in the weeks or months leading up to a big event, carry around a photo or some other reminder of their chief competitor. They are psyching themselves up for the contest, building up their anger, their pride, their *thumos*.

The ancient Greeks had a kind of "hydraulic" understanding of *thumos*, as a sort of fluid that builds up pressure in the soul.[14] Here is how Socrates characterizes the power of *thumos* in the case of righteous indignation: "and what about when a man believes he's being done injustice? Doesn't his spirit in this case boil and become harsh and form an alliance for battle?"[15] This image of *thumos* boiling captures something essential in the ancient Greek understanding of the phenomenon—the sense of an energy building up that needs to be discharged and that may explode when it is finally released. We share this conception today when we talk about athletes "blowing off steam" in the heat of the contest. If *thumos* is what fuels athletic competition, then we can picture it in three stages: (1) the calm buildup of *thumos* before the event; (2) the stormy release of all the pent-up *thumos* in the heat of competition; (3) the calm after the storm once all the *thumos* has been discharged.[16]

The athletic pattern of "calm before the storm–storm–calm after the storm" fits the story of Achilles in the *Iliad* very well. When Achilles indignantly withdraws from battle, he imposes upon himself what for him is an unnatural regime of inactivity. He is a man who lives for warfare and is used to expending *thumos* on a daily basis, warring with opponents and getting what we today would call an adrenaline rush.[17] He needs warfare to satisfy his pride and his aggressiveness; he is a combat junkie. Once he ceases fighting, with no outlet for his *thumos,* pressure starts to build up in him to return to the fray. Achilles sulking in his tent is like an athlete on the sidelines itching to get back into the game. Thus once Achilles finally goes back into combat, his *thumos* explodes in a monumental rage and a murderous frenzy. His combat with Hector is the main event he and everyone else have been anticipating, just as if it were a world championship boxing match. Everything hinges on this one supreme moment of contest, and Achilles, like a great athlete, focuses all his thumotic energy on triumphing over Hector.

That Achilles should experience a kind of calm after this colossal discharge of *thumos* is only natural. In one moment of overwhelming tension, Achilles has expended all the energy, mental and physical, he had been building up in his days of inactivity.[18] Thus it is not surprising that after killing Hector, he behaves differently from the way he did before. With his great purpose accomplished and all his energy expended, he has calmed down and become disposed to listen to messages from the gods that he would have angrily dismissed just days earlier, during the buildup to his confrontation with Hector. Having satisfied his thumotic need for revenge in the most vicious and complete way possible, Achilles becomes almost a different person and can behave like a gentleman for a change. To press our athletic analogy further: think of the peculiar pattern of behavior characteristic of boxers, especially champions and contenders. Leading up to their big fight, two boxers will "bad-mouth" and "trash talk" each other at press conferences, much the way the heroes in Homer verbally spar before their combats. With boxers today, much of this behavior is for the benefit of the television camera, and is clearly part of a publicity campaign designed to sell tickets. But at least some of this animosity is real, and when a fight breaks out between boxers at a ceremonial weigh-in, it is not always fake. Boxers really do have to work up hate for each other before their confrontation in the ring, and once their fight begins, their savagery in attacking each other can become frightening. And yet, in many big boxing contests, a seeming miracle occurs when the final bell rings. Two men who looked as if they were trying to kill each other for twelve rounds suddenly embrace and hug. From being the worst of enemies, they suddenly appear to become the best of friends. Having discharged their *thumos* in the most direct way possible, the boxers can start behaving like ordinary, decent human beings again and no longer like savage warriors. The same logic governs Achilles' treatment of Priam and his ability to reach out to a man who is his enemy.

To carry our athletic analogy even further: Think of the typical victorious athlete in a post-fight or post-game interview: "I'm going to take a few days off, just relax, enjoy the moment." But when athletes speak this way, it does not mean that they are ready for retirement. They are not expressing a lesson they have learned that athletic competition is not really for them. On the contrary, the typical athlete enjoys the warm afterglow of a great victory for a while, but sooner or later longs to reenter the ring or the stadium.[19] Similarly in the case of Achilles, even as he appears to be reconciled with Priam, he calls for what amounts to only a cease-fire, not a full-scale end to warfare between Greeks and Trojans. An undercurrent of hostility runs beneath his dialogue with Priam; he feels he needs to remind the suppliant king of what might happen if his *thumos* were aroused and his anger flared up again: "So don't anger me now. Don't stir my raging heart still more. / Or under my own roof I may not spare your life, old man."[20] Clearly in Book XXIV Achilles is already thinking of returning to the battlefield. Given his thumotic nature, he has no choice.

We hope that no one will think that we are making light of Homer and the *Iliad* by suggesting this kind of athletic analogy for the story of Achilles. The ancient Greeks took their athletic competitions very seriously, and treated their victorious athletes as heroes just the way they did their victorious generals. Thus to speak of Achilles in athletic terms is not to belittle or make fun of him. Nor is it to reject completely the lesson about common humanity that many interpreters would like to read out of the *Iliad*. One can question whether Achilles really learns a moral lesson in the course of the poem without denying that the poem as a whole embodies a sobering teaching about humanity and the need to control *thumos*. The ancient Greeks, from Homer to Plato, thought of what they called *thumos* as an essential part of human nature. That Achilles' conduct in the *Iliad* can be explained in terms of the working out of *thumos* in his soul is thus in ancient Greek terms a lesson in humanity.

The way athletics takes on increasing importance toward the end of the *Iliad* is evidence for this understanding of Achilles. In its grand architectonic pattern, the poem begins with *thumos* at work in an army camp and concludes with *thumos* at work on an athletic field. Opening with the quarrel between Achilles and Agamemnon, the *Iliad* shows *thumos* at its most divisive. Forced to give up his own concubine, Agamemnon decides to take Achilles' concubine Briseis as recompense. The problem is that Briseis was a prize of war for Achilles. He becomes enraged at Agamemnon, not because he deeply desires Briseis or profoundly cares for her, but because she is a badge of his honor, his triumph as a warrior.[21] Above all, he begrudges relinquishing her to Agamemnon, which would be a sign of his inferiority to him. The affront to his honor is so great that Achilles is on the verge of killing Agamemnon on the spot—only the intervention of the goddess Athena prevents this violent outcome. Still, this quarrel, as we have seen, leads to all the carnage in the *Iliad*. Once the *thumos* of the Greek and Trojan warriors is released and set in motion, they kill each other with enthusiasm and a kind of joy in the competition. Only when the display of thumotic aggressiveness culminates in the spectacular confrontation of Hector and Achilles are the warriors ready for a brief cessation of hostilities and a little rest and recreation.

Accordingly, Homer devotes Book XXIII of the *Iliad* to the funeral games Achilles ordains to commemorate the death and burial of Patroclus. These athletic contests are a remarkable anticipation of the ancient Olympic Games. They include many of the classic Olympic events: chariot racing, boxing, wrestling, foot racing, and javelin throwing.[22] Many of the institutions of formal athletic competition are already in place in Homer's account. A race course has been laid out, umpires or referees are on the scene, some rules of competition are in effect, prizes have been set up. There is even some coaching and the possibility of cheating. Virtually every element of athletic competition as we know it today comes up in the *Iliad*, including betting on the outcomes. Perhaps all that is missing is product endorsements by the victors (if they happen to cry "Nike" when they win, that is *not* a brand name, but simply the Greek word for "victory"). It says something about the centrality of the Olympics in ancient Greek culture that, already in its foundational poem, we see such a detailed blueprint for what was to become Olympic competition. If Homer was the teacher of the Greeks, then one thing he taught them was the need for the Olympics to channel *thumos* away from the deadly combat of war.

Already in the *Iliad,* Homer offers athletic competition as an alternative to war, a different way of expending *thumos.* We see all the aspects of thumotic behavior in the funeral games—the overwhelming desire to be first, the aggressiveness of the competitors, their pride in victory, their bitter shame and anger in defeat.[23] Even in what is supposed to be the alternative to deadly combat (and part of a religious rite), the Greeks apparently cannot help risking their lives to be first. The chariot racers behave like NASCAR drivers today. At the risk of crashing, they push their vehicles to their limits of performance, and jockey dangerously for the most advantageous positions on the turns. Even the spectators get so caught up in the excitement of the competition that Ajax and Idomeneus feel that they must place bets and are on the verge of coming to blows when Achilles intervenes to calm them down.

Achilles' role in the funeral games is especially instructive. In the calm that has descended upon him in the aftermath of his overwhelming and deeply satisfying defeat of Hector, Achilles has made a deliberate and seemingly uncharacteristic decision not to compete. Still, he cannot help pointing out that if he were to do so, "surely I'd walk off to my tent with first prize."[24] But because Achilles is not competing, his *thumos* is not engaged, and he can play the unfamiliar role of mediator in the disputes that arise between the intensely competitive participants in the games. He very diplomatically settles conflicts over such contentious issues as order of finish, and even manages to juggle the prizes to satisfy contestants who feel they have been cheated or slighted.[25] Achilles invents what we would call consolation prizes, and thereby reveals what distinguishes athletics from warfare. There are no consolation prizes on the battlefield. Indeed Homer presents military combat as the classic zero-sum game. Typically in the *Iliad,* the result of combat is that one hero lives and the other dies. The Homeric epic is the ultimate example of the principle that the last man standing wins. As the Achillean American general Douglas MacArthur said in his famous Farewell Address to Congress on April 19, 1951: "In war there is no substitute for victory."

The principle of "no substitutes" is what created the original problem between Achilles and Agamemnon. Agamemnon could offer no replacement for Briseis in Achilles' eyes because what was at stake between them was not an object for which something else could substitute but rather a pure matter of honor. It is therefore significant that in the funeral games, the Greek heroes are willing to accept substitutes for the prizes they initially believe they deserve; they are actually willing to settle for second prize or even lower.[26] Perhaps most significant of all is the way Achilles chooses to treat Agamemnon in the funeral games. He speaks to him courteously and makes sure that the great king is honored without even having to compete. The way both Achilles and Agamemnon are generous with giving away prizes at the end of Book XXIII contrasts sharply with their behavior in Book I, where their proud clinging to their possessions provokes their disastrous argument. The contrast between Book I and Book XXIII in this respect must be deliberate. In the funeral games, we can see Homer's hope that the volatile force of *thumos* might somehow be moderated among the fiercely competitive Greeks, by channeling it into athletic competition. And yet the way Homer's Greeks compete furiously even on the athletic field, and the way that, even in play, their contentiousness almost leads to deadly results, reminds us how powerful and dangerous the force of *thumos* was in the ancient Greek world.

We normally think of philosophy and athletics as occupying opposite ends of the spectrum of human activity, with the former exercising the mind and the latter the body. But as we have seen in examining texts by Nietzsche, Plato, and Homer, philosophy and athletics have much in common and much to teach each other. The Greek concept of *thumos,* most fully articulated in Plato but already present in Homer, reveals an aspect of human nature in which the mind and the body intersect, and which therefore can manifest itself in both philosophy and athletics. We have seen that Plato's philosophic discussion of *thumos* can help us understand the competitive spirit that motivates athletes. By the same token, as Nietzsche shows, athletic competition provides a useful model for what occurs when philosophers enter into spirited dialogue with each other. As we saw in Homer's *Iliad,* from the earliest moments we can observe in Greek culture, concern with athletic competition is bound up with larger concerns about the human condition. The kinds of athletic competition we associate with the ancient Olympic Games were already being played out in Homer's imagination on the plains of Troy. As Nietzsche, Plato, and Homer show, the competitive spirit, the *thumos,* that animated the Olympics pervaded the whole of the ancient Greek world.

# Notes

The epigraph is from *The Portable Nietzsche,* Walter Kaufmann, ed. and trans. (New York: Viking, 1954), 37.

1. *Nietzsche,* 37–38. On the pervasiveness of competition in ancient Greek culture, see John J. Hermann Jr. and Christine Kondoleon, *Games for the Gods: The Greek Athlete and the Olympic Spirit* (Boston: MFA Publications, 2004), 145, and M. I. Finley and H. W. Pleket, *The Olympic Games: The First Thousand Years* (Mineola, NY: Dover, 2005), 21–22.

2. The Greek word is often transliterated into English as *thymos.* For a wide-ranging series of essays on the philosophical importance of *thumos,* see Catherine H. Zuckert, ed., *Understanding the Political Spirit: Philosophical Investigations from Socrates to Nietzsche* (New Haven: Yale University Press, 1988). For other philosophical reflections on *thumos,* see Francis Fukuyama, *The End of History and the Last Man* (New York: Free Press, 1992), 162–191, and Harvey C. Mansfield, *Manliness* (New Haven: Yale University Press, 2006), 206–208, 220–221, 228, 230–231, 236.

3. For a careful attempt to discriminate among the many meanings of *thumos* in Homer, see Julian Jaynes, *The Origin of Consciousness in the Breakdown of the Bicameral Mind* (Boston: Houghton Mifflin, 1976), 69, 258–259, 261–263, 274–275. For the archaic meaning of *thumos,* see also Bruno Snell, *The Discovery of the Mind: The Greek Origins of European Thought,* trans. T. G. Rosenmeyer (New York: Harper & Row, 1960), 8–22; Snell stresses that we must distinguish between the meaning of *thumos* in Homer (where it is a very concrete term) and its meaning in later Greek literature, such as Plato (where the term becomes more abstract). On the meaning of *thumos* specifically in Homer, see also James M. Redfield, *Nature and Culture in the Iliad: The Tragedy of Hector* (Durham, NC: Duke University Press, 1994), 171–179.

4. In fact, in the *Republic,* Plato uses the even stranger word *thumoeides* ("thumos-formed") in addition to the more normal Greek word *thumos.* For the use of the words *thumos* and *thumoeides* in the *Republic* and throughout Plato's dialogues, see Leon Craig, *The War Lover: A Study of Plato's Republic* (Toronto: University of Toronto Press, 1994), 96 and 381–383, note 10. This book is one of the most thorough and insightful studies of the importance of *thumos* in the *Republic* and specifically relates it to athletics on 66–67.

5. Jaynes, *Origin of Consciousness,* 263.

6. As difficult as it may be to believe, this full range of meanings is indeed comprehended under the Greek word *thumos.* Here is a partial listing of the translations of *thumos* in the authoritative Liddell and Scott Greek-English lexicon: the soul, breath, life, spirit, heart, mind, the seat of sorrow or joy, temper, will, courage, the seat of anger, wrath (*An Intermediate Greek-English Lexicon* [Oxford, UK: Clarendon Press, 1889], 371).

7. On the connection between gymnastics and philosophy, see Craig, *War Lover*, 72–73.

8. Allan Bloom, ed. and trans., *The Republic of Plato* (New York: Basic Books, 1968), 119–120 (440b,e in the standard Stephanus numbering of Plato's dialogues).

9. Ibid., 120 (441a).

10. For detailed analysis of the dramatic action of the *Republic,* see Leo Strauss, *The City and Man* (Chicago: Rand McNally, 1964), 50–138, and the "Interpretive Essay" in Bloom, *Republic,* 307–436. For the specific issue of *thumos,* the problem of educating the guardians, and Socrates' relation to Glaucon and Adeimantus, see Strauss, *City and Man,* 85–112, and Bloom, *Republic,* 337–343, 348–365, 375–378.

11. For a systematic analysis of the connection between *thumos* and philosophy in the *Republic,* see Craig, *War Lover.* For a different view of the subject, see Mary P. Nichols, "Spiritedness and Philosophy in Plato's *Republic,*" in Zuckert, *Political Spirit,* 48–66.

12. See, for example, what Bernard Knox says of this scene in his introduction to Robert Fagles's translation of the *Iliad:* "This is a new Achilles, who can feel pity for others, see deep into their hearts and into his own. For the first time, he shows self-knowledge and acts to prevent the calamity his violent temper might bring about. It is as near to self-criticism as he ever gets, but it marks the point at which he ceases to be godlike Achilles and becomes a human being in the full sense of the word. . . . It is an admission of mortality, of limitations, of the bond that unites him to Priam, and all men" (Homer, *The Iliad,* trans. Robert Fagles [New York: Penguin, 1990], 60–61). See also Redfield's comment on this scene: "At this point Achilles . . . becomes himself a moralist" (*Nature and Culture,* 217; see also 215–216). On this point, see also Arlene W. Saxonhouse, "*Thymos,* Justice, and Moderation of Anger in the Story of Achilles," in Zuckert, *Political Spirit,* 44. This essay is one of the best treatments of the role of *thumos* in the *Iliad.*

13. In the epic cycle, Homer's *Iliad* was followed by the *Aethiopis,* traditionally ascribed to Arctinus of Miletus. This poem evidently carried the story of the Trojan War through the death of Achilles up to the quarrel between Odysseus and Ajax over the arms of Achilles, which resulted in Ajax's suicide. In the course of the *Aethiopis,* Achilles once again goes on a rampage: he kills the Amazon warrior Penthesilea, as well as the scurrilous Thersites within the Greek camp, and is finally himself killed by Paris with the aid of Apollo in the course of his attempt to assault Troy to avenge the death of Antilochus (an episode that appears to recapitulate his avenging of Patroclus). Of course none of this legendary material is presented within the *Iliad,* but Homer was undoubtedly aware of at least some of it. At a minimum, he registers throughout the *Iliad* his awareness that Achilles was soon going to die in battle. For what we know of the *Aethiopis,* see Hugh G. Evelyn-White, ed. and trans., *Hesiod, The Homeric Hymns and Homerica* (Cambridge, MA: Harvard University Press, 1914), 506–509. For an imaginative attempt to retell these legends (nevertheless grounded in the ancient sources), see Gustav Schwab, *Gods and Heroes of Ancient Greece,* trans. Olga Marx and Ernst Morowitz (New York: Random House, 1974), 498–529.

14. Redfield makes the point this way: "*thumos* is not an organ; rather, it is a substance which fills an organ, namely, the *phrenes*" (Redfield, *Nature and Culture*, 173; *phrenes* is another Greek word meaning "mind," from which we get words like *phrenology*; in Homer, as Redfield points out, the *phrenes* is identified with the lungs and the *thumos* with the breath that fills the lungs).

15. Bloom, *Republic*, 120 (440c). The image of boiling is in the original Greek.

16. Redfield develops a similar understanding of another key term in the *Iliad*—*cholos*, the word that is used to describe Achilles' "rage." Redfield characterizes *cholos* as a force that builds up and then must be discharged: "*Cholos* is a whole-body reaction, the adrenal surge which drives men to violent speech and action. . . . There are two ways of dealing with *cholos*. It can be poured into violent action and in that way 'healed' (IV.36). Or it can be 'digested' (I.81; cf. IX.565); in the course of time the body will consume the *cholos* and the man will be calm again" (*Nature and Culture*, 14–15; Redfield's book/line references are to the original Greek text of the *Iliad*).

17. For the "physiology" of *thumos* and its association with adrenaline, see Jaynes, *Origins of Consciousness*, 262: "*Thumos* then refers to a mass of internal sensations in response to environmental crises. It was, I suggest, a pattern of stimulation familiar to modern physiology, the so-called stress or emergency response of the sympathetic nervous system and its liberation of adrenalin[e] and noradrenalin[e] from the adrenal glands. This includes the dilation of the blood vessels in striate muscles and in the heart, an increase in tremor of striate muscles, a burst of blood pressure, the constriction of blood vessels in the abdominal viscera and in the skin, the relaxing of smooth muscles, and the sudden increased energy from the sugar released into the blood from the liver, and possible perceptual changes with the dilation of the pupil of the eye. This complex was, then, the internal pattern of sensation that preceded particularly violent activity in a critical situation. And by doing so repeatedly, the pattern of sensation begins to take on the term for the activity itself. Thereafer, it is the *thumos* which gives strength to a warrior in battle, etc. All the references to *thumos* in the *Iliad* as an internal sensation are consistent with this interpretation." Since Jaynes is talking about Homer here, he is referring to activity in warfare, but the physiological responses he describes are equally involved in athletic exertion. For a simultaneously mythological and physiological view of Greek athletics, see Hermann and Kondoleon, *Games for the Gods*, 22: "Divine intervention was considered a major factor in the outcome of athletic contests. In Homer, gods give extra rushes of adrenaline to their favorites."

18. For Achilles' exhaustion after his battle with Hector, see Homer, *Iliad*, 23: 11. 74–75: "his powerful frame was bone-weary from charging Hector / straight and hard to the walls of windswept Troy" (Achilles' *thumos* is mentioned in the preceding line in the Greek: 23, 1. 62). On Achilles' exhaustion, see also Homer, *Iliad*, 23: 11. 266—he "sank down, exhausted. Sweet sleep overwhelmed him." We quote the *Iliad* in English from Fagles's translation (cited in note 12), and give book and line numbers. Since these line numbers differ in the original, when we cite the Greek text, we are

referring to the Loeb Classical Library edition, *Homer: Iliad*, 2nd ed., trans. A. T. Murray, rev. William F. Wyatt (Cambridge, MA: Harvard University Press, 1999).

19. This change in mood after athletic competition may not simply be a mental phenomenon; it apparently has a physiological component. The idea that strenuous physical exertion can by itself produce a feeling of contentment is embodied in the common expression "runner's high." Recent medical studies have uncovered and documented a physiological basis for this well-known feeling. Strenuous exercise evidently leads the body to release its natural opiates, endorphins, into the bloodstream, thus producing a general feeling of well-being. This research was carried out at the Technische Universität München and the University of Bonn and is reported in the journal *Cerebral Cortex* 18 (November 2008): 2523–2531, in a paper entitled "The Runner's High: Opioidergic Mechanisms in the Human Brain." For popular accounts of this research, see Gina Kolata, "Yes, Running Can Make You High," *New York Times*, March 27, 2008, and "Runners' High Demonstrated: Brain Imaging Shows Release of Endorphins In Brain," *Science Daily*, March 6, 2008. Achilles' famous change of mood at the end of the *Iliad* may thus be the result of his extraordinary physical exertion in chasing down Hector around the walls of Troy. It is, after all, not improbable that "swift-footed" Achilles might provide the all-time greatest example of runner's high.

20. Homer, *Iliad*, 24: 11. 667–678. On this point, see Saxonhouse, "*Thymos*," 43. Where Fagles translates "heart" in this passage, Homer's original Greek is in fact *thumos* (24: 1. 568 in the Greek).

21. But see Saxonhouse, "*Thymos*," 36, for the puzzling moment when Achilles refers to Briseis as his "wife" (*alochon*) at IX: 1. 336 in the Greek.

22. For a list of the events at the ancient Olympics, see Finley and Pleket, *Olympic Games*, 43. For the relation of the *Iliad* to the Olympics, see 19–20.

23. See Homer's description of the participants in the chariot race: "the heart of each man raced, / straining for victory" (*Iliad*, 23: 11. 418–419). The word Fagles translates as "heart" is *thumos* in the Greek (23: 1. 370).

24. Homer, *Iliad*, 23: 1. 316.

25. See Saxonhouse, "*Thymos*," 40.

26. See Redfield, *Nature and Culture*, 209, where he says of the funeral games: "The competition is not zero sum." Redfield provides a very thorough and illuminating discussion of the funeral games in general, 204–210. In contrast to the athletic competition in the *Iliad*, "only first place counted at the ancient Olympics . . . ; second- and third-place finishers were just losers" (Hermann and Kondoleon, *Games for the Gods*, 26). See also Finley and Pleket, *Olympic Games*, 22.

*Jesús Ilundáin-Agurruza*

# GO TELL THE SPARTANS

## Honor, Courage, and Excellence in the Ancient Olympic Games

*Editors' Note:* The following essay intersperses comical fragments from an imagined Greek play with ancient Greek and
modern Olympic history and philosophy. The elements are linked
with spunky narration to inspire a Hellenic rethinking of the
Olympic creed and motto.

## Scouting Skirmishes

Fragments from a recently discovered ancient Greek play, *Olympia,* have
puzzled experts, who can't agree even on the genre (tragedy? comedy?
first tragicomedy?). Worse, a number of anachronisms suggest textual
corruption. Pertinent excerpts supplement our text.

*Dramatis Personae.*
Aristodemus: Spartan warrior
Brundy Average: former IOC president[1]
Nastasius: Persian sympathizer of Greek stock
Cyniska: Spartan princess
Chorus of Thespians

Location: Hades (twenty-first-century life makes it look like a
Copacabana resort). Absurdly, Brundy Average and Aristodemus strike
up a chat to kill time where eternity is but the beginning of an endless
supply of ennui.

*Brundy Average* ("Average" hereafter): Greetings, my good fellow. Very pleased to meet—

*Aristodemus:* Pleasure or chagrin, that's to be seen. Aristodemus. Roughly "best of the people" in your barbarian language. The gods know I tried to live up to it.

*Average:* How Greek of you! The tragic counterpoint where the human hopelessly pursues the unattainable. That French tart Camus was enamored of such absurd enterprises. But I wane sentimental. Honored to meet the famous Spartan general—

*Aristodemus* (cuts him off, drily): I'm the infamous *tresante*, "trembler," who shamefully survived Thermopylae.

*Average* (unconcerned): Oh, how sad indeed.

*Aristodemus:* And, Mr. Average, your name means—what?

*Average:* Well, it doesn't translate well. Call me Brundy.

*Aristodemus* (mischievously): I prefer to observe propriety, Mr. Average.

*Average* (curt): Fine. Let's discuss something more inspiring . . . the Olympics?

To begin without a warm-up: What *should* Olympism, the theoretical framework of the movement, be about philosophically? Intellectual sprinters may single out Baron Pierre de Coubertin's iconic Olympic motto: *Citius, altius, fortius* (swifter, higher, stronger), and the popular (with condescending winners and consolable whiners) Olympic creed: "The most important thing in the Olympic Games is not to win but to take part. . . ." Such swift answers, lacking understanding, unerringly trip. A philosopher's long-distance-thinking gait reveals the tension between the former slogan's record-driven ethos and the second's cheerfulness. To those impatient who mock slow-poked philosophers, I offer four words: Achilles versus the Tortoise. Today's Olympic ideals show more wear and tear than Athens' Parthenon, and we know what that looks like. Here we tour the Greek world for alternative ideals to restore the Olympic Movement's worn-out conceptual architecture, beset by the modern challenges that Average conveniently presents.

*Average:* See, the Olympics are plagued by evils you wouldn't have tolerated any more than a barbarian at a symposium back in the day: an unhealthy obsession with records, fame, and money, dubious performance-enhancing means, cheating, a consumerist circus where *everything* is for sale, rampant nationalism, Eurocentric ideals, unsustainable development, environmental issues. Appalling!

*Cyniska:* Gentlemen—some of you anyway. Don't forget women, whose Olympic aspirations have faced obstacles you'd be unable or unwilling to leap! I could win my medal only by sponsoring a chariot. Sure, it was common practice: Alcibiades entered seven chariots to win his! But I'd have kicked any male charioteers' butt—

*Nastasius* (rudely cuts in): So melodramatic! Nastasius, call me *Naste*—

*Chorus* (drowning Naste's voice): Swifter, higher, stronger. What'd you do to run faster than Apollo, soar higher than Athena, and wrestle down Heracles?

## Olympic Clash at the Hot Gates

In 480 BCE a Persian army threatened ancient Greece—its numbers being more disputed than Wall Street's ledgers, let's just say it was huge. Herodotus tells how the Persians were baffled when only 7,000 Greeks showed up to fight, then amazed to learn the small numbers were due to the celebration of the Olympic festival, and finally thunderstruck when told the prize was a wreath of olive leaves. What topped this was learning, as Herodotus's *Histories* recounts of the Spartans, that on the eve of the battle, when they expected to be creamed and pureed, "some of them were stripped for exercise, while others were combing their hair. The Persian spy watched them in astonishment. . . . Xerxes was bewildered" (489).

Indeed, what sort of men were the ancient Greeks who, *supposedly* just for honor and the sake of a festival, Olympic or not, risked being conquered and sent thousands of men, many amazingly nonchalant, to their death? A suitably scorching question. This is the stuff of legend, or madness—or both. We can learn much from people with such bizarre (to our "civilized" eyes) behavior.

Herodotus's words intimate several things. As Paul Cartledge explains, Xerxes thought that warriors tending to their hair like vain women weren't worth worrying about. The Mede ruler pictured a bunch of sissies who, the moment they broke a nail, would drop their weapons and run away screaming. Moreover, their actions also bespoke men ready to die for their ideals, something utterly unfathomable to the king (Cartledge, 209). To tie this analysis to the Olympic motif, it's striking that those who weren't preoccupied with coiffing their long, gorgeous locks were exercising—naked, of course.[2]

To put ourselves in their sandals (loinclothed if self-conscious): if we knew that we wouldn't survive tomorrow's fight, what do we choose to do? Exercise?! Getting in one last workout doesn't fit most normal people's agenda today. Spartans weren't oddballs in their cultural context. What follows reveals why exercise and competition were so intrinsically important for them.

Continuing with our cross-cultural impersonation and comparison, imagine delaying our country's defense from imminent invasion because of a festival. Inconceivable! Well, unless this coincided with an *American Idol* final (what this says about us is better left alone). Strategically, stalling allowed events to play out before making a move either for or against Persia. But Athens and Sparta's jockeying doesn't discount the credibility of the reason not to muster the army: the Games had to be the sort of event that could be preferred to homeland defense. Stephen Miller, in his book *Ancient Greek Athletics*, writes, "that these games went on as Athens was burning tells us much about the position of athletics in Greek society" (4). Ironically, Miller proceeds to say virtually nothing about this. The rest of this chapter will.

Shielded by our shiny new *hoplon* (Greek shield), let's pass through the Hot Gates (Thermopylae) to find out.[3] Three critically engaged citations from Herodotus anchor the narrative, one for each day the Greeks fought off the Persian onslaught. We just encountered the first. Two themes run this mercifully "less-than-Marathonian" course: a triad of virtues and their role in Greek life and athletics, and the insights this virtuous athletic mélange affords on the spirit that fought at Thermopylae and vice versa. Fittingly, this narrative ends with one cryptic message from the Oracle.

Straining as we are with the *hoplon*'s twenty pounds—we're definitely not Spartan material—let's set it down to reflect and illuminate how ancient Greece may inspire a new Olympic creed and motto. Once again, almost 2500 years after fighting the Persians at Thermopylae, Spartan king Leonidas and his warriors come to our rescue here.

## Tragic Drama Queens

Tough as they were, ancient Greeks were drama queens: they embraced a tragic sense of life, to echo Miguel de Unamuno's coinage. The bellicose age they helped to create promoted this outlook: fight the Myrmidons on Monday, battle the Thracians on Thursday, if still alive brawl on Sunday with the Smyrnians, and monthly mess with the Medes. Besides, an irrational world and godly fickleness wrested control from their hands: fickle fate struck rich and poor, good and bad alike. They fought this uncertainty with a reasoned principle *(logos)*, the charms of art, and athletic brawn. Armed with these, they actually relished life.

Unlike Unamunian broodiness, the Greeks' sunny temperament balanced the calamitous with the "keenest appetite for activity of all kinds—physical, mental, emotional; a never-ending delight in doing things and in seeing how they were done" (Kitto, 59). Greeks reveled in exploring life, mindful of its inherent "take no prisoners" harshness from which everyone *must* exit eventually. What mattered was one's conduct before that exit: a lucid acceptance of the situation without self-help sugary coatings. To boot, they sported a keen sense of humor, as their comedies show.

Sports and the Games added richly to this ancient Greek zest for life, bringing a kind of order and satisfaction through competition and achievement. Another fragment presents this:

*Average:* I just realized! I never understood *why* you Greeks were so bloody competitive athletically.

*Cyniska:* In a world riddled with chance and divine whim, we wanted to be in charge in whatever small way we could.

*Average:* But athletics is fraught with chance and luck at its most interesting.

*Aristodemus:* Rational conditions for competition, without external elements influencing the event, meant champions were determined objectively (Miller, *Ancient Greek Athletics*, 43). We wanted champs, not chumps.

*Naste:* Pfft! Many other contests—team competitions, musical events in non-Olympic festivals, chariot races—lacked such objectivity.

*Aristodemus:* Those didn't exemplify *aretē.*

*Cyniska:* In athletic competitions it was a matter of who was stronger, faster, quicker on the day. *Aretē* and objectivity were feasible, if only for a moment.

*Average:* Lots of pain endured and energy spent in pursuit of *aretē* . . .

*Naste:* Zeus! I'm Greek, but I don't get this *aretē* business.

For a tragic fate look no further than mythological Sisyphus, condemned by the gods to absurdly push a rock for eternity—he's shoving it over there. Incongruously, Albert Camus concludes that "one must imagine Sisyphus happy" because of his lucid hubris (123). Athletic effort—the Olympics as its paragon—allows for the construction of a more tantalizing possibility.

## No Pain, No Gain

The dawn of the Olympic Games (their 776 BCE date is more disputed than the 2000 U.S. elections) coincides with the start of a period of spectacular flourishing in Greece at all levels: artistic, political, economic, military, and indeed sporting. This coalesced into a sense of Greekness that saw its apogee in Pericles' Athens. Some may sneeringly compare Ancient and Modern Games: the former were a provincial affair among city-states with a handful of events and "crowds" a few thousands strong, whereas the gargantuan Beijing Games in 2008, for example, were followed by billions and involved 11,000 athletes from 200 countries. True, but this smugness will go once we see how meaningful athletics were for the average ancient Greek.

Competition quickly pushed its way to the fore of Greek cultural traits. To understate it, ancient Greeks were the most competitive bunch on earth, *ever.* They devised all sorts of events to see who was best. Preferably such that rivals would be embarrassed, say by besmirching their name in memorable couplets coined to that effect. It was all about agony. *Agōn,* competition, comes from *agora,* "a meeting or assembly, [which] came to refer to an assembly to watch games" (Miller, *Ancient Greek Athletics,* 13). Whoever coined the slogan "No pain, no gain" surely had Greek blood. *Nikē,* victory, is a triumph predicated on suffering. With plenty of hurt to go around, Nike's "Just do it" slogan is especially apt.

Despite all the pain that sports involved, asking "Were sports popular in Greece?" is like asking "Are koalas cute?" As Miller puts it, "The games run hand-in-hand with Greek cultural development" (*Ancient Greek Athletics,* 4). Athletics and the Olympics were an integral part of Greeks' identity as Greeks. Our athletic debt to Hellas is patent. Sure, many current sporting values emigrated from the British Isles, but to skip the foggy lands of Albion and Hibernia for the sun and surf: Greece had a "calendar" bursting to the brim with hundreds of athletic events. Even the smallest *polis* (city-state) had one or more religious festivals where athletic competition was the fun part. Let's shatter some myths.

*Average:* The scourge I fought all my life, professionalism, began all Olympic evils. It undercuts aristocratic amateur values. Greece competed for the love of the game!

*Cyniska:* David Young, a scholar I just met—fine chap—says your IOC presidential agenda polarized the debate, promoting a myth of class-based amateurism (76ff.), whereas in our time you'd be hard pressed to find evidence of amateurism (147–148).

*Naste:* Old man, you're disarmingly gullible. Greek athletes weren't amateurs. Ask our friend the trembler here! (Moves at a safe distance.)

*Aristodemus:* The word *athlete* comes from *athleon,* to contend for a prize; *athlon* means "prize" or "reward." To contend in games is a secondary meaning. Nuff said.

*Naste:* Always so damn pithy, Ari. In the crown games—Olympic, Isthmian, Delphic, Nemean—manifest prizes were different kinds of wreaths, but winners received juicy rewards. Like free meals for life at their city's expense.

*Cyniska:* And with so many festivals and increasing appreciation for athleticism, many could train full-time, making a plush living in the "sports circuit" [equivalent to hundreds of thousands of today's dollars].

*Naste:* If that's not professionalism, Zeus thunderclap . . . Smite me!
(A loud clap is heard—Aristodemus slapping Naste's nape.)

*Aristodemus:* I cleared my name by dying first at Plataea after sending many Persians to Hades.

*Average:* Gardiner and other scholars support the idea of Victorian-type amateurism. So, there!

*Cyniska:* Speaking of scholars, Pleket was closer to the truth, as Young argues (148). Your social elitism equates amateurism with gentlemanly birth status, and professionalism with having to work for a living, Sir.

(Tense silence.)

To wrap this up like a Greek boxer's leather-bound fist (or a gyro, your pick): fans of amateurism would object to Greek athletics' princely rewards. We can defend amateurism, but not claim that the Ancient Games validate it. A better way lies with a noninstrumental interest in activities, as we'll see.

*Agōn* revalues athletic victory because it goes beyond mere gloating over vanquished opponents. It brings honor, the aspiration to excel, and the valor to endure, thereby sublimating pain into joy. But ultimately, triumphs are earned at the expense of lots of physical, intellectual, and emotional energy, an expenditure that must be fed well.

## The Ancient Greek Diet

In Herodotus's *Histories* (508), one of Xerxes' generals exclaims, "Good heavens . . . what kind of men are these you have brought us to fight against—men who compete with one another for no material reward, but only for honour!" (royally pissing off his king). In the original text, "honor" is a declination of "*aretē,*" a direct passage into our argument.

Gastronomically, ancient Greek cuisine deliciously exhibits the virtues of a healthy Mediterranean diet. Ethically, their fare was no less wholesome and more awesome. To sample Aristotle's outstanding moral recipes: his concept of virtue ethics is built on finding the mean. For example, the virtue of courage lies between recklessness (an excess of courage) and cowardliness (a deficiency of courage)—and both extremes can be vices for a particular person under certain circumstances. One develops the right character through habit and good judgment.

Virtue ethics has *eudaimonia* as its bull's-eye (don't cross champion marksman Aristotle on this).[4] Oft equated with happiness, *eudaimonia* transcends it. Is there more to life than happiness? If your idea of a good diet is fast food, stick with it. But life offers healthier, tastier treats. *Eudaimonia* nurtures a wholesome, flourishing life where excellence and well-being are vital. Its goal is to live the best possible life. This idea is very Greek: they thought, with no little hubris, that they had indeed "found the best way to live," as Hellenophile H. D. F. Kitto avows (11). We'll chew on three delicious complementary ingredients of this virtuous diet: *aretē, andreia,* and *kalon.*

*Aretē.* Excellence, virtue, skill, prowess, valor, nobility . . . and more we fail to convey, as Stephen Miller ruefully avows (*Aretē,* ix). *Aretē* drove Greeks madder with excitement than dropping a bucket of blood amid famished sharks. The U.S. Army's slogan "Be all that you can be" is the pessimist's low-expectations version. The Greeks put their whole being on the line, seeking personal distinction and excellence all around: athletics, politics, arts, warfare, business. It involved desert, what one has rightfully earned (it might mean a tasty dessert too). Helping others, battlefield feats, or outfighting a wrestler were not done simply to succor, impress, or beat others, but out of a sense of duty to oneself: to realize one's best. *Aretē* gave the Greeks their reason for being. The Thebans, Thespians, and Spartans who died at Thermopylae exhibited *aretē* to the man.[5] *Aretē* also has a dark side, which we'll explore below.

*Andreia.* Courage—literally "manliness." These were definitely macho times. Given their busy battlefield agenda, *andreia* was critical for the Greeks. To get a fuller taste:

*Naste* (sarcastic): You *must* be an expert in courage, Ari. Care to elaborate?

*Aristodemus:* Even the village idiot—you fit the bill—could see courage's usefulness for war: survival of self, kin, our way of life depended on one's companions holding hoplite formation.

*Average* (conciliatory): It'd also handily fulfill one's *aretē* on and off the athletic field. To paraphrase my academic bane, Young, one needed to be fearless to risk all in athletic contests, dear (174).

*Cyniska:* Men weren't the only ones embodying courage. My pal, Princess Artemisia, her countryman Herodotus tells, commanded a ship on the Persian side at Salamis. Xerxes himself held her counsel and valor above that of most men (522–523, 535–536). So much for testosterone!

*Aristodemus:* And not all men embraced it. Naste, here's a role model for you. Archilochos of Paros said, "Some Barbarian is flashing my shield, a perfectly good tool that I left by a bush unwilling, but likewise unwilling to face death. To hell with that shield! I can buy a new one just as good." (fragment 6, Miller, *Ancient Greek Athletics,* 3).

*Kalon.* The quality of *kalon* has to do with beauty garnished with ethical connotations. Calling actions or people *kalon* connotes the beautiful, honorable, noble. Athletes' bodies, beautiful in the density of their somatic expression as carved by repetitive motion, are the fitting vessels for actions meriting the *kalon* epithet. In the sports world this refers to honorability in competition. At the 1963 Innsbruck Winter Olympics sledding event, Italian Eugenio Monti and his teammates lent mechanical parts or expertise to other teams that would otherwise have been excluded. Both times they did this resulted in their winning a bronze instead of a gold medal. They didn't wish to win unless they beat the best (Ecenbarger, 103). True *aretē* wrapped in *andreia* and adorned by *kalon!* Shinier, worthier than gold.

Let's taste the unpalatable. Ancient Greek athletes often didn't compete *just* for honor—many reaped substantial material and social benefits; some were willing to cheat. Concerning the first unsavory issue, Homer cooks two appetizing counterpoints in the *Iliad* when Achilles quarrels with Agamemnon over sexy vestal Briseis first (he gets plenty of booty, girl included) or Antilochos later (he's got a spoon in all stews) because Antilochos deems he has earned the prize mare Achilles gives to someone else (IX 105–140; XXIII 530–585). In neither case is it about the lass or mare per se, but about the "prize" as a symbol of their *aretē:* their claim to hard-earned excellence (Antilochos gives the mare away after getting it). Epic poetry incarnates the values to which the Greeks aspired.

With regard to the insalubrious issue of cheating, violators were punished by flogging. To get in their skin and understand the significance of the punishment: it wasn't about the physical pain but the psychological humiliation. Whipping reduced Greek citizens, inordinately proud of their status as free men, to the condition of slaves (the only ones expected to cheat) or animals.

Simmering *kalon, andreia,* and *aretē* concocts an IOC legal Olympic potion that results in athletic and overall excellence through noble, beautiful performances where athletes truly take risks testing their mettle. It also makes *eudaimonia* more likely. Besides, the blend tastes great. This triad, exemplified by Leonidas's soldiers and Olympic athletes alike, gives us insight into the inspiring Greek spirit, revealing a view of life for which risking our own may well be worth it, or at least merit being memorialized with a good tragedy (times being what they are, a Hollywood blockbuster will do).

## Shield against Shield

Hoplite warfare involved two eight-rank deep or more phalanx-arranged armies brutally shoving against each other until one gave way and a rout ensued, with winners chasing losers. This modus operandi explains the small number of casualties among the winners and the carnage in the loser's camp (Warry, 37). The Persians' tactics, ill-suited for the terrain, and their less efficient weapons spelled doom in any language. But Greek martial prowess met its match when it failed to evolve. Cunning Iphicrates' reforms of hoplite accoutrement made for very mobile troops, giving an edge over the lumbering Greek phalanxes to Philip of Macedon and his badass son Alexander. The point? One must engage Greek values critically, minding contemporary needs, to avoid becoming a shish kebab. An examination of noninstrumental value and an apology for collaborative competition should do the trick.

Time to grit your teeth. Appreciating something, an activity, or someone noninstrumentally implies doing so for what or who they are. We play tennis because we enjoy hitting the ball with economical movement and precise racket handling. We still aim at achieving an end, but the emphasis is on the process. We're less likely to lie or cheat: we are invested in minding the rules of the game because they *are* the game.

Instrumentality, by contrast, tends to turn interests into means. We might play billiards, for example, to make money or boost the pool of attractive date candidates. Exaggerated instrumentalization brings a troupe of troublemakers. If the end is all that matters, it justifies all means and makes rule-breaking more probable. True appreciation of swimming rules out the use of water-scooters. Using drugs or bending the rules are scooters in disguise with a pretense to *aretē*. Making the Olympic Games about glory of country exploits sport and athletes for political ends, and encourages illegal or ethically dubious means, as with the Chinese swimmers of 2000 or the U.S. cyclists of 1984. This isn't conducive to *aretē* but to baseness: we don't find *kalon* but sordid Olympics and sports; *andreia* is supplanted by spinelessness. Still, many find the temptation irresistible: the cheats' (dis)honor roll is longer than the Great Wall.

Although noninstrumental and instrumental values can fight on the same side, the idea is to give precedence to the noninstrumental side of the formation when push comes to shove on the battlefield of human pursuits. The litmus test: will we act according to noninstrumental concerns when it costs us? *Kalon* is beautifully congruent with a noninstrumental conception of sport the way the angles of equilateral triangles are: without room for wiggle. We compete minding rules or others' interests even when we stand to lose. Japanese equestrian competitor Shunzo Kido, worried for his horse's well-being (interests don't concern humans alone), quit while leading the obstacle race at the 1932 Games (Ecenbarger, 101). At their best, sports and competition are pursued noninstrumentally.

Often, our strengths are our Achilles' heel. The ancient Greeks' agonic and aretaic approach to competition was their own accursed heel. At the Olympic Games, the marquee testing ground, while all might have exhibited *aretē*, only one person per event *fulfilled* it. The rest were losers who probably would have appreciated Prozac: they were disgraced, trodden on, and spat upon—and this from caring family and friends. Today's games follow suit with their "take no prisoners" attitude.

This agonic competitive model, ironically a "virtuous extreme," is a zero-sum game where wins are achieved at the expense of others' losses. Vince Lombardi's creed that "winning is the only thing" condones abuse and cheating. A strong interpretation of the Olympic motto, *Citius, altius, fortius,* suits this. On the other extreme, the Olympic creed at its weakest suggests a purely recreational notion of sport, where the spirit of enjoyment rules: what matters is participation. Show up for the 100-meter butterfly at the Games, then float like a cork. Win, lose, sink; it doesn't matter. Hardly inspirational, this approach is missing the drive for excellence.

The alternative? A collaborative, noninstrumental conception of competition. Collaboration means undertaking a project as a common goal. This approach integrates adversaries as essential for our own success. Since the goal is shared, cheating, (mis)using others, or humiliating those clearly not up to par undercuts our own chances of success, and this works to celebrate a victory like horseflies make for great pets. And, like an Aikido technique (only nicer), here's the pincer move: we win even if we lose because our interest isn't only or primarily victory, but engaging the activity to the best of our ability. Our focus rests on performing as well as we can. Better, we develop those skills integral to enjoying the sport, enhancing competition. If we win, we get to stand on the podium and show off the medal!

To shove harder: we must best the best at their best to claim *aretē*. Winners' victories are all the worthier *because of* the defeated athletes, as this means beating *great* opponents. Cecil Healy, in the 1912 Olympics, would have easily won the 100 freestyle had he not argued in favor of allowing the tardy U.S. team to compete; the Hawaiian Duke Kahanamoku bested him (Ecenbarger, 100). Healy understood what was best for the competition and posed a truer challenge even if it meant a loss.

This line of attack might improve today's Olympics, which, to echo Allen Guttmann's seminal work *From Ritual to Record,* have gone from ritual to record obsession (think "Phelpsmania"). The primary source of interest in Olympic events nowadays is not the pursuit of *aretē,* but an instrumental practice centered on records—results external to and removed from the competitive moment. To prophesy: today's record-craze will be the dodo of sports. Sigmund Loland argues that the very notion of athletic records is an unsustainable practice: premised on a limited system where human capacity will eventually reach its limits, it requires unlimited growth (147). Rule alteration changes the activity, making genuine comparison to previous efforts dishonest or impossible. Overcoming our limits via technologically or biologically suspect means impales itself on a pointy ethical spear. The alternative is simply to stop chasing records. This allows for interesting redefinitions of athletic competition that dispose of the sustainability issue. Cognizant of the prevailing merit and luck in sport, we can cultivate complexity and diversity in our Olympics by lengthening and shortening courses, including different surfaces, and such (Loland, 148–152).

Records are recorded, but feats are fêted—as Pindar's unforgettable odes did. Which one we favor and which we emphasize will prove fateful for Olympism and the Games. (Of course, what goes for records applies to other problems, many arising from instrumentalizing athletes, events, and the Games). We are ready to join the scrum with resolve, and kick some gluteus maximus.

## The Last Stance at Thermopylae

Herodotus's famous epitaph from Thermopylae, "Go tell the Spartans, you who read: We took their orders and here lie dead," laconically both encapsulates honor and duty to a higher cause no matter the cost and celebrates a set of values that nurtured a people who, on their last night alive, chose to either coif their hair or exercise.[6] It brings us back to that first sortie where the Spartans' behavior begged to be explained.

Behind the heroism of those who died at Thermopylae lies an enthusing conception of life: those values most worth living for are worth dying for. More important, the purest expression of this isn't found on the battlefield, but on the "sportsfield," as we'll argue with José Ortega y Gasset. His aesthetic conception of life was personified in the metaphor of the warrior or the archer because it introduced an element of danger in life that elicits a deep joy and exuberance best thought of as a sporting affair (*El sentimiento estético de la vida*, 26).

What's up with this Spartan penchant to engage in pre-demise exercise on their last night alive? Ancient Greeks cultivated the body kinesthetically: embodied movement became valued and enjoyed in the very doing. Paradoxically, it incarnated something transcendental. The Spartans' actions expressed the meaning of the present moment with the harmonious movements of their glistening bodies. Utterly poetic till the sweat splatters, then it's nasty—be forewarned. This connects with some invigorating perspectives on sport that conceive it in terms of energy spent "just because."

Living is based on our management of energy, which is a limited resource we intake, process, and spend. But even the Energizer Bunny eventually runs out of juice. In life's rhythm, from moment to moment (is there any other way to live?), we spend our energy in a tidal ebb and flow of plethoric expressions and fatigued withdrawals. Two divergent extremes sharpen our perspective: a practical, utilitarian ethos that seeks to maximize payout for one's exertions, embodied by the Persians; and a festive spirit that fritters energy away, like the Greeks, that may result in creative windfalls, or wipeouts.

Fanning the fire, Roger Callois writes: "Play is an occasion of pure waste: waste of time, energy, ingenuity, skill" (5–6). David Sansone finds that the common denominator among rituals, games, and sports lies in the squandering of energy. Accepting that one must give energy to receive energy (as in hunting) has two consequences: eventually it doesn't matter on what the energy is spent, and there is a tendency toward repetition and exaggeration (training regime, anyone?) (63). Sport is the poster boy of exuberance, and the ancient Greeks fostered it. They reveled in their festivals come what may: rain or shine, Persians or Titans.

Our three virtues support this philosophy of life. The honorably beautiful agony of sporting competition is bravely built on this, for endeavors that really matter are not "serious" business but a game, where what is most important is that it "be played as well as it may be possible" (Ortega, "Carta," 469). Sport and the Olympics excel at this. The Spartans' activities on their last night might make more sense now. And (coincidence of coincidences) Ortega explains that culture grows out of joviality, from the god Jove (Jupiter). When we play, we emulate the Olympic Jupiter (*¿Qué es filosofía?* 100). Need we say more?

Sisyphus can push his rock with hubris, as Camus says . . . or do it in the spirit of *aretē,* aware of the futility but embracing it as sport. The punishment becomes reward. And there isn't a damned thing the rancorous deities can do about it.

## The Oracle Speaks

The Greeks—*this* is bizarre—consulted the murkier-than-mud Oracle of Delphi when facing tough situations. If IOC luminaries were to ask, the following divination would be fitting: "No gold medal will hang from your neck, no olive wreath will crown you, yet you will attain victory" (Oracle of Delphi—apocryphal).[7] Its meaning is best left to sibyls. But to give it a whirl . . . it may involve *aretē, andreia,* and *kalon* collaboratively, noninstrumentally intertwining in a sportive way with that exuberant life, joyfully spent just for the heck of it.

Sports are the kind of practice that can enhance our lives. Olympism, concretely incarnated in the Olympic Games, may be a repository of values as inspiring as the stuff of legend we are wont to admire—like the actions of a bunch of warriors in a narrow pass twenty-five centuries ago, or the grimace of simultaneous ecstasy and agony on competitors' faces giving their all.

To paraphrase Camus, a lover of Greek culture: the struggle to achieve, the process itself, should be enough to fill a person's heart (123). A final fragment closes matters.

*Naste:* Humor me, Ari. Do you go to the sea for pleasure?

*Aristodemus:* Spartans weren't close enough to be a seafaring bunch. Yet I'd have fought at Salamis.

*Average* (piping in after nodding off): I'd like some of that Salami too! Where's the vittles?

*Naste* (annoyed): Old fart. I ask because the French have a proverb: "He who would go to sea for pleasure would go to hell for a pastime."

*Aristodemus:* We're at the right place, then. To cite a Frenchman—he kicks a football up and down a hill nearby: "I have always felt I lived on the high seas, threatened, at the heart of a royal happiness"(Camus, 181). Ah, Sisyphus! Defying the gods to enjoy life but for a full moment.

*Naste:* That's a loser's loser, Sissy-phus! Nothing like our tomboy Cyniska!

*Cyniska:* Get out from behind Mr. Average and I'll show you, Persian panderer!

*Aristodemus:* No need for that. He's trembling already.

*Average* (sarcastic): Shocking Mr. Naste! The epitome of *andreia, aretē, and kalon.*

## Notes

To my mother, María Agurruza-Echavarren, "Chaco." Tough, brave, disciplined like a Spartan. She thoroughly embodies the quest for *aretē*, and would integrate a "formidable badass sisterhood" alongside Cynisca, Artemisia, Atalanta, and our fearless editor Reid.

1. The name plays on Avery Brundage, former IOC president (in)famous for his adherence to a class-based elitist amateurism at odds with historical evidence.

2. Not to disappoint titillated readers by the risqué overtones, let's shed some sartorial and academic layers now. Olympic and Pythian athletes competed stark naked. Ignoring apocryphal stories about the fashion originating in a bared runner's win, this wasn't an anomaly (if sartorial absence could be a fashion at all). Gymnasia, places for cultivating mind and body, say it all with the name—*gymnos* means naked.

Besides steamy academic prospects, this exposes plenty about how ancient Greeks viewed the body: not to be shamefully covered, but nurtured and celebrated alongside mathematical, oratorical, or philosophic abilities. Moreover, it revealed one's true self to gods and others. Before Plato, the view was that mind and body were an indivisible unity. But even Plato, a once mighty wrestler who could win disputes by either reason or headlock, made much of athletics and their role in education. Heather L. Reid argues that Plato thought abilities and attitudes developed by physical exercise, such as tenacity, could transfer to philosophical and ethical pursuits (166).

3. For an unrated, longer director's cut edition see www.atisbos.com. Undaunted readers will find additional juicy excerpts, more intellectual forays, an anachronistic joke and, of course, more gore.

4. Aristotle urges us to be like archers to hit the ethical target in book I of his *Nichomachean Ethics*, p. 2.

5. This is also a redemptive text for ignored feats and tragic figures: Aristodemus, the 1000 Thespians, maybe the 700 Thebans (if they stayed willfully and not under compulsion).

6. "Laconically" is fitting: it derives from the Spartans, a.k.a. Laconians or Lacedaemonians, noted frugal speakers—as Aristodemus exemplifies.

7. The Oracle has seen better days, but with dwindling offerings and no vestal virgins, it's as good as it gets. The source of this revelation lies in an oxygen-deprived state undergone by the author after a very painful athletic contest he did not win, if you must know.

# Bibliography

Aristotle. *Nichomachean Ethics*. Trans. D. P. Chase. New York: Dover Publications, 1998.

Callois, Roger. *Man, Play and Games*. Trans. Meyer Barash. Urbana: University of Illinois Press, 2001.

Camus, Albert. *The Myth of Sisyphus*. New York: Knopf, 1958.

Cartledge, Paul. *Thermopylae: The Battle that Changed the World*. New York: Vintage, 2007.

Ecenbarger, William. "El espíritu olímpico." In *Selecciones de Reader's Digest*, July 2008. 98–105.

Guttmann, Allen. *From Ritual to Record*. New York: Columbia University Press, 2004.

Herodotus. *The Histories*. Trans. Aubery de Selincourt. London: Penguin Classics, 2003.

Homer. *The Iliad*. Perseus Digital Library. Trans. Samuel Butler. http://www.perseus. tufts.edu (accessed March 26, 2010).

———. *The Iliad*. Trans. W. H. D. Rouse. New York: Signet Classic, 1999.

Kitto, H. D. F. *The Greeks*. London: Penguin, 1954.

Loland, Sigmund. "Olympic Sport and the Idea of Sustainable Development." *Journal of the Philosophy of Sport* (2006): 144–156.

Miller, Stephen G. *Ancient Greek Athletics*. New Haven: Yale University Press, 2004.

———. *Aretē: Greek Sports from Ancient Sources*. Berkeley: University of California Press, 2004.

Ortega y Gasset, José. "Carta a un joven argentino que estudia filosofía." In *Obras Completas*. Vol. 2, 1916. Madrid: Santillana Ediciones Generales, 2004.

———. "El origen deportivo del Estado." In *Obras Completas*. Vol. 2, 1916. Madrid: Santillana Ediciones Generales, 2004.

———. *El sentimiento estético de la vida*. Ed. J. L. Molinuevo. Madrid: Editorial Tecnos S.A., 1995.

———. *¿Qué es filosofía?* Madrid: Alianza Editorial, 2001.

Reid, Heather. "Sport and Moral Education in Plato's *Republic*." *Journal of the Philosophy of Sport* 34 (2007): 160–175.

Sansone, David. *Greek Athletics and the Genesis of Sport*. Berkeley: University of California Press, 1992.

Warry, John. *Warfare in the Classical World*. Norman: University of Oklahoma Press, 1995.

Young, David C. *The Olympic Myth of Greek Amateur Athletics*. Chicago: Ares Publishers, 1984.

*Heather L. Reid*

# THE SOUL OF AN OLYMPIAN
## Olympism and the Ancient Philosophical Ideal of *Aretē*

What was it like to be an ancient Olympic athlete? A visit to the ancient stadium at Nemea, site of another Pan-Hellenic athletic festival, can help us to imagine the experience. You begin at the ruins of the *apodyterion*, literally the "undressing room," where athletes removed their clothes in preparation for their events—and a favorite setting for Socrates' spiritual undressing of Athenian youth. Like the otherworldly Greek sanctuaries themselves, the *apodyterion* was a place to shed your attachment to the mundane world of the everyday, to prepare to reveal and celebrate the higher dimensions of your humanity. Next you walk down the long stone tunnel, where ancient athletes stood in cool and quiet darkness, waiting for their names to be called. Eyeing the bright light and shimmering heat of the track outside, hearing the muffled rumblings of the crowd, it must have been a moment of deep uncertainty, a delicate spot of aloneness. Finally, your name is called, and you burst out into the light, naked both literally and metaphorically, ready to face the challenge and be tested in front of everyone: your competitors, your family, your friends and enemies; ready to submit your soul, under the brilliant Mediterranean sun, to be inspected by the gods themselves.

In a society where shame and failure were unmercifully disdained, where there were no consolations for losers or rewards for simply taking part, one has to ask: What drove a person to do this? What is that force that makes an athlete want to test himself in this way—to risk the humiliation of failure, to strive for unattainable heights? It was more than recreation, more than social custom, even more than professional obligation. It was a burning drive for excellence that transcends the practical considerations of everyday life and strives to discover what's best in humanity. It is a philosophical and humanistic force, something fundamental to the human character and, although less pervasive than it was in ancient Greek culture, it's a force that I believe is still alive today. Indeed, I will show that the drive to achieve excellence is foundational to the origin and nature of sport itself. The purpose of this chapter is to unleash that force among contemporary athletes and sports enthusiasts generally, providing us with a goal both alternative to and nobler than the prevailing sports objectives of entertainment and revenue: the goal of an Olympian soul.

It's no secret that the ideals of ancient Greece were what inspired the modern Olympics' founder, Baron Pierre de Coubertin. Neither is it a secret that his vision of ancient sport was romanticized and in some details inaccurate.[1] There's little doubt that professionalism, entertainment concerns, and even cheating were present in ancient sport. Not all ancient athletes and fans were consciously driven by the higher ideals in their society. The point is not simply to revive the idealistic vision of antiquity that motivated the Games' founders, but to revisit the connections between ancient Greek philosophical texts and the metaphysical realities of sport itself—realities that were as apparent in the world of Homer as they are in today's high-tech stadiums. These connections will reveal that while money and entertainment may forever be a part of the popular conception of sport, they are not its true purpose: the acquisition and celebration of human excellence are. Because this purpose is something intrinsic to the structure of sport itself, athletes who experience competition don't have to be pushed hard to understand that.

A bit of a nudge is necessary, however, to engender a value for the ancient ideal of *aretē* in modern practitioners (and spectators) of sport. I propose to provide that nudge by interpreting the stated ideals of modern Olympism in terms of the ancient philosophical ideal of *aretē*, then to show how that ideal may be profitably cultivated though the practice of sport. I will do this first by interpreting the Olympic Charter's first Fundamental Principle of Olympism in terms of the ancient Greek ideal of *aretē*. Second, I will briefly explain the general connection between philosophy and sport. Finally, I will connect five of the virtues traditionally associated with *aretē* to the metaphysical structure of sport. The hope is that these connections can reveal the philosophical pursuit of *aretē* as something possible within, and even fundamental to, the practice of sport.

## Connecting Olympism and *Aretē*

Perhaps the first thing to remember when comparing modern Olympic sport with ancient Greek thought is that the ancient Olympians were not athletes, they were gods. It is not such a mistake to call our greatest athletes "Olympians," however, because the ancient Greek gods symbolized and exemplified the kind of perfection for which human beings strive. The philosophical ideal of *aretē* was envisioned as a godlike perfection of body, will, and mind. From this perspective, we can see how the connection between the modern ideals of Olympism and the ancient ideal of *aretē* is apparent in the first Fundamental Principle of Olympism, which reads: "Olympism is a philosophy of life, exalting and combining in a balanced whole the qualities of body, will, and mind. Blending sport with culture and education, Olympism seeks to create a way of life based on the joy found in effort, the educational value of good example and respect for universal fundamental ethical principles."[2] Combining this statement with several other Olympic symbols and ideals, one can derive many concepts important to the ancient Greek ideal of *aretē*: general principles such as *kalokagathia* (the connection between beauty and goodness), and specific virtues such as *eusébeia* (respect), *andreia* (courage), *sōphrosynē* (self-discipline), *dikaiosynē* (justice), and *sophia* (wisdom).

But understanding the connection between Olympism and *aretē* requires much more than a translation of the ancient words; it also requires an appreciation of the concepts behind them, and *that* requires a grasp of ancient Greek philosophy, especially the thought of Socrates, Plato, and Aristotle. Beyond the ideas of specific thinkers, however, we must become aware of the connection between philosophy, understood as the pursuit of wisdom, and athletics, understood as the pursuit of excellence. This connection is much tighter than it may first appear because for most classical Greek philosophers, *aretē* cannot be separated from wisdom.[3] In fact, *aretē* is often understood as the health of the *psychē* (mind or soul); but the soul is the source not just of thought, but also of *kinesis*, physical movement.[4]

Indeed Plato, who was himself a competitive wrestler, makes extensive physical training part of his educational programs for *aretē* as described in the *Republic* and *Laws,* and states specifically that these gymnastics are for the *benefit of the soul.*[5] Although his explanation of just how gymnastics develops the soul is limited,[6] connections can be made between athletics and philosophy beyond their common goal of improving the soul. Indeed, in the *Republic* (539d), Plato has Socrates compare as "counterparts" proper engagement in philosophic argument with proper participation in physical training. His point here is that those who use argument for the "sport" of defeating others rather than the higher goal of finding truth and leading a virtuous life are akin to those who practice athletics for *philonikia,* the love of victory, rather than the pursuit of personal excellence, or *aretē.*[7] Plato feels that the former are not worthy of the name "philosopher"—are the latter worthy of the name "Olympian"?

## Looking at the Metaphysics of Sport

While it may be clear that using argumentation for anything less than the pursuit of truth is an abuse, the use of sport for the purpose of "beating the next guy" might seem entirely appropriate. Indeed it may seem that sport is structured just for the purpose of declaring one competitor superior to the others, and the Olympic Games organized for the purpose of declaring one nation superior to the others. No doubt, Olympic sport is frequently used for just that purpose. But in line with Plato's claims about argumentation, I would contend that the metaphysics of sporting contests suggests that their purpose is in fact something much greater than beating the next guy or showing national superiority, much less providing entertainment or generating revenue. A look at the basic structures of sport, structures which haven't changed since ancient times, will reveal that their fundamental goal is to cultivate and celebrate human excellence (i.e., *aretē*).

What do I mean by the "basic structures of sport"? If we look all the way back to Homer's *Iliad,* written around the eighth century BCE and set nearly half a century earlier, we find athletic contests that were sufficiently familiar to the practitioners to suggest that such games were already a long-standing tradition by the time of the Trojan war.[8] The events include a footrace, a chariot race, a weight-throw, and contests in wrestling and boxing. Their formats reflect modern sport: competitors volunteer to participate, the criteria for victory and defeat are articulated, valuable prizes are offered, and there are extensive discussions about the justice of the races' outcomes. But what's most important about these and all sporting events is that the challenges they create serve no practical purpose. Even though the skills tested are sometimes useful in combat, the games are distinguished from combat precisely in that there is no practical purpose to them: the runners, for example, end up where they started, having carried no message or cargo from point to point. Modern sports like golf and figure skating are even farther removed from practical concern. Bernard Suits's famous definition of game playing as "the voluntary attempt to overcome unnecessary obstacles" applies just as much to ancient sport as it does to modern.[9]

So if the contests themselves lack intrinsic purpose, we must ask where their meaning comes from. I would submit that it comes from the human *excellences,* or *aretai,* demanded by these tasks. Sporting contests set up challenges that act as a mechanism for cultivating and celebrating the very human qualities that enable a person to excel in life's (meaningful) challenges. Achilles and his friends make it clear that they are celebrating their fallen comrade Patroclos's excellences, excellences that have served them well on the very serious field of battle. At the same time they are pushing each other to demand more of themselves, to test their *aretē* against that of their comrades as part of a community drive to achieve ever higher levels of excellence. The prizes are rewards and incentives for the cultivation of such excellences, but they are not the reason for, or goal of, each contest.[10] Nor is the goal simply to "beat the other guy." If it were, then it wouldn't matter who the other guy was; but Achilles insists that the most noble and skilled men should take part in each contest. The purpose is not simply to set one man above the rest, but to test and to *celebrate* the excellences that the contests elicit and thereby to honor Patroclos and the gods themselves.

## Sport and the Parts of *Aretē*

So sporting contests derive their meaning not from such acts as putting balls into nets, but from the human excellences that actions like putting balls into nets demand. And those excellences are themselves valuable because *aretē* is understood as a *dynamis,* a power in the soul that can be applied to such meaningful tasks as being a good citizen or achieving *eudaimonia* (happiness).[11] The specific virtues implied by the ancient concept of *aretē* varied in ancient times (as it would across different cultures today), but generally it includes *eusébeia* (respect), *andreia* (courage), *sōphrosynē* (self-control), *dikaiosynē* (justice), and *sophia* (wisdom). Furthermore, there is a strain of thought in Hellenic philosophy that these virtues are at least interrelated, if not completely unified: to have one is, to some degree, to have them all, and to perfect one entails, in some sense, perfecting them all.

Now this last claim is sure to elicit a myriad of counterexamples involving athletes who excel in sports but display few, if any, of the virtues on the list just given. Likewise there are many thinkers skilled in debate and argument who nevertheless fail to pursue knowledge or live virtuous lives. Both cases demonstrate the limitations of the activities (athletics and philosophical debate) to reliably elicit the excellence they are designed to reward. It is a failure of sport, noted by many including Plato, that it sometimes rewards skills in the absence of true *aretē*. But this doesn't diminish sport's potential to cultivate *aretē* nor does it refute the observation that sporting contests do and should be intended to elicit those cardinal virtues. What follows is a brief account of these ancient Greek ideals accompanied by an explanation of how the practice of sport may help us to cultivate them.

*Eusébeia,* often translated as piety or reverence, may best be understood as respect for and duty to some ideal beyond oneself.[12] For the Ancient Hellenes, the commitment to excellence, including the practice of sport, was ultimately religious. Their stadia were within religious sanctuaries, and the games were part of festivals to honor the gods. Olympia was a Pan-Hellenic religious sanctuary long before it hosted games, and indeed the first Olympic contest is said to have been run in order to select someone to light the sacrificial flame.[13] It has even been argued that ancient Greek athletics generally, and even the athletes' sweat, were themselves items of ritual sacrifice.[14] While modern sport need not be subsumed by any particular religion, the sense that athletic pursuits are aimed at ideals that transcend mundane existence remains. The Olympic prize of a *kotinos* (olive wreath) symbolically blends the idea of divine perfection with the short-lived nature of victory and human life; it was just as relevant at the 2004 Games in Athens as it was in ancient Olympia. Furthermore, the venerated Olympic *ekecheiria* (truce), adopted and endorsed by the modern United Nations, places sport above commerce and political quarrels. Both practices show reverence for a higher standard of excellence reflected in the mystery of the divine realm. Both ancient and modern Olympic athletes compete not just for worldly goods but also to honor higher ideals by displaying what is best and most noble in themselves.

Along with this appreciation for the divine ideal, *eusébeia* requires an awareness of our imperfection with respect to the ideal, and some doubt about our ability to live up to it. This combination yields a desire to test oneself against the ideal, or at least against others who may approximate it. I take Socrates' *eusébeia* to be a paradigm example. Famously, he appreciates the ideal of divine knowledge, acknowledges the fact that he doesn't have it, and sets about testing his ideas against the "wisest men" of Athens in order to try and achieve it. It's no coincidence that Socrates compares himself to an Olympic athlete in this effort and claims that he deserves the prizes routinely awarded to Olympic victors for the benefits he has provided to the city (*Apology*, 36d–e).

Of course Socrates' fame lies not in his athleticism, but rather his humble and reverent admission of ignorance in comparison to the perfect knowledge of gods (*Apology*, 23b). This reflects the situation of athletes, who almost by definition seek perfection while constantly facing up to their imperfections. Even the world's best athletes are often dissatisfied with their record-breaking performances, because they appreciate and are trying to attain an even higher excellence. For many of us, sport provides our first experience of conceptualizing an ideal and measuring ourselves against it. Often the ideal begins as some champion athlete, but for most of us it evolves beyond a particular person to a more abstract idea such as "the perfect game." In both cases it is that tension between the person we are and the person we want to be that motivates us to train, compete, and strive for otherwise meaningless goals. Although our victories may be accompanied by prizes and popularity, those spoils are not the true objects of our striving. We are trying to find out something about ourselves, about ideals, and about the capacities of humanity itself. In short, we are showing respect and duty toward ideals greater than ourselves—we are exercising the virtue of reverence.

*Andreia,* translated as "bravery" or "courage," is grounded in the view of life as *agōn,* or struggle.[15] The idea that life is *agōn* grows directly out of *eusébeia,* since recognizing one's imperfection with respect to an ideal and then striving to attain it is by definition a struggle. *Andreia* generally is that power that enables us to endure and even to excel in that struggle. Plato took pains to show in *Laches* that *andreia* is less an absence of fear than a kind of wisdom about what should and should not be feared. Socrates eventually describes it as wise endurance in the pursuit of noble goals.[16] In *Republic, andreia* is the quality of the spirited part of the soul that enables it to follow reason's lead.[17] Plato's point is that it's not enough to be willing to take risks and face danger, because many risks and dangers are not worth taking. Nor is it *andreia* to fight one's way toward victory at any cost. Socrates' historic retreat in the battle of Delium saved many lives and so enabled the Athenians to fight another day.[18] Aristotle likewise defined courage as a midpoint between the excesses of cowardice and rashness (*Nicomachean Ethics,* 2.8). What *andreia* demands is a willingness to follow through with what we discern to be right, and this includes the courage to risk one's wealth and reputation in order to pursue higher ideals.

Now, to the ancient Hellenes, there could be no such thing as *aretē* without struggle, since *aretē* must be exercised and life itself *is* struggle. The problem is that life's meaningful struggles—whether they take place in the individual, the family, or the greater community—often come along when we're least prepared for them. It makes sense, therefore, to prepare ourselves by establishing and engaging in "artificial" struggles that cultivate qualities like *andreia.* This is exactly what sporting contests, ancient and modern, do. They manufacture *agōn,* challenges that test our ability to follow rules and execute plans. When Plato designed competitive games for his ideal city (*kallipolis*) in the *Laws,* he specified that the fighting contests be real enough to incite fear and reveal bravery.[19] The cultivation of *andreia* demands that we take risks—not merely physical risks, but also, and even more important, the psychological risk of trying and failing, of revealing embarrassing truths about ourselves in public. To take part in competitive sport is by definition to risk losing.[20] But not to take part is to lack the courage to strive beyond what's predictable and safe. Without the courage to face challenges in and out of the stadium, man cannot hope to achieve excellence in any endeavor.

*Sōphrosynē,* usually translated as "temperance" or "self-control," contains a sense of power and control that is not easily communicated by those words. Nevertheless it is a concept easy for those who love and participate in sports to understand. *Sōphrosynē* applies the aesthetic qualities of harmony and balance to the metaphysical understanding of man as a limited combination of mind, body, and spirit. It views *aretē* in terms of the harmonious balance and dynamic function of these three elements. In *Charmides,* Plato's Socrates rejects definitions of *sōphrosynē* as modesty or quietness by using counterexamples from sports such as running and boxing.[21] Beauty, the central criterion for *sōphrosynē,* requires a dynamic and harmonious tension between power and control.

Power and control are precisely the qualities demanded by both the aesthetic ideal and the practical objectives of most sports. In fact, much of Olympic sports' entertainment value may be traced to the aesthetic pleasure we take in athletes' displays of controlled power. But the purpose of sport is not to market such beautiful displays; rather, it is to elicit such human excellence as *sōphrosynē,* that reflects our human nature as powerful but inevitably limited beings. An important metaphysical characteristic of sport is that it quite consciously is constructed to impose limitations and boundaries on space, time, and action. Ironically, these boundaries carve out a space apart from the mundane world where we can "go all out" and express unprecedented freedoms.[22] I can scream as loud as I want on the racquetball court, but not in my classroom. What's fascinating about sports is the dynamic human power displayed within extreme limits—gymnasts do things on a four-inch balance beam that seem to defy gravity. Surely Plato had *sōphrosynē* in mind when he emphasized dignity and control in dancing and wrestling contests.[23] While modern sport is often characterized by excesses and "winning ugly," the ideal remains a harmonious tension between power and control.

*Dikaiosynē,* or justice, is easy to translate but very hard to explain. There were many different ideas of justice in ancient times, just as there are now. Fortunately, Olympic sport accommodates and celebrates a variety of theories of justice. The term *dikaiosynē* is roughly contemporary with the introduction of written laws and was meant initially to describe a man who obeyed these laws.[24] This ideal fits well with sports, since sports are made up of rules, so to break a rule is in some sense not to play the game at all.[25] But in both sport and philosophy, justice cannot simply be reduced to rule obedience. What about the possibility of unjust rules or minor violations such as an unintentional handball in soccer that may nullify a justly deserved victory?

In *Republic,* Plato came to understand justice in the individual and in the city as the proper ordering and harmonious function of the various parts of the soul or of the citizenry. For the soul, this means that the rational part must lead, with the spirited and appetitive parts following. Isn't this just the thing demanded of an athlete by sport? Think of a martial arts form, a complicated dance move, or even an offensive play in American football. One must rationally conceptualize the proper moves, then have the "heart" and "guts" to perform the action with power and enthusiasm. Justice in Plato's city depended on the citizens who were best suited to particular tasks performing them for the good of the community at large. This is also the distribution of labor demanded of athletic teams, which always perform best when the work is distributed according to talent and skill. While it may be difficult to isolate a single theory of justice in the ancient world, sport seems well suited as a mechanism for eliciting most of our conceptions of it; so much so that we often refer to sports to illustrate important aspects of justice—for example, the concept of a "level playing field."

*Sophia,* or wisdom, evolves in ancient thought from something like prudence to a philosophic understanding of good and evil. For Socrates at least, *sophia* seems to be that element of *aretē* that renders the individual virtues useful for the pursuit of happiness—which is the ultimate prize in the game of life. Just as a doctor's skills may be applied to help or harm the patient, athletic skills such as courage and self-discipline can be used in the pursuit of either base or noble ends. The ability to discern what's best for oneself, one's community, and one's environment is the linchpin of any athletic program aimed at personal excellence. This ability is also the goal of philosophy: the love of wisdom, as practiced by Socrates, Plato, and Aristotle. But despite its intellectual nature, *sophia* can and should be pursued with the whole soul. Practiced thoughtfully, athletics themselves can be understood as the pursuit of wisdom.[26]

The key here is the attitude and intellectual engagement of the athlete within the sports experience. Just as the philosopher recognizes truth (and not victory in argument) as her true goal, the Olympic athlete should focus on the ideals of excellence and perfection. The philosopher, like the scientist and the detective, tries to discover some truth about the world. The athlete tries to discover some truth about what he himself and humanity in general are capable of. In this sense, athletic contests are like science experiments that must be conducted according to the rules and with a willingness to accept the truth of the results they render, even when the results are not what the scientist (or her sponsor) was hoping for. It also requires an effort to reflect upon and evaluate the meaning of those results in the context of one's greater goals.

Most of this process is already in place for successful athletes. They see their sport, say a 100-meter dash, as a "lived question," a complex problem to be solved.[27] And they bring all their resources (physical, intellectual, and spiritual) to bear in their attempts to solve it. To progress, they must analyze and evaluate their results, searching for ways to inch closer to perfection within the limits imposed by their human nature. When things are going well, they experience states of beauty and elation referred to as "flow" or "being in the zone." These are fleeting experiences of the truth they are seeking, akin to the beauty and elation experienced by musicians and theorists.

Modern sport tends to fail in developing *sophia* among athletes when it disengages them from solving the "problem" of their performance and fails to place athletic pursuits in service of the larger projects of personal excellence and happiness. Many coaches and athletic programs focus narrowly on the (intrinsically meaningless) objectives of the sport itself, viewing athletes as means to their own career or fund-raising goals. In many sports, tactics, strategies, and even particular moves are conceived and dictated by coaches through small radios. Athletes uncritically follow prescribed training programs, without understanding the theories behind them or reflecting on their role in a balanced and happy life. Even student-athletes competing in institutions that claim to be driven by the mission of education are provided little or no opportunity to reflect on their sports experience in such a way as to decipher values and meanings that might be applied to other aspects of life. These and other short-sighted practices in modern sport help to explain why athletes so often fall short of the virtues that sport is designed to develop. By recognizing the wisdom-seeking nature of sport itself, *sophia,* the virtue that renders all others valuable, might again become the recognized end for athletes and coaches alike.

## Conclusion

In 2004, the modern Olympic Games returned to Greece, and their connection to the ancient world was briefly recalled and appreciated. But the Olympic movement needs to do more than remember its Hellenic heritage; it must also come to understand the ancient conception of *aretē* and its eternally valuable components, such as *eusébeia, andreia, sōphrosynē, dikaiosynē,* and *sophia*. Sport can be a mechanism for cultivating and celebrating such human excellence. By refreshing the ancient connection between sport and philosophy, we may revive in today's athletes an appreciation and drive for sport's greatest reward: the Olympian soul.

## Notes

1. For a detailed account, see Dikaia Chatziefstathiou and Ian Henry, "Hellenism and Olympism: Pierre de Coubertin and the Greek Challenges to the Early Olympic Movement," *Sport in History* 27:1 (2007): 24–43.

2. International Olympic Committee, *Olympic Charter* (Lausanne: International Olympic Committee, 2010), 11.

3. For the connection between wisdom and *aretē*, see any of Plato's Socratic dialogues and Aristotle's comments at *Eudemian Ethics*, 1216b and *Nicomachean Ethics*, 1145b. There is an extensive secondary literature on this subject; see, for example, Terry Penner, "The Unity of Virtue," *The Philosophical Review* 82 (1973): 35–68.

4. For the connection between *kinesis* and *psyche*, see Plato, *Phaedrus*, 245c–246a; *Laws X*, 894c; *Sophist*, 254d; and Aristotle, *De Anima*, 413a–b, 432a–433b.

5. Plato, *Republic*, 410c.

6. Plato, *Republic*, 410b–412a. Plato explains that physical training is used in combination with music and poetry to balance and harmonize the rational and spirited parts of the soul. In particular, gymnastics arouses the spirited part of the soul and keeps a philosopher from becoming too weak and soft. In *Phaedrus*, 246a–257a, he offers an illuminating illustration of this ideal with his analogy of a charioteer who coaxes the best performance from his team by balancing noble and wicked horses, which represent the rational and appetitive parts of the soul. For a detailed analysis of Plato's use of gymnastic education, see Heather Reid, "Sport as Moral Education in Plato's Republic," *Journal of the Philosophy of Sport* 34:2 (2007): 160–175, and Heather Reid, "Plato's Gymnasium," *Sport, Ethics, and Philosophy* 4:2 (2010): 170–182.

7. For more on Socrates' use of competitive techniques, see Heather Reid, "Wrestling with Socrates," *Sport, Ethics, and Philosophy* 4:2 (2010): 157–169.

8. Homer, *Iliad*, 23.256–24.6. Scholars debate the Bronze Age authenticity of Homer's games; Mark Golden identifies several suspected anachronisms in *Sport and Society in Ancient Greece* (Cambridge: Cambridge University Press, 1998), 93.

9. Bernard Suits, *The Grasshopper: Games, Life, and Utopia,* 2nd ed. (Peterborough, Ontario: Broadview Press, 2005), 55.

10. For more on the role of prizes in the ancient games see Ben Brown, "Homer, Funeral Contests, and the Origins of the Greek City," in *Sport and Festival in the Ancient Greek World,* ed. David J. Phillips and David Pritchard (Swansea: The Classical Press of Wales, 2003), 123–162.

11. For more on the nature of *dynamis* and its connection to *aretē,* see Plato, *Republic,* 477bc and 430b.

12. For a detailed account of this virtue, see Paul Woodruff, *Reverence: Renewing a Forgotten Virtue* (New York: Oxford University Press, 2002).

13. See Panos Valavanis, "Thoughts on the Historical Origins of the Olympic Games and the Cult of Pelops in Olympia," *Nikephoros* 19:1 (2006): 137–152. For a philosophical analysis of the religious heritage of the games, see Heather Reid, "Olympia: Running towards Truth," *Sport, Ethics, and Philosophy,* 4:2 (2010): 136–145.

14. See David Sansone, *Greek Athletics and the Genesis of Sport* (Berkeley: University of California Press, 1988).

15. The view that *agōn* characterized the Greek outlook on life is generally attributed to Jacob Burkhardt; see his *The Greeks and Greek Civilization,* trans. Sheila Stern (New York: St Martin's Press, 1998).

16. See Plato, *Laches,* 196d and 192e ff.

17. Plato, *Republic,* 430b, 442c.

18. A historical event recounted at *Symposium,* 221a–b.

19. *Laws,* 830e–831a.

20. For a detailed explanation, see H. Reid, *The Philosophical Athlete* (Durham, NC: Carolina Academic Press, 2002), Chapter 5.

21. *Charmides,* 159c–d.

22. An observation made by Eleanor Metheny in "The Symbolic Power of Sport," in *Sport and the Body: A Philosophical Symposium,* 2nd ed., ed. Ellen Gerber (Philadelphia: Lea & Febiger, 1979), 231–236.

23. *Laws,* 814e–f.

24. F. E. Peters, *Greek Philosophical Terms: A Historical Lexicon* (New York: New York University Press, 1967), 39.

25. This "formalist" account of rules and games is a subject of hot debate among sports philosophers. For a sampling, see Kathleen Pearson, "Deception, Sportsmanship, and Athletics," *Quest* 19 (1973): 115–118; and Warren Fraleigh, *Right Actions in Sports: Ethics for Contestants* (Champaign, IL: Human Kinetics, 1984), 79–81.

26. For more on this connection, see Heather Reid, "Sport, Philosophy, and the Quest for Knowledge," *Journal of the Philosophy of Sport* 36:1 (2009): 40–49.

27. The concept of the "lived question" is explained in Heather Reid, *The Philosophical Athlete,* section 1.1.

**Part 3**

# MODERN IDEALS

*Douglas W. McLaughlin and Cesar R. Torres*

# MORE THAN GAMES
## Olympism as a Moral Approach to Sport

The modern Olympic Games have dramatically increased in scope and significance since their inception in 1896. More than just a sporting festival, the Games are imbued with a complex philosophical vision that entails ethical principles. Pierre de Coubertin, the chief founder of the modern Games, called this philosophical vision "Olympism," and his elaboration of it not only influenced the Games' growth but also identified the rich social and ethical grounds of the Olympic movement. When the Olympic Games are approached as merely sporting championships, however, the significance of the Olympic movement and its inspiring ideals are neither fully understood nor appreciated. Similarly, it is often difficult to determine how Olympism clarifies ethical conflicts that arise in and through sporting contests.

Concurrent with the development of the modern Olympic Games was the elucidation of a concept called "intersubjectivity" by phenomenologists such as Edmund Husserl, Maurice Merleau-Ponty, and Emmanuel Levinas. Intersubjectivity identifies the grounds of human experience and expresses a philosophical vision that is in concert with the notion of Olympism. Indeed, understanding intersubjectivity proves beneficial for fully comprehending the significance of Olympism and appreciating why the Olympic Games are so captivating. Intersubjectivity provides a valuable resource for enriching our understanding of the Olympic movement and addressing any shortcomings and ambiguities pertaining to Olympism.

This chapter begins with an elucidation of Olympism. Due to the complexity of its philosophical underpinnings, it is important that we determine the importance Olympism plays in framing the meaning and values embedded in the Olympic Games and identify shortcomings and ambiguities. To address these issues, we present an account of sport and intersubjectivity. As a rich description of human experience that reveals important aspects of our human condition, intersubjectivity allows for a deeper appreciation of Olympism. In addition, our understanding and appreciation of sport itself can be enhanced when Olympic philosophy is informed by intersubjectivity. The goods and values that have come to be associated with sport are most fully intelligible from an intersubjective approach and are most readily realized through the philosophy of Olympism. We support this claim by looking at how Olympism and intersubjectivity inform two very important philosophical inquiries: what the nature of athletic excellence is and how ethical concerns are resolved in sport.

By the conclusion of this chapter, we will have addressed three primary questions. First, are the Olympic Games best understood when informed by its moral vision? Second, what does an intersubjective moral approach to sport look like? Finally, how is it that this approach informs the Olympic movement and its practices?

## Olympism

The modern Olympic Games have already spanned three centuries. From humble beginnings in the late nineteenth century to their gigantic proportions at the dawn of the twenty-first century, the Olympic Games have established themselves as one of the greatest shows on earth. In spite of criticism bestowed upon the Games since their inception in 1896, they are widely honored and valued. The interest in hosting the Games, the number of participating nations, as well as the staggering TV audiences, among other indicators, confirm this. Although the Games are an international multisport event for elite contestants held every two years, they are, despite what many like to believe, more than sports. Coubertin did not hesitate to express this idea. Discussing the uniqueness of the Olympic Games in comparison with world championships in 1908, Coubertin stressed that though the Olympics include international sport competitions, they "are 'something else' as well, and it is just this 'something else' that matters, as it is not to be found in any other variety of athletic competition."[1]

For Coubertin, this "something else" was a complex philosophical vision he referred to as Olympism. Arguably, his Olympism provided the raison d'être not only for the Olympic Games, setting them apart from other sporting events, but also for the entire Olympic movement. In other words, Olympism was the driving force behind the universal fascination with all things Olympic. In his day, Coubertin complained that people misunderstood his project. The crowds, he wrote in 1920, "had seen five successive Olympiads held with increasing pomp and circumstance, and yet we felt that they still had only a vague grasp of the meaning and import of the Games."[2] Although Coubertin's assessment seems accurate, he might not have realized that a very important reason for the misunderstanding was based on his own inability to concisely conceptualize a clear account of Olympism, rather than in people's failure to grasp it.

Coubertin wrote several articles discussing Olympism and mentioned it in many more, but he never articulated it in a comprehensive theory that facilitated its grasp. Indeed, Coubertin continued adding ideas to, and even reformulating, Olympism throughout his life. The complexity of the concept might reflect the fact that Coubertin was influenced by different worldviews, ranging from classic Hellenism to English muscular Christianity to French social reformism to classic nineteenth-century liberalism.[3] Coubertin's radical eclecticism and unsystematic written production make the understanding of Olympism a challenging project.

Nevertheless, reading Coubertin's writings and the International Olympic Committee's (IOC) rendition of Olympism elucidates what lies at the core of Olympism. For instance, the Olympic Charter, the fundamental text of the Olympic movement, advances that "Olympism is a philosophy of life, exalting and combining in a balanced whole the qualities of body, will and mind. Blending sport with culture and education, Olympism seeks to create a way of life based on the joy found in effort, the educational value of good example and respect for universal fundamental ethical principles."[4] It also states, "The goal of Olympism is to place sport at the service of the harmonious development of man, with a view to promoting a peaceful society concerned with the preservation of human dignity."[5]

What comes to light when considering these passages is that the uniqueness of Olympism resides in its ambition to explicitly pursue moral values through sport and especially through the Olympic Games. Although there is no unanimous consensus on the specific content of Olympism, several scholars have noted that, as one commentator put it, "values such as holistic human development, excellence, peace, fairness, equality, mutual respect, justice, and nondiscrimination among others are repeatedly emphasized."[6] For instance, sport philosopher Jim Parry recently wrote that Olympism "emphasizes the role of sport in global culture, international understanding, peaceful coexistence, and social and moral education."[7] Clearly, because of the ostensible moral values tied to the Olympic Games and sport, Olympism becomes a program for moral and social improvement. Since the advancement and materialization of the values propounded by Olympism require action, the Olympic Games and sport become imbued with an educational rationality and purpose. After all, referring to its educational role, Coubertin noted that "Olympism is a destroyer of dividing walls."[8] Devoid of their moral values as well as educational rationality, the Olympic Games would just be, to use Coubertin's phraseology, world championships, or "simply games."

Despite the fact that Olympism demands that the Olympic Games be understood not merely as "simply games," at the core of Olympism resides a species of games: competitive sport. Indeed, sport is the undisputed medium through which Olympism's program for moral and social improvement is implemented. It is precisely through sport, most conspicuously the Olympic Games, that Olympism seeks to materialize its moral values. Perhaps this is why Coubertin repeatedly endorsed a rather broad and vague definition of sport proposed by M. Milliaud in the early 1910s: "Ultimately, sport is a kind of activity that ranges from games to heroic acts, covering all the stages in between."[9] If sport covers the whole gamut of possibilities ranging from games to heroism, it can certainly be used to spread the universal values inherent in Olympism. The problem is that such a definition of sport is so porous that it excludes activities that it should include and includes activities that it should not. Despite the fact that Olympism takes sport seriously, the lack of specificity regarding the internal logic and central purpose of competitive sport might exacerbate some of Olympism's enduring ambiguities. Consider, for example, Olympism's uncertainty in relation to the role and significance of athletic excellence in the face of its emphasis on participation. Another example comes from the apparent tension in Olympism's goal to promote peace and internationalism through competitive sports. Which vision of the Olympic Games should prevail, and why?

Given the intimate connection between sport and Olympism, and in light of the latter's enduring ambiguities, a coherent account of sport could only assist in clarifying Olympism as well as in tempering the stupefying effects of potential and current conflicts. In other words, focusing on the internal logic and central purpose of competitive sport is necessary in order to make better sense of Olympism. Is competitive sport a rich enough activity to fulfill the promise and actualize the hopes that Coubertin invested in Olympism and the Olympic movement?

If the inconsistencies and lack of clarity could be addressed so that a richer account of Olympism is realized, then perhaps the values of Olympism would be more fully realized in the practice of the Olympic Games. Even if Olympism entails ambiguities that make it difficult to determine what recommendations should be made in Olympic practice, it is not necessary to accept that as the end of the story. Just as the Olympic Games have grown and flourished, so too can our understanding of Olympism. Just as Coubertin's account of Olympism was informed by multiple sources, those interested in the Olympic Games can and should draw on all relevant sources that prove beneficial in elucidating Olympism and resolving any ambiguities.

## Sport

Because competitive sports are a form of games, it is worth beginning with a definition of games. Philosopher Bernard Suits argues that "to play a game is to engage in activity directed towards bringing about a specific state of affairs, using only means permitted by rules, where the rules prohibit more efficient in favor of less efficient means, and where such rules are accepted just because they make possible such activity."[10] This definition identifies the necessary and sufficient conditions of game playing: a goal, a limitation of means, rules, and a lusory attitude.

It is this last condition that Suits argues is the linchpin of his definition. The lusory attitude makes game playing an intelligible practice because it provides the rationale for voluntarily abiding by means-limiting rules in attempting to achieve a goal. The permissible means for achieving a goal can be limited based on many different reasons. One such limitation of means is based on ethical grounds. A person may want to become a millionaire, but will not rob or steal to gain that money due to moral prohibitions. Even when there are no explicit rules or limitation of means directly related to the activity itself, mandates of morality can supersede goals and prohibit certain actions. Another example of limited means is bureaucratic in nature. Some bureaucratic rules seem to have no understandable justification or purpose, such as some arcane and complicated tax laws. Although the rules are explicitly stated and make it more difficult to achieve a goal, they seem to lack any clear rationale. In games, however, carefully limiting the means to achieve a goal is precisely what makes game playing intelligible. For instance, while it might be easier to use one's hands in soccer, field players are not permitted to handle the ball simply because of the challenge that limitation creates. This gratuitous logic, and its concomitant free acceptance of unnecessary challenges, is what makes game playing a meaningful and interesting activity. Notice that in sports, the gratuitous logic also requires accomplishing a goal through the demonstration of highly specialized physical skills.

The gratuitous logic of sports not only makes game playing intelligible, but it also determines what counts as achievement and makes meaningful an athlete's devotion to developing skill and becoming excellent in a particular game. It also makes evident how games can serve as the framework for Olympic values. Athletes must be disciplined in their practice and development of skills. This discipline in turn leads to the development of individuals oriented toward the appreciation and pursuit of excellence. To seriously participate in sports is to care deeply about the values of discipline as well as human development and excellence more generally: values that are part and parcel of the Olympic philosophy.

But the Olympic Games are comprised of a particular subset of sports, competitive sport, that provide fertile ground for the realization of additional Olympic values. In addition to testing their abilities, athletes are also *con*testing—setting out to determine their abilities in comparison to one another. Contesting athletes are members of a "testing family" who share an interest in and appreciation for a particular test.[11]

Appreciating what constitutes achievement in a given sport, athletes are engaged in what sport philosopher Robert L. Simon calls a "mutual quest for excellence through challenge."[12] By recognizing the role of testing families and the mutuality of excellence through contesting, we can properly understand Olympic values such as mutual respect, nondiscrimination, fairness, and peace. Athletes are considered equal under the rules of the sport and the Olympic Charter. This serves as a basis for mutual recognition and respect among athletes and the demand that achievement be determined in a nondiscriminatory and fair manner. How the Olympic Games can serve to promote peace is discussed in greater detail later in this chapter, but in part the interaction among individual athletes of various backgrounds forms the basis of a peace-making program.

## Intersubjectivity

A more concrete account of competitive sport alone may not seem sufficient to account for the central role it plays in promoting the values of Olympism. There are a myriad of counterexamples of sporting behavior that seem to call into question the Olympic vision. But examples of cheating, injustice, or disrespect, though they may identify how sport is sometimes practiced, do not define how it should or can be practiced. These counterexamples are not a reason to abandon Coubertin's ambitions pertaining to Olympism. Rather, we must determine how such ambitions can be met in the face of these challenges. One possible answer is to establish how the philosophical concept of intersubjectivity can illuminate the practice of sport and the concept of Olympism.

Philosopher Edmund Husserl is a central figure in the development of intersubjectivity and is in many ways a parallel figure to Coubertin. Like Coubertin with the Olympic Games, Husserl is generally considered the founder of phenomenology, a branch of philosophy that studies the structure of people's conscious experience as experienced by them. And, also like Coubertin, Husserl was not without his critics. Some responding to his early writing objected to his account of phenomenology because they felt it amounted to a solipsistic account of the world. Husserl (like Coubertin) was not discouraged by criticism. Rather than a failure of his philosophical thought, he understood it as a failure of his expression of that thought. His goal was to elaborate the nature of human experience in a manner more consistent with our lived experience. Husserl's notion of intersubjectivity played a vital role in his response to the critics of his early writing, and its subsequent development by other philosophers has further elucidated the nature of human experience.

Intersubjectivity elucidates the relationship between the self and others. It establishes the social nature of persons and explains our ability to empathize with others. Husserl wrote, "I *experience* the world . . . *not* as . . . my *private* synthetic formation but as other than mine alone, as an *intersubjective* world, actually there for everyone."[13] Because our experience is always already intersubjective, our values and meanings are forged in and reflect this actuality. One way in which intersubjectivity provides an enhanced account of our humanity is by resolving philosophical concerns that pertain to purely subjective or purely objective moral accounts of persons. From an intersubjective standpoint, there is no pure subjectivity, for "I" am always already being in the world, influenced and informed by others, and negotiating meaning with others. In turn, there is also no pure objectivity, for "it" or "the other" is also always already immersed in a network of relations in which the other's meaning is determined through interactions between itself and a myriad of others.

Concerns about the philosophical difficulty of reconciling the self and the other are resolved through the notion of intersubjectivity because, rather than beginning with theoretical abstractions that create an unbridgeable gap between subjectivity and objectivity, it begins with an account of our coherent experience in the world, "our undergoing, our involvement in the world, our lending or withholding ourselves, keyed to our responsiveness, our sensibility, our alertness, or our deadness."[14] An accurate account of our experience expresses how we are tethered to one another. Whether from the perspective of the collective or of the individual, "there is implicit a *mutual being for one another.*"[15] Our intersubjectivity weaves through all that we are and do.

The significance of an intersubjective account of sport is supported by sport philosopher William J. Morgan, who argues that in moral considerations of sports neither a subjective nor an objective account of sport is sufficient. Rather, an intersubjective account is necessary, "an interpersonal moral take, one that combines critical reflection with an appreciation of the cultural and historical situatedness of sports."[16] Morgan even identifies "international athletic festivals such as the Olympic

Games" as examples of a communicative moral approach to sport in which "some overlapping consensus about how sports should best be treated and regulated is required just to be able to stage such global events."[17]

Before turning directly to intersubjectivity in the Olympic movement, we must elucidate several considerations pertaining to what intersubjectivity consists of. The first is that humans are always already social beings. As philosopher Maurice Merleau-Ponty noted, "I find myself already situated and involved in a physical and social world."[18] Failure to account for this social dimension does not diminish its presence or its purchase. As philosopher John Russon wrote, the recognition that "the substance of our lives is to be found in our dealings with other people" requires that we take seriously the social character of our being.[19]

Although our identity, values, and concerns are forged within a social matrix, it is important to bear in mind that our understanding of our social being is developmental. It is in our engagement with others that we establish our identity and learn to tell our stories. Russon describes this process as entering into intersubjectivity by "becoming familiar with particular others, and these familiars are our originary vision of intersubjectivity, of 'who we are.' It is our family . . . that first defines for us where we fit into intersubjective relations and, consequently, what will count as the values by which 'we' must approach the world, by which we must contact reality."[20] This developmental character of intersubjectivity corresponds with the Olympic value of human development.

An intersubjective moral approach now has some purchase, because it recognizes how morality arises out of our intersubjective being. The most ardent advocate for the moral implications of intersubjectivity is philosopher Emmanuel Levinas, who advanced that "access to the face is straightaway ethical . . . before the face I do not simply remain there contemplating it, I respond to it . . . to greet the Other is already to answer for him. It is difficult to be silent in someone's presence."[21] Running shoulder to shoulder or facing off over a puck, our very interaction with others compels us to be responsible to them. This responsibility, a moral imperative, is born out of our social encounters in which we must always be held in check by our "initial interpersonal relation."[22] Recognizing the necessity of our opponents to make our participation in sport possible is a recognition of our need to answer to them. An intersubjective moral approach must always trace back through our meanings and values as they are developed in our intersubjective and developmental being in the world.

When the Olympic Games are understood as a communicative moral approach to sport, intersubjectivity accounts for cultural and narrative pluralism and makes necessary an interchange of competing viewpoints. The very basis of knowledge and morality is dependent on the authority of our human projects being intersubjectively scrutinized. As Russon argues: "to be an intersubjective body is to be already implicated in issues of authority, and our study of the path of intersubjective life has shown why it is that we are necessarily beholden to a project of universal answerability, of having our own measuring of significance measure up to the standards of others."[23] Because an intersubjective account of sport attends to the authority and examination of moral claims, it is clear how the values of justice, fairness, and equality are central to Olympism.

Before addressing what an intersubjective moral account of sport means for the Olympic movement in particular, we must identify the limitations of this approach. While it is important that inquiries into the nature of sport, values, and ethics take seriously the intersubjective nature of sport and persons, even an intersubjective approach to ethical deliberations can go wrong. For example, when we fail to fully bear in mind that our social being is developmental, our intersubjective judgments are incomplete.

Also, an examination of our intersubjectivity will not result in universal agreement on all matters. An intersubjective approach, says Russon, "does not mean that our dealings with others are inherently smooth or happy; it means only that we inherently inhabit the interhuman sphere of communication and contact."[24] The recognition of our intersubjective character is not the end or fulfillment of communication, but rather it facilitates the possibility of authentic communication.

Furthermore, a community with shared values, such as a testing family, by its very nature "opens us to an intersubjective horizon in which who we and our family members are is subject to redefinition."[25] Whereas objectivity may amount to a more static view of human meaning and values, intersubjectivity allows for an unfolding that takes place as our experience and relationships develop. Sport is a realm of ever-unfolding horizons, a social network in which meanings and values are dynamic as new possibilities are realized, new opportunities are opened, new family members arrive, communities merge or collide, and so on.

## Intersubjectivity in the Olympic Experience

Both a precise account of sport and an intersubjective moral approach to sport are important for a full appreciation of Olympism. Not only does an intersubjective moral approach to sport seem to be inherent in Coubertin's Olympic vision, but it also reveals how moral values can flourish in and through competitive sport. Let us now consider how Olympism, as an intersubjective moral approach to sport, interprets the nature of excellence in sport and illuminates moral considerations.

The pursuit of excellence through sporting contests is a central concern in the Olympic Games. But competition, understood only as a quest for victory, presents many difficulties for Olympism when the individual's or the team's interests are emphasized to the exclusion and at the expense of other contestants, such as when athletes cheat to attain a favorable result. A correction to this negative and divisive approach to sport, with its overemphasis on winning, is an approach that emphasizes the importance of excellence and participation. While these two qualities seem incompatible, they are both recognized as significant within the Olympic movement. The Olympic motto, *Citius, altius, fortius,* represents the aspirations of achievement and excellence. Conversely, the Olympic creed, which emphasizes the value of participation, asserts that "the most important thing is not winning, but taking part." Is this an internal contradiction within Olympism?

From an intersubjective lens, these seemingly contradictory notions can be readily reconciled. When an individual becomes concerned with participation, it is almost always participation in a particular activity—in this case, a particular sport. Identity, values, and a life narrative are informed by and wrapped up in the sport and sporting community a person participates in, generating a shared concern for a particular set of skills and an appreciation for the excellent execution of those skills. Therefore participation, in the fullest sense of the word, necessarily leads to a recognition, appreciation, and concern for excellence, including the expression of victory in sporting contests even when the victory is not one's own.[26]

An interest in winning, however, is only fully justifiable when understood in an intersubjective manner. The significance of one's victory is in part dependent on the quality of one's opponent. So if one truly cares about winning, then one must care about one's sport and the values and excellences that make up that sport. Appreciating winning demands an appreciation for the contesting that makes winning intelligible, which necessarily demands a concern for the sport and its community of practitioners. To jump higher, run faster, and become stronger requires effort and devotion to that endeavor. When one has achieved excellence in a sport, it is normal to look for validation and appreciation from others. In order for one's excellence to be meaningful and appreciated, there must be others to provide a significant challenge, recognize skillful achievement, and validate that achievement in proper measure. Excellence and winning occur within the network of relations of those participating in a given sport. Intersubjectivity reconciles participation and winning because it shows how they are inextricably bound, that they logically entail the other.

As mentioned earlier, competitive sports are more than just simply games. Coubertin recognized that sports served as a basis for developing deeper engagements with others. The Olympic Games are a means to make connections that transcended sport itself, not to mention nationalistic or political ideologies. While excellences are honored through contesting, the Olympic Games also serve to recognize social and moral values. These values are neither assumed as given nor are they taken for granted. Olympism recognizes the distinction between how sport is actually practiced and how it can be ideally practiced. Additionally, it takes seriously that by being well intentioned and deliberative, our involvement in sport can more closely approximate that ideal.

As an intersubjective moral approach to sport, Olympism takes seriously an inclusive approach to sport. That is represented by the Olympic symbol, which, as defined in the Olympic Charter, "consists of five interlaced rings of equal dimensions" and "represents the union of the five continents and the meeting of athletes from throughout the world at the Olympic Games."[27] The "union" and the "meeting" recognize our intersubjective involvement. The linking of the rings signifies how people are inextricably related to one another in the act of participating in the Olympic Games and beyond.

What is represented in the Olympic symbol is enacted in Olympic governance, which is conducted through interactions between the International Olympic Committee (IOC) and its respective commissions, the National Olympic Committees (NOCs), the International Sport Federations, and the Organizing Committees of the Olympic Games. So structured, the multiple representative bodies negotiate and collaborate the identity, implementation, and meaning of the Olympic movement. Although at different times some parties have wielded more influence than others over the modern Olympic Games, clearly the intent is for the multitude of interested parties to have a voice in the Olympic movement. This is perhaps best expressed through Olympic Solidarity, a branch of the IOC that provides financial and other kinds of assistance to the NOCs, especially those with the greatest need. Olympic Solidarity, being both responsive and empowering, represents Olympic values related to inclusiveness, equality, and mutual respect. While it could be argued that it does not go far enough, Olympic Solidarity continues to be an influential and positive factor that provides greater opportunities for Olympic involvement by all nations.

Perhaps the most ambitious claim regarding Olympism pertains to promoting peace. One of the roles of the IOC is "to cooperate with the competent public and private organisations and authorities in the endeavour to place sport at the service of humanity and thereby to promote peace."[28] Therefore, organizations wishing to become involved in the Olympic movement must be guided by principles that are compatible with Olympism's intersubjective moral approach to sport. Just as our humanity is only actualized through intersubjectivity, so too is peace only possible when individuals, organizations, and nations recognize their reciprocity and mutuality to one another. Coubertin expressed this very notion when he wrote, "This is why every four years the revived Olympic Games must give the youth of all the world a chance of a happy and brotherly encounter which will gradually efface the people's ignorance of things which concern them all."[29]

Indeed, internationalism has been the focus of the promotion of peace through Olympism and the Olympic movement. But for Coubertin, peace would be promoted fundamentally at the level of individuals engaged in the common practice of sport. As argued by anthropologist John J. McAloon, for Coubertin "true internationalism certainly involved the discovery and experience of social and cultural differences. However, far from dividing and repelling men from one another, national differences were to be celebrated as different ways of being human; their recognition was the first step toward peace, friendliness[,]" and mutual respect.[30] While peace, friendship, and mutual respect can be conferred between nations, it is at the level of intersubjectivity that they become meaningful; it is here that differences can be negotiated and reconciled, and commonalities can be recognized and forged.

It has been suggested that sport is a universal language.[31] Such a claim, often used to support, for example, the role of sport in efforts to promote peace, often lacks sufficient justification. However, an intersubjective account of humanity makes apparent that humans share a common ancestry that provides common concepts and thus informs our understanding of humanity. Indeed, sport is a universal language that allows people to recognize their intersubjective nature and negotiate values and meaning. It becomes clear, then, why Coubertin was so committed to sport as a means of promoting humanistic goals.

Intersubjectivity is not an addendum or amendment to Olympism; it is, rather, a concept that assists in the elucidation of the Games' complexity, allure, and power. At the same time, it underlies the complex Olympic philosophy and the way human beings negotiate the meaning of that philosophy as well as live it out in the actual practice of the Olympic Games. Coubertin would probably have been amenable to the use of intersubjectivity in elucidating his notion of Olympism. In fact, had he himself made use of this concept, perhaps we would have avoided some of the ambiguity regarding Olympism that exists to this day. Because intersubjectivity allows us not only to understand sport and competition more completely but also to understand ourselves as relational beings more fully, an intersubjective moral approach to sport promotes a better understanding and implementation of Olympism.

## Notes

1. Pierre de Coubertin, "Why I Revived the Olympic Games," in *Olympism: Selected Writings*, ed. Norbert Müller (Lausanne: International Olympic Committee, 2000), 542–543.
2. Pierre de Coubertin, "The Contribution of the Seventh Olympiad," in *Olympism*, ed. Müller (Lausanne: International Olympic Committee, 2000), 477.

3. For an account of how these ideas influenced Coubertin, see Sigmund Loland, "Coubertin's Ideology of Olympism from the Perspective of the History of Ideas," *Olympika: The International Journal of Olympic Studies* 4 (1995): 49–77; and John J. MacAloon, *This Great Symbol: Pierre de Coubertin and the Origins of the Modern Olympic Games* (Chicago: University of Chicago Press, 1981).

4. International Olympic Committee, *Olympic Charter* (Lausanne: International Olympic Committee, 2007), 11.

5. Ibid.

6. Cesar R. Torres, "Results or Participation? Reconsidering Olympism's Approach to Competition," *Quest* 58 (2006): 242. See also, for example, Warren P. Fraleigh, "Competition Olympique et Valeurs Dominantes," in *Valeurs de L'Olympisme*, ed. Bertrand During (Paris: INSEP, 1989), 107–121; Vassil Girginov and Jim Parry, *The Olympic Games Explained: A Student Guide to the Evolution of the Modern Games* (London: Routledge, 2005), 1–15; Hans Lenk, "The Essence of Olympic Man," *International Journal of Physical Education* 21 (1984): 9–14; idem, *Social Philosophy of Athletics* (Champaign, IL: Stipes, 1979), 119–199; Loland, "Coubertin's Ideology of Olympism"; Mike McNamee, "Olympism, Eurocentricity, and Transcultural Values," *Journal of the Philosophy of Sport* 33:2 (2006): 174–187; Jeffrey O. Segrave, "Towards a Definition of Olympism," in *The Olympic Games in Transition*, ed. Jeffrey O. Segrave and Donald Chu (Champaign, IL: Human Kinetics, 1988), 149–161; and Jim Parry, "Sport and Olympism: Universals and Multiculturalism," *Journal of the Philosophy of Sport* 33:2 (2006): 188–204.

7. Parry, "Sport and Olympism," 190.

8. Pierre de Coubertin, "Olympic Letter III: Olympism and Education," in *Olympism,* ed. Müller, 548.

9. Pierre de Coubertin, "Educational Use of Athletic Activity," in *Olympism,* ed. Müller, 193. See also Coubertin, "Olympia: Lecture Given in Paris, in the Festival Hall of the 16th Arrondissement Town Hall," in *Olympism,* ed. Müller, 564.

10. Bernard Suits, *The Grasshopper: Games, Life, and Utopia* (Toronto: University of Toronto Press, 1978), 34.

11. R. Scott Kretchmar, "From Test to Contest: An Analysis of Two Kinds of Counterpoint in Sport," in *Philosophic Inquiry in Sport*, ed. William J. Morgan and Klaus V. Meier (Champaign, IL: Human Kinetics, 1995), 36–41.

12. Robert L. Simon, *Fair Play: The Ethics of Sport* (Boulder, CO: Westview Press, 2004), 70.

13. Edmund Husserl, *Essential Husserl: Basic Writings in Transcendental Phenomenology,* ed. Donn Welton (Bloomington: Indiana University Press, 1988), 136.

14. Henry Bugbee, *The Inward Morning: A Philosophical Exploration in Journal Form* (Athens: University of Georgia Press, 1999), 41.

15. Husserl, *Essential Husserl,* 157.

16. William J. Morgan, "Why the 'View from Nowhere' Gets Us Nowhere in Our Moral Considerations of Sports," *Journal of the Philosophy of Sport,* 30:1 (2003): 51.

17. Ibid., 65.

18. Maurice Merleau-Ponty, *Phenomenology of Perception* (New York: Routledge, 1998), 360.

19. John Russon, *Human Experience: Philosophy, Neurosis, and the Elements of Everyday Life* (Albany: State University of New York Press, 2003), 51.

20. Ibid., 65.

21. Emmanuel Levinas, *Ethics and Infinity* (Pittsburgh, PA: Duquesne University Press, 2000), 85, 88.

22. Ibid., 90.

23. Russon, *Human Experience*, 73.

24. Ibid., 56.

25. Ibid., 67.

26. See Torres, "Results or Participation?"

27. International Olympic Committee, *Olympic Charter*, 21.

28. Ibid., 14.

29. Quoted in McAloon, *This Great Symbol*, 188.

30. McAloon, *This Great Symbol*, 266.

31. See, for example, former United Nations Secretary-General Kofi Annan's remarks when launching the International Year of Sport and Physical Education in 2004. "Universal Language of Sport Brings People Together, Teaches Teamwork, Tolerance, Secretary-General Says at Launch of International Year." United Nations' Press Release SG/SM9579, available at http://www.un.org/News/Press/docs/2004/sgsm9579.doc.htm (retrieved on February 21, 2010).

*Milan Hosta*

# OLYMPISM BETWEEN INDIVIDUALISM AND TRANSNATIONALISM

Sport as a manifestation of popular culture is among the effects of global-ization, a driving force that dictates our everyday existence. Every four years, the eyes of the world turn to a spectacle beyond compare: the Olympic Games. For any state worth its name, it is not to be missed; a sporting festival that has grown in political, economic, social, and envi-ronmental significance—a truly important cultural phenomenon.

It is no coincidence that such a "banal" thing as sport attracts so much attention. Pierre de Coubertin devoted much of his time and many writings to asserting the culture of sport among the French youth of the Third Republic. His well-known pedagogic motives and academic au-thority combined with his sociopolitical activities to promote the values of sport for national and personal fulfillment within elite society, and gave birth to a movement that has yet to be matched.

The ideas of democracy and liberalism were starting to flourish at the time when Coubertin's career was on the rise. Industry and science were on display at World Expos;[1] international political cooperation was in-tense; and, as a by-product of such rapid changes, indulgence and even decadence were taking hold in European culture. What at first glance seems utopian—the rehabilitation of ancient Greek ideals—was in fact appropriately rooted at the end of the nineteenth century. Philhellenic enthusiasm and courage, focused on the body, is even today the driving force and endless resource of Olympism. Coubertin's idea that sport could take an important role in international cooperation, leading to mu-tual understanding, order, and peace among nations, is now manifest as a spectacle of its own. As such it is a source and target of many colorful images and interpretations.

Our focus in this chapter is internationalism, a bridge between Coubertin's nationalism and the transnationalism that has almost become an organizational standard in our time. We begin with a discussion of individualism—giving the athlete the main role, for without the athlete no such story leading toward transnationalism could be born.

Our theme is an ambitious one, but the Olympic movement itself is complex, with many meanings that cannot be explained in one fell swoop, if superficiality is to be avoided. This discussion is therefore only one part of the larger whole that is the philosophy of Olympism. Our justification for this approach can be summed up in the words that anthropologist John J. MacAloon said of Olympism: "He who tries to swallow the thing whole will find himself swallowed by it instead."[2]

## Olympic Identification

The need for a feeling of identity comes from the very foundation of our existence. People are willing to do and to risk many things in order to gain or preserve contact with "alikeness"' or, as T. Praprotnik says, "to be able to be in the herd."[3] He goes on to develop a thesis about the necessity of creating *artificial* identities that are constitutive of subjective existence.

Today, when "big stories" (whether of ideology or religion) are moving off the world's stage, postmodern pluralism is calling for stories with heroes. If there is no single and eternal truth anymore, then everyday heroes (sport stars, movie stars, music stars, politicians, etc.) are good enough. But these heroes, under the sway of postmodern logic, are heroes just for today, to be replaced by new ones immediately. The Olympic Games are a wonderful generator of such small stories, personal dramas, and short-term identities.

From the viewpoint of the individual, sports spectacle—as any other sport activity—is based on single-person agency. From the wider social point of view, however, sport creates new laws that, in the case of the Olympic Games, become global or transnational. If, in concise and in dialectical manner, we draw a line from individualism and nationalism toward internationalism and transnationalism, we come in some sense back to the beginning—to the individual or, more specifically, to the subject-athlete—to justify our inner consistency of discourse.

## Individualism

We must give first place, the place of honor, to corporal identity (and once again express our affinity with sports culture) since, as the philosopher S. Južnič says, "Without corporal identity any other identity cannot exist."[4] The body is part of us; it is fundamental and unavoidable. Corporal identity is therefore always present. It can be manifested in many different forms of bodily techniques or bodily projects—and in this sense it allows a certain degree of modification. Through the bodily techniques known as sport a special kind of corporal identity is created: power, endurance, agility, beauty, elegance, discipline, health, and an identity that serves the particular movement patterns or required skills of individual sports.

When we talk about the Olympic Games, or, better, Olympic competition (Olympic *agōnes*) we need to consider the basic characteristics of competition. Sigmund Loland (2002) talks about the structural goals of competition: to measure, to compare, and to rank. Competition is, immanently, a conflict situation where, according to explicit criteria and cooperative agreements, the quality of competitors is measured, compared, and ranked. Ranking ultimately has the role of defining the most successful—the winner.

The athlete, therefore, is pushed to seek a competitive advantage. This today has become institutionalized behavior that permeates sport practice, sport science, sport reporting, and so on. Regardless, in the end, the sportsperson is an agent of activity responsible to himself and to others for his success and failure. Given the structure of sport, the logic behind seeking an advantage that leads to winning is obvious. But at the top there is not much room, obviously. This competitive structure sets the foundations for an ethical logic that follows the imperative of being the best and outdoing others. The struggle for the top is cruel and allows no slacking. That is why we can talk about the ethics of maximization in competitive sport. For further reflection we offer these thoughts from Jelica Šumič-Riha: "To call the subject to fully realize what he is capable of means that he is capable of doing something that he was not able to

before, or to realize what he thought he was not able to realize before."
And: "If we place ethics of law in opposition to ethics of proper measure,
we do it because ethics of law doesn't know the measure, not even thinking about the proper measure. The ethics of law is distinguished for its
excessiveness and immoderation."[5]

It would not be fair if we did not mention Coubertin's view on the
sports elite. The following quote of his from 1911 makes clear that even
Coubertin accepted the starkly competitive ethic inherent in sport: "The
athletes, for their part, will have to maintain quite a delicate balance between the exuberant zeal of the mind and the daring suppleness of the
body. Their effort will be a bit like flying in airplanes. Sometimes people
fall out of them and die, but it is a glorious end. On such wings, however,
those who remain on board have a shot, at least, at reaching the highest
peaks of pure Olympism." And to convince even the "last of the Mohi-
cans" who still think that elite sport is a practice that embodies such
values as moderation, sustainability, and the like, consider Coubertin's
words from 1935: "To try to make athletics conform to a system of mandatory moderation is to chase after an illusion. Athletes need the 'freedom of excess.' That is why their motto is *Citius, altius, fortius:* faster,
higher, stronger, the motto of anyone who dares to try to beat a record!"[6]

Olympic philosopher Hans Lenk's dynamic anthropology reveals a
paradox (a dynamic openness) in the essence of the human being.[7] He
understands and justifies the devotion of athletes to a purpose, to excellence, and to the imperative of going beyond limits. The personal inten-
tionality of athlete and the art of dynamic harmonization of human
potential are worthy of deep exploration at another opportunity. Here we
offer one more proof to support our claim about the importance of individualism in the context of free agency: "The Olympic record man is the
symbol reminding [us] of man's transcendental dimensions. It is mirroring
man's eternal quest for the best."[8] The excellence shown by the athletes,
then, is fascinating and results in some sort of comfort (material, social,
self-fulfilling, etc.). Any excellence presupposes effort; and, when the goal
is reached, some kind of institutional support is usually guaranteed (schol-
arships, awards, etc.). Still, we should not avoid the dynamic of human
existence. When there is excellence in one aspect, there usually is some
lack in others. This is only logical: not every practice can be driven to the
same level of excellence due to physical limitations of time and space.

Above all, when talking about individualism, we should emphasize the value of self-knowledge and self-realization through sport. Alienation seen and practiced in sport is an ideologically questionable phenomenon. The sports act influences our body in a way that precludes alienation (others can manipulate and regulate the achievement/result but no one can take away the athlete's self-experience). The ancient motto "Know thyself" has found in sport a good partner—one that reflects all the depth and paradox of the human being.

Olympism does not simply reflect social circumstances; it is also rooted deeply in the individual desire to succeed, to win, and to be recognized among others. In its symbolic sense it is similar to religion, and this is no coincidence. Religion, in order to exist, must sustain the irrational, which it does through fulfilling experiences and different interpretations of the symbolic. That is why the Olympics are full of small stories that are of great importance to humanity.

The words of runner Paavo Nurmi from Finland support again our thoughts about constructed reality, which finds itself somewhere between the subjective and objective, between self-centeredness and the view from nowhere. Said Nurmi: "I run for myself, not for Finland."[9]

There is much more we could say about individualism in sport; but because our concern here is the relation of individualism to internationalism, let us move forward to consider individualism in that larger context.

## Nationalism and Internationalism

Before the eyes of the world, the Olympic Games offer to big countries a chance to show their power, and to the smaller ones the chance to become known for "special effects." The opening ceremony is a wonderful opportunity for recognition, since the national symbols visible at such international gatherings prompt strong emotions for many.[10]

Coubertin, when he realized that there would be some difficulties in the Stockholm Olympics in 1911, wrote that the Games should include "all games, all nations." Finns and Czechs didn't want to compete under the flags of Russia and Austria. Finnish runner Hannes Kolehmainen, pointing to the Russian flag, stated: "I would almost rather not have won than see the flag up there."[11] By allowing Finns and Czechs to walk in the opening ceremony with their national symbols, Coubertin expressed his so-called sports geography: the notion that the nation is not necessarily an independent state. That is why sports geography sometimes differs from political geography.[12]

It was not only Coubertin who viewed the nation through the lens of sport. Earlier individuals (e.g., Jahn, Guhts-Muts) and movements (e.g., Sokol) promoted the development of strong, healthy, and powerful individuals who would represent the nation. But Coubertin saw in sport the values of democracy and freedom that were starting to flourish in France's Third Republic.

To honor the flag as a national symbol is one of the main aims of Coubertin's concept of *religio athletae*. The athlete, whether he likes it or not, is representing his own nation, and Coubertin was aware of this. The power of national identification is gained as differences are exposed on an international stage. If this is done in the context of international confrontation, which is what the Olympics are about, then the drama (although only a game) affects the mass of people and their sense of collective identity.

To illustrate the zeitgeist when nationalism became an important political force, consider the following excerpt from Prince Albert's Mansion House speech addressing the first World Exposition in London in 1851:

> Nobody . . . who has paid any attention to the peculiar features of our present era, will doubt for a moment that we are living at a period of most wonderful transition, which tends rapidly to accomplish that great end, to which, indeed, all history points—the realisation of the unity of mankind. . . .
>
> The distances which separated the different nations and parts of the globe are rapidly vanishing before the achievements of modern invention, and we can traverse them with incredible ease. . . . On the other hand, the great principle of division of labour, which may be called the moving power of civilisation, is being extended to all branches of science, industry, and art.[13]

Integrating the nations seemed, after the times of colonialism, when the world was already possessed by a few, a logical move. But, with the development of a political culture that valued democratization and liberalization, strong divorcing movements in the guise of nationalism occurred. Despite all efforts to sustain the myth that sports (the Olympics especially) have nothing to do with politics, the political activities of the International Olympic Committee (IOC) are the driving force that joins the world every four years. Therefore, let us now focus on an understanding of Olympism through the national and international context.

## Coubertin's Internationalism

In 1935, Coubertin wrote:

> To ask people to love one another is merely a form of childishness. To ask them to respect each other is utopian, but in order to respect each other they must first know each other. The only true basis for peace will come from taking into account the precise chronological and geographical outlines of World History as it can now be taught.[14]

William Morgan describes Coubertin's internationalism as a kind of moral epistemology; knowing others (their core beliefs, values, and forms of life) is the prerequisite to treating them with the proper approach and respect. He questions whether we can reasonably hope to achieve solidarity with others, and not suppress or deform their cultural identity or "turn them into something they are not: clones of us."[15]

Coubertin was aware of different interpretations of internationalism. In order to follow the global aims of world order and peace he distinguishes between true or sincere internationalism and its insincere simulacrum: "There are two ways of understanding internationalism," he wrote in 1901. "One is that of the socialists, the revolutionaries, and in general, of theoreticians and utopians. . . . The second is that of men who make observation without prejudice and take reality, rather than their favourite ideas, into account. For a long time now, these men have realized that national characteristics are an indispensable precondition for the life of a people and that, far from weakening them, contact with other people makes them sharper."[16]

The other way of understanding internationalism has evolved into a cosmopolitanism that can be also seen in two ways. One way, in Coubertin's explanation, was of a cynical character: "An English company—the same one which owns the Hotel Metropole in London—has built very near Cannes an enormous hotel which is filled with English people. Why do they go there instead of to other hotels equally as well, or even better, situated? Because the wallpapers, the furniture, the staffs, even the fenders, all come from London; because they gave bacon for breakfast in the morning and toast and muffins at afternoon tea; because, in short, they provide themselves with the illusion of being on the shores of the Mediterranean without having left England."[17]

Certainly, this way of understanding internationalism leads to a false recognition of other nations/cultures. Coubertin also commented on the new culture of tourism, which can be afforded only by an aristocratic elite and is, from the elites' point of view, justified. MacAloon ingeniously grasps the spirit of those times of multicultural cooperation, especially in its representation of exotic people/cultures, with the phrase "popular ethnography." The flourishing science and technology that were on display at world expositions were also, under the guise of public education, exhibiting "primitive" tribes.

Imported "savages" displayed their culture on the stage in front of the exposition visitors on the streets of London, Paris, and other cities. Rituals that were supposed to be kept away from the public's eyes, and should have been undertaken only in the context and circumstances prescribed by the tribe's tradition and mythology, were deconstructed and completely devalued (sold off).

Cosmopolitanism manifested as modern tourism has the same influence on authentic culture as spectacle does on ritual. It is unaccomplished, deficient, unaccustomed, unengaged observation based on distance and apparent objectivity, which creates an opportunity for uncritical interpretation of what is seen, and for the culture to be manipulated in any touristically profitable way.

The epistemological emphasis on properly understanding others should have been one of the key messages of modern Olympism, and today the Games openly emphasize their role in such understanding. Multiculturalism is one of the core promotional mottos of the Olympic movement, which is one of the most successful (if not the most successful) organizations at generating international networking in the form of interaction among representatives from all the countries of the world.

The contemporary Olympic idea combines the political and social power of the United Nations with the universally binding strength of sport manifested through spectacle. The problems produced by (to paraphrase President George W. Bush) the axis of Olympic evil—professionalism, gigantism, and cultural imperialism—can only be counterbalanced through critical reflection and self-restrictions of these "evils," together with the promotion of symbolic and actual networking.

The fact that over two hundred nations gather for the Games, as witnessed in Beijing in 2008, speaks for itself, and is worth preserving—though not at any price, of course, and maybe not in the exact form that it is now. True internationalism demands the recognition of social and cultural differences, but not the broadening of the gap between them. National differences, as MacAloon suggests, should be celebrated as various forms of living, which is the first step toward peace, friendship, and mutual respect.

Patriotic nationalism, defined by Coubertin as a love of country, demands a critical approach, not a blind love that sees no defects. Love of one's country does not exclude an interest in, and attraction to, other countries. False nationalism, by contrast, is deeply rooted in hostility toward others, which fosters an uncritical, irrational relationship with one's home country, leading to conditions of conflict contrary to the international spirit.

The second part of Coubertin's nationalism has to do with meeting others, since only in this way is it possible to come to know others, and to develop the respect that comes from that knowledge. This is the important role of the Olympics as a cultural event transcending mere sport.

Morgan emphasizes the value of Coubertin's sincere internationalism as an ideal, since it requires not only tolerance, but also respect for another's worth. On this point we must acknowledge the depth of Coubertin's thinking (conscious or not), which still resonates today. In the words of Ante Debeljak, "Tolerance, namely, is nothing else than the form of superiority to which the explicit instance or subject allows (the thing, person, viewpoint etc.) to exist, not being valued equal to himself. In Hegelian words it is about the right to be different, which is known, but not recognized, i.e. it doesn't come to be a constitutive part of the viewer's horizon. Inside of the horizon of tolerance, the language games are equal in principle, but not as a matter of fact."[18]

Sincere nationalism and sincere internationalism, following Morgan, constitute the core of Coubertin's theory, which tends toward peace and dynamic international order sustained through the existence and development of pluralism, and not, as it might be interpreted, mere tolerance. Sport plays a special role in this context.

First, to quote Morgan, sport can provide an "opportunity for im-passioned soaring that evinces a healthy drunkenness of the blood" while raising and intensifying human experience.[19] Second, athletic standards of excellence are the motivation given by the structural organization of sport; this motivation does not sanction the comfortableness of everyday routine but, rather, forces the athlete to push as far as possible, to engage fully in the practice and, ultimately, with his competitors.

This and much more is experienced by the athlete, and it does not allow the spectator to remain high above the happening, unaligned. That sport is much more than the game—that it possesses the depth of narra-tion—is seen in the words of the grandmother of the famous boxer Joe Louis. Listening to a live radio report of his match, when Louis was in trouble or seemed about to lose, she said: "It was not just one black man against the ropes, it was our people falling. It was another lynching, yet another black man hanging on a tree. One more woman ambushed and raped. A black boy whipped and maimed. . . . We didn't breathe. We didn't hope. We waited."[20] Internationalism, then, presupposes national-ism, and not just any kind of nationalism, but the sincere one we have described. But there is one more identifying line, which does not require a national quality, since it is established independently from it. Here we start with the notion that the IOC is a transnational organization, whose members represent Olympic interests, not, as often misinterpreted, na-tions on the board of the IOC—at least not in a formal, organizational way.

## Transnationalism

The International Olympic Committee was established in the late nine-teenth and early twentieth centuries, a period that spawned several great international organizations (the Red Cross in 1863, the Esperanto move-ment in 1887, and the Scouts movement in 1908, to name only three). New ideas sprang up about world citizenship, environmental concerns, social and peace movements, the elimination of economic and political borders, and the importance of human rights. These new movements were apparently independent of national interests, as is the Olympic movement, which engages individuals through sport regardless of national origin. It is clearly defined in the Olympic Charter that the IOC is the highest authority of the Olympic movement, and that "any person or organisation belonging in any capacity whatsoever to the Olympic Movement is bound by the provisions of the Olympic Charter and shall abide by the decisions of the IOC."[21] The IOC is also, however, dependent upon the support of multinational corporations and media attention. The international characteristics of the Olympic movement should therefore be understood also from the viewpoint of transnationalism. While acknowledging that the movement is affected by a variety of interests (nongovernmental, governmental, national, transnational, corporate, and media interests, to name a few), we focus here on the transnational dimension of the Olympic movement.

We begin with the set of characteristics of transnational organizations offered by Macintosh and Hawes, who define such organizations as:

1. having a relatively large, hierarchically organized, centrally directed bureaucracy;

2. performing a set of relatively limited, specialized, and, in some sense, technical functions; and

3. performing these functions across one or more international boundaries and, insofar as is possible, in relative disregard of those boundaries.[22]

To support the idea of transnational organizations, Huntington contrasts them with international organizations.[23] First, an international organization requires identification with, and a basis for, common interests among nations, whereas a transnational organization follows its own interests, which do not necessarily relate to the national. Second, the purpose of an international organization is to facilitate or safeguard the common interests of nations, while a transnational organization pursues a single interest among many national units. And third, an international organization requires consensus among nations, whereas the transnational one only requires access to the nations.

That third contrast ingeniously grasps a difference that can serve as our point of departure for explaining the logic of the Olympic movement on the transnational level. Access to nations is the key to the movement's existence.

How is it, then, that the Olympic movement manages to bring the entire world together without being denied by a single nation (excepting here the occasional exemption). Something has to produce this "irresistible impulse" that goes beyond borders, wars, and truce. "The Games must go on!" said Avery Brundage when tragedy happened in Munich in 1972, thereby transcending the merely political.

Thirty years later, however, Brundage's fellow American, President George W. Bush, declared the Salt Lake Games open even as the hosting nation was at war with Iraq, which certainly is not in accordance with Olympic ideals and breaks the symbolic sacredness of Olympic truce.[24] But the symbolic values of the Olympics are probably best exemplified by the spectacular show in which the individual, the nation, and humanity itself performs as one. This is the magic formula for success.

The concepts of equality, a fair fight, the chance for little heroes to win their games, world peace, and united humanity are ideals that allow different interpretations and can touch every human being to the deepest layers of the soul. As MacAloon tells us, the Olympics are the celebration of storytelling.[25]

Being an elite club, the IOC from its very beginning was devoted to the ideology of progress. Following socioeconomic trends, it has evolved into a real multinational corporation that has transcended its original nonprofit nature. Yet at the same time it has acted as a defensive mechanism, trying to stop unarticulated growth and leading the anti-doping movement. It is too early to reach conclusions about the consequences of the IOC's forceful anti-doping campaign. But we mention it here to show the power that the Olympic movement has. In just a few years the World Anti-Doping Agency (WADA), established under the initiative of the IOC, has succeeded in convincing international sport federations and the governments of many states to follow its rules about doping in sport—in some cases even inspiring new public laws.

The mythological dimensions of Olympism also evolve on a transnational level, although this aspect of its transnationalism may be seen negatively, as cultural-ideological imperialism. The fascination with sports drama of the highest degree is at the same time inspiring to athletes and spectators; it inspires passion and reveals the immanent paradoxical nature of human beings. Because of this, sport plays an important role in the imperative to "know thyself," since it is obviously both a physical and a moral activity.

## Conclusion

Through symbolic struggle, the transnational organization depends on the efforts of the individual. It is, as written in the ritualized formula of the Olympics, the celebration of the individual, the nation, and humanity. The winner is objectively always the winner for himself, for the nation, and for humanity. Spectators and participants alike are free to interpret and identify with one or with all of the above. But the values of ritual, if taken seriously, don't allow manipulation of the fundamental idea. The idea is branded as a seal onto the athlete, who becomes an Olympian forever. To be an Olympian means to have suffered the requirements of ritual, to have gone successfully through the tasks of the sport maturity test (i.e., Olympic competition), and to have entered the new dimension of the Olympic family.

Olympic transnationalism, we conclude, is pragmatic: the Olympic movement is constantly being reshaped and reinterpreted through its broadly conceived idealistic values. Nowadays, for example, a concern with multiculturalism and environmentalism is fashionable and attracts interest. Not by chance, the Olympic ideologists are leading the promotion of the Olympic movement in this direction. What we need now is an institution that follows these ideas, leaving the old (now false) concepts behind and setting a new paradigm of the Olympics as a human and nature-friendly organization.

Through continuing discussion, many new avenues for interpreting Olympism have been opened. Certainly, one of the more thought-provoking is the analogy between the Olympics and Empire, which could be addressed through transnationalism.

Individualism, going through transnationalism, turns into itself again. The reproduction of the ruling order, no matter how abstract it may seem, is effected by the individual. And the power for change lies in the hands of that same individual, if only he or she is capable of recognizing this fact.

In closing, we quote the conception of Empire given by Hardt and Negri: "Finally, although the practice of Empire is continually bathed in blood, the concept of Empire is always dedicated to peace—a perpetual and universal peace outside of history."[26] That paradox is among the core issues of the modern Olympics. The practice of elite sport devoted to the logic of spectacle begins with the record-seeking and backbreaking individuals who follow the narrow goal of winning, while inspiring the rhetoric of an institution devoted to health, peace, and understanding.

## Notes

1. The first such exposition was held in London in 1851. Twenty-five countries were represented, and in the period of five months more than six million visitors had been counted (Roche 2000, 48).
2. MacAloon 1981, xi.
3. Praprotnik 1999, 21.
4. Južnič 1993, 17.
5. Šumič-Riha 2002, 12.
6. Coubertin 2000, 212, 581.
7. Lenk 1984.
8. Ibid., 333.
9. Nurmi quoted in Senn 1999, xv.
10. Senn 1999.
11. Kolehmainen quoted in ibid., 30.
12. Coubertin 2000, 590.
13. Albert quoted in MacAloon 1981, 129.
14. Coubertin 2000, 583.
15. Morgan 1994, 12.
16. Coubertin quoted in MacAloon 1981, 264.
17. Ibid.
18. Debeljak 1989, 90 (my translation).
19. See Morgan 1994.
20. Quoted in Guttmann 1986, 182.
21. Olympic Charter 2004, General organization article 2, p. 10.
22. Macintosh and Hawes 1992, 6.
23. Huntington 1973.
24. Here we cannot fight the cynicism: it is obviously about the transnational organization that, when appropriate, transcends also itself.
25. MacAloon 1981.
26. Hardt and Negri 2000, xv.

## Bibliography

Coubertin, P. de. 2000. *Olympism—Selected Writings*. Lausanne: International Olympic Committee.

Debeljak, A. 1989. *Postmoderna sfinga* [Postmodern sphinx]. Celovec: Wieser.

Gebauer, G. "Citius–Altius–Fortius and the Problem of Sport Ethics: a Philosopher's Viewpoint." In *Sport, the Third Millennium,* ed. F. Landry, M. Landry, and M. Yerlès. Sainte-Foy: Laval, 1991.

Gruneau, R., and D. Whitson. 1993. *Hockey Night in Canada: Sport, Identities, and Cultural Politics.* Toronto: Garamond.

Guttmann, A. 1986. *Sports Spectators.* New York: Columbia University Press.

Hardt, M., and A. Negri. 2000. *Empire.* Cambridge, MA: Harvard University Press.

Huntington, S. P. 1973. "Transnational Organizations in World Politics." *World Politics* 25 (April): 333–368.

Južnič, S. 1993. *Identiteta.* Ljubljana: Fakulteta za družbene vede.

Lenk, H. 1984. "The Essence of the Olympic Man: Toward an Olympic Philosophy and Anthropology." *International Journal of Physical Education* 21, no. 2: 9–14.

Loland, S. 1995. "Coubertin's Ideology of Olympism from the Perspective of the History of Ideas." *Olympika* 4: 49–78.

———. 2002. *Fair Play in Sport.* London: Routledge.

MacAloon, J. J. 1981. *This Great Symbol.* Chicago: University of Chicago Press.

———. 1989. "Olympic Games and the Theory of Spectacle in Modern Societies." In *Rite, Drama, Festival, Spectacle,* ed. J. J. MacAloon. Philadelphia: Institute for the Study of Human Issues.

Macintosh, D., and M. Hawes. 1992. "The IOC and the World of Interdependence." In *First International Symposium for Olympic Research,* ed. R. K. Barney and K. V. Meier. London, ON: International Centre for Olympic Studies.

MacNeill, M., P. Donnelly, and G. Knight. 2000. "Contested Nationalisms: Canadian Athlete–Media–Sponsor Relations and Preparations for the Sydney Olympic Games." In *Bridging Three Centuries: Intellectual Crossroads and the Modern Olympic Movement—Fifth International Symposium for Olympic Research,* ed. K. B. Wamsley, S. G. Martyn, G. H. MacDonald, and R. K. Barney. London, Ontario: Centre for Olympic Studies, University of Western Ontario.

Miller, T., G. Lawrence, J. McKay, and D. Rowe. 2001. *Globalisation and Sport.* London: SAGE.

Morgan, J. W. 1994. "Coubertin's Theory of Internationalism: A Critical Reinterpretation." In *Critical Reflections on Olympic Ideology: Second International Symposium for Olympic Research,* ed. R. K. Barney and K. V. Meier. London, Ontario: Centre for Olympic Studies, University of Western Ontario.

———. 1995. "Cosmopolitanism, Olympism, and Nationalism: A Critical Interpretation of Coubertin's Ideal of International Sporting Life." *Olympika* 4: 79–92.

Olympic Charter. 2004. http://multimedia.olympic.org/pdf/en_report_122.pdf.

Parry, J. 1999. "Globalisation, Multiculturalism, and Olympism." Paper delivered at 39th International Session of the International Olympic Academy, Olympia.

Praprotnik, T. 1999. *Ideološki mehanizmi produkcije identitet* [Ideological mechanisms of identity production]. Ljubljana: ISH in ŠOU.

Roche, M. 2000. *Mega-Events and Modernity: Olympics and Expos in the Growth of Global Culture.* London: Routledge.

Senn, A. F. 1999. *Power, Politics, and the Olympic Games.* Champaign, IL: Human Kinetics.

Šumič-Riha, J. 2002. *Mutacije etike: od utopije do neozravljive resnice* [Mutations of ethics: from Utopia to incurable truth]. Ljubljana: ZRC.

Vodeb, R. 2001. *Šport skozi psihoanalizo* [Sport through psychoanalysis]. Trbovlje: FIT.

*Jeffrey P. Fry*

# CITIUS, ALTIUS, FORTIUS, VIRTUOUS

Imagine that you have just been transported through time to an Olympic Games in the not-too-distant future. You arrive at an athletic venue as three women are ascending a victors' stand, where they will be festooned with gold, silver, and bronze medals, respectively. Soon you realize that these Olympic Games have a new twist. Medals are being awarded in these Games not only for athletic excellence, but for moral excellence as well. Indeed, the three women in question are being recognized for their morally virtuous performances. These awards go hand in hand with a recently revised Olympic motto, which was formerly *Citius, altius, fortius*. Due to proclaimed heightened interest among the custodians of the Olympic movement in moral virtuosity, the new Olympic motto reads "Citius, Altius, Fortius, Virtuous."

Is this scenario plausible or feasible? Is it a worthy goal? These are questions that I consider in this chapter. The motives behind a desire to reward virtuous sporting performances with Olympic medals might be understandable, and even laudable. Rewards for moral virtue might even seem especially fitting in the context of the Olympic Games. After all, the ancient Greeks gave us the Olympics, and ancient Greek philosophers such as Plato and Aristotle were deeply concerned about moral virtue. In addition, coinciding with the fact that the Olympics currently occur on a worldwide stage, in recent decades there has been a revival of virtue ethics. Despite these seemingly serendipitous factors, however, I argue that an attempt to implement such reforms would face tall, if not insuperable, hurdles. While it is now customary to bestow encomiums and awards for sportspersonship and courageous comebacks in sports, the Olympic

Games are a peculiar institution, and attempts to award virtuous performances in Olympic competitions in a widespread fashion would face significant challenges in addition to those encountered in other sporting contexts.

In the first part of this chapter, I suggest some possible rationales for the contemplated Olympic reforms, and I show that each of these has attendant problems.[1] I derive these concerns, in particular, from the moral philosophy of Immanuel Kant. In the second part, I examine some issues of a practical nature that would complicate an attempt to implement such proposals in the Olympic Games. While I do not claim to have exhausted all of the potential problems associated with awarding Olympic medals for virtue, I raise sufficiently significant concerns so as to call into question the feasibility of the contemplated reforms. In concluding, I offer a scaled-back proposal in keeping with the spirit, but not the letter, of the reforms considered for the Olympic Games.

## Arguments Pro

Why consider the proposed reforms at all? What might motivate the issue at hand? Here I examine the merits of three related rationales for the reforms considered for the Olympic Games. Stated concisely, these rationales focus respectively on the expectation, encouragement, and recognition of virtue at the Olympics. The first rationale highlights standards. The second rationale focuses on consequences. (The first rationale could also take this form, but it need not.) The third rationale is a claim that it is fitting to acknowledge virtuous performances. Each of these rationales raises concerns.

### Raising Expectations

The Olympic Games and other sporting competitions are made possible under the condition of mutual expectations and professions. Among them are the expectation and profession of fair play. This is a peculiar, hybrid form of expectation, combining prescriptive and descriptive elements, with varying weights assigned to each of the components, depending on local circumstances.[2] Of course, the expectation of fairness is frequently unmet, and few of us are naïve enough to believe that Olympic athletes never cheat. But in the absence of at least an aura of fairness, one arguably significant rationale for sporting competitions—the determination of the relative excellence of competitors under shared conditions—vanishes.[3]

Suppose that International Olympic Committee members determined that the expectation of fair play is too minimalist. Olympic officials might decide to send the more robust message that in addition to fairness, various other virtues (such as courage or compassion) are expected of Olympic competitors.[4] Furthermore, they might conclude that they could promote this message by bestowing medals on individuals who exemplify the relevant virtues in their Olympic performances.

This scenario raises a number of issues. One initial difficulty with this approach is that it would require that Olympic officials determine which virtues should be rewarded. Assuming they were able to resolve the issue of relevance, and were also able to detect and measure the relevant virtues (more about these issues below), the awarding of medals for virtuous performances might still be counterproductive, due to unintended consequences. If a select few are awarded for virtuous performances, athletes might conclude that only members of an elite group are able to attain a medal level of virtue.[5] Notwithstanding Garrison Keillor's Lake Wobegon, the received message might be that not all children can be "above average," even in virtue, and this might have a deflationary effect on motivation.

Further, if the expectations of virtue were understood in a strongly prescriptive sense, then they would translate into commands. But should Olympic officials be licensed to command virtue in the context of athletic competition? To single out one issue in this regard, what would determine the line of demarcation between expected and perhaps prescribed behavior on the one hand, and what is supererogatory (above and beyond the call of duty) on the other?

There are significant, real-life consequences to the responses given to such questions. For example, in recent years there has been debate among mountain climbers as to one's moral obligation to fellow climbers who fall ill or are injured while climbing mountains at high altitudes. Climbers have faced well-publicized situations under these conditions in which life-and-death decisions have been made. Some climbers have risked their

own well-being and sacrificed their dreams in order to assist fellow climbers. Other climbers, however, have held to a sterner ethic. They have been
unwilling to risk their own well-being for others, and some have held that
it is unreasonable to expect them to do so.

In general, of course, the stakes are lower in the Olympic Games.
Even so, Olympic athletes would likely balk at a robust idea of virtue on
command. In light of such likely resistance, a more accommodating approach might be taken. Instead of expecting virtuous performance in a
strongly prescriptive sense (at least beyond a requirement of fair play),
Olympic officials might reframe their rationale in terms of encouraging
virtuous performances. This revised, "softer" rationale for rewarding virtuous performances on the medal stand would be that these awards could
elicit virtuous performances.

## Encouraging Virtue

Some have argued that the offer of inducements for virtuous athletic performances in the Olympic Games would foster virtue. In order to evaluate this argument I borrow from the work of the German philosopher
Immanuel Kant. While Kant was not himself celebrated for athletic
prowess, he was purportedly a faithful and methodical walker in his
hometown of Koenigsberg. As we will see below, Kant believed that virtue deserved a reward. But at the same time, he perceived a problem in
the linkage of virtue and reward.

In Kant's view, people should not seek to live virtuous lives in order
to receive rewards, even though their virtuosity deserves to be rewarded.[6]
For Kant, the issue of motive was of singular importance in moral action,
and he held that for an action to have moral worth, it must be motivated
by duty, and not by the prospect of reward.[7] One plausible interpretation
of Kant's view is that although other motives might also be in play when
one acts, the motive of duty would have to be sufficient for the action to
occur in order for the action to have genuine moral worth.[8] Adherence to
this view might, however, complicate efforts to foster morally praiseworthy actions in the Olympics and in sports generally.

In the ESPN film *Winning Time: Reggie Miller vs. the New York Knicks*,
former NBA great Patrick Ewing tells what it was like playing under then–
Knicks coach Pat Riley. According to Ewing, any Knicks player who

picked up an opposing player who had been knocked to the ground was subject to a fine. But imagine a different scenario. Suppose that in order to encourage sportspersonship, officials added a new rule such that a basketball team would be awarded a point whenever one of its players helped up a fallen opponent. Players might then assist opponents, though their act might be primarily motivated by the desire to score a point, rather than by a sense of duty or out of compassion. Players knocked to the floor might even refuse assistance in an attempt to prevent their opponents from being awarded a point.[9]

On the one hand, Kant's rather stringent conditions for the moral worth of an action seem to collide with what we think are reasonable expectations for creatures with the psychological makeup of human beings. But on the other hand, there is something unsettling about the prospect of individuals consumed with obtaining rewards for being "virtuous." We would rightfully question whether such individuals were truly virtuous. Would such persons, in the absence of the prospect of reward, still act as virtuous persons would? If not, might such persons be aptly characterized as opportunistic rather than as virtuous? It might then be the case that attempting to encourage virtuous performances by offering medals would be counterproductive. This practice might actually lead to a reduction of virtue, particularly if virtue is constituted by an inner condition of the moral agent and not simply by outward behavior.[10]

Not to be deterred from their goal of awarding medals for morally virtuous performances, Olympic officials might opt for a third rationale. Rather than prescribing virtue or offering enticements for virtuous performances, they might argue that it is simply fitting to recognize virtuous performances. One conspicuous way to bestow this recognition would be by awarding medals.

## Recognizing Virtue

Once again I turn to Kant, in the first place to offer support for this position, but ultimately to call it into question. As already noted, Kant held that an action could not be truly morally praiseworthy unless performed from the motive of duty. Yet he also believed that virtue and reward are logically connected.

Kant held that virtuous people deserve a reward of happiness. In a realized state of the highest good, people's happiness would be commensurate with their virtue. In our present existence, however, this correlation is not found. Instead, in our world righteous individuals suffer and scoundrels sometimes prosper. As a result, in order to make sense of morality Kant postulated a future existence in which we finally receive what we deserve.[11]

With Kant in mind, we might say that the awarding of medals for virtue at the Olympics provides a partial realization of the highest good in this world. Virtue would be rewarded, as is fitting—and in the here and now.[12]

But this approach also raises some concerns, some of which have already been touched on, but which reappear here. Kant believed that virtue deserves to be rewarded; but, as already noted, he was also concerned about the motives that propel one's actions. Given this concern, how would judges ascertain the motives behind athletes' actions? Might the awarding of medals for virtuous performances foster an environment in which athletes performed "virtuously" in order to receive recognition? How would one know?

In Kant's philosophy there is a final arbiter who ultimately sees to it that a reward of happiness is properly allocated for virtue. Kant postulated the existence of God, along with immortality and freedom, in order to make sense of morality. In an existence beyond this life God sees to it that one's happiness is properly apportioned in light of one's virtue. God has the requisite knowledge and power to do this. But human beings do not possess the requisite power to justly apportion happiness in systematic fashion; and, more to the point for present considerations, we do not possess the requisite knowledge of people's motivations to ensure that virtue is fittingly recognized.

Perhaps no single difficulty that I have pointed out is of sufficient force to rule out the imagined reforms that I have depicted. Taken together, however, they do pose a nontrivial challenge to the proposed reforms.

## Practical Complications

I turn now to some practical concerns. Some of these are relevant to any enterprise in which virtues are singled out, acknowledged, and measured in individuals. But, as I intimated earlier, the Olympic Games pose some special challenges for such endeavors.

## Epistemological Obstacles

Among the practical obstacles to successfully instituting the proposed Olympic reforms are some epistemological issues.[13] In the first place, given the global nature of the Olympic movement, there would have to be cross-cultural agreement about which characteristics to recognize as virtues. Different virtues have been emphasized at different times and in different cultures. Christianity places emphasis on a kind of humility. But Aristotle, one of the great expositors on virtue in the ancient world, did not catalogue humility as a virtue.[14] More recently, Friedrich Nietzsche offered sharp criticisms of Christian virtues.[15]

Nevertheless, while acknowledging a degree of cultural relativity with respect to the virtues, we might attempt to find areas of agreement to avoid the controversial cases.[16] Something like this strategy is contemplated in Plato's celebrated dialogue *Euthyphro*.[17] After announcing that piety is what the gods love, Euthyphro is confronted with the claim that the gods sometimes disagree with one another. Some gods hate certain things that the others love. Thus, Euthyphro's definition of piety seems unworkable. As a result, Euthyphro revises his position. Focusing on the area of agreement among the gods, he then suggests that piety is that which *all* of the gods love.

Perhaps some level of widespread cross-cultural agreement can be found. As already noted, fairness seems to be an underlying value of the Olympic Games. Perhaps if we probed the idea of fairness deeply enough it would lead us to the advocacy of other, related virtues.[18] Suppose that these possibilities were realized. Still, this would not settle all of the epistemological challenges, including those concerned with the detection and measurement of virtue.

I have already discussed the issue of opaque motivations, and how some individuals might act "virtuously" for a reward. But there is another issue related to the opaqueness of our inner states. We might fail to take note of athletes who are inconspicuously performing virtuously. We can determine, albeit at times only by enlisting the help of technology, who crosses the finish line first, who jumps highest, and who throws the farthest. Although their decisions are at times highly controversial, judges also assess the excellence of dives, tumbling routines, and skating performances. But would the process of detecting and quantifying virtues such as courage share a similar degree of difficulty? Surely not. The process of detecting and measuring virtue would entail vastly greater difficulty. Often we lack critical information about the athlete in question. What is happening in the athlete's life? How much physical and emotional pain is the athlete enduring? What innate abilities does the athlete possess?

At times we may feel confident, if not certain, that we are observing truly courageous performances. Consider a grueling duel between two front-runners who are racing at record-setting pace over the last several laps of the 10,000-meter run. Something like courage or fortitude is surely on display here. But how would we measure their courage? Could we automatically assume that the winner was the more courageous of the two? This does not seem self-evidently true. Beyond this issue, how would we compare the courage of the winner of this event with that of a participant in another running event, such as the marathon, or in an altogether different event, such as the discus throw?

I have considered here some epistemological challenges to the proposed reforms. But there are also political issues. These issues might turn out to be among the most intractable ones.

## Political Obstacles

Who would constitute our panel of expert judges, and how would they be selected? Would we want ethics professors to serve as judges? Or perhaps former athletes? Would the judges need expertise in both ethics and sport? The Olympic Games have already known their share of well-publicized problems in connection with events in which the judgments of Olympic officials are determinative in awarding athletic excellence. Wouldn't the judgment of character be fraught with even more problems? Could we count on the objectivity of the judges? What judges would want to see their countrymen and -women consistently out of the running for medals for virtue? Isn't it likely that there would be intense political pressure from above to render biased judgments? What if a handful of countries consistently captured most of the virtue medals? Because the Olympic Games are highly symbolic, this might be interpreted as signifying the moral superiority of those countries. But this would surely mean a loss of face for those left out. It is implausible that in the arena of global politics these results would be deemed acceptable. How would these issues be resolved?

Once again, the argument for awarding Olympic medals for virtue faces serious hurdles. In place of the suggested Olympic reforms, I want now to suggest a more modest approach.

## A Scaled-Back Scenario

Perhaps the concern about awarding medals for virtue has been much ado about nothing. Could it be that the awarding of medals for virtuous performances in the Olympics would be redundant? It could be argued that winners and other top finishers are the most virtuous in a sense highly relevant to athletic competition. Since they already receive medals, there is no need for further recognition.

But surely this argument is flawed. It is plausible that consistent winning requires special excellences, perhaps even certain moral virtues.[19] Nevertheless, there is something to be said for the maligned notion of moral victories. These are not victories in the customary sense, hence their maligned nature. But they can be remarkable. Athletes are at times pitted against opponents whose natural abilities are far superior. Yet sometimes the lesser athletes give those with superior overall skills a strong test, as when a 1,500-meter runner who does not possess a strong finishing "kick" strategically pushes the pace early in the race, but is caught in the end after a courageous effort.[20] Stunning upsets are even known to occur, as when Billy Mills won the 10,000-meter race in the 1964 Tokyo Olympics in a time of 28:24.4, which was 46 seconds faster than he had previously run the distance.[21] In any case, there are surely occasions in which athletes exhibit exemplary character in losing efforts. Even leaving cheating aside, we cannot count on an exact correspondence between winning and virtue.

Given that we cannot count on a simple correlation between athletic success and virtue, and in light of the caveats previously raised in this chapter, what might we do if we wished to acknowledge virtuous sporting performances? One possible approach is to embrace a practice already found in the sporting world. This is to acknowledge seemingly candidates for virtue, such as honesty or courage. Finally, it seems to be the case that from the time of the ancient Olympic Games Olympic athletes have been esteemed for embodying a variety of virtues, and that there have been hopes and expectations regarding virtuous performances. What to my knowledge distinguishes the current proposal is that medals for moral virtue would be awarded in addition to the medals awarded to winners and other top finishers of events.

5. One might object here that, following this logic, athletes wouldn't be motivated to pursue Olympic medals for athletic excellence either. But there are significant differences between rewarding athletic excellence and rewarding moral excellence. For one thing, in tests to determine athletic superiority, athletes can actually see how close they came to winning a medal.

6. See Immanuel Kant, *Critique of Practical Reason*, trans. Lewis White Beck, Library of Liberal Arts (New York: Macmillan, 1956).

7. On acting from the motive of duty see Immanuel Kant, *Groundwork of the Metaphysics of Morals*, trans. H. J. Paton (New York: Harper & Row, 1964), 64–69.

8. For this point I am indebted to John Beversluis, "The Connection between Duty and Happiness in Kant's Moral Philosophy," PhD diss., Indiana University, 1972.

9. I am indebted to Heather Reid for this apt example.

10. For example, see Aristotle's stringent qualifications for truly virtuous actions in Aristotle, *The Nicomachean Ethics*, trans. David Ross, rev. J. L. Ackrill and J. O. Urmson ([1925] Oxford: Oxford University Press, 1980), p. 34. Aristotle writes: "The agent must also be in a certain condition when he does them; in the first place he must have knowledge, second he must choose the acts, and choose them for their own sakes, and thirdly his actions must proceed from a firm and unchangeable character."

11. For Kant's views on the highest good, and his postulations of God, freedom, and immortality discussed below, see Kant, *Critique of Practical Reason*.

12. In theological parlance, this represents "realized eschatology." Something like the Kingdom of God is realized in this world here and now.

13. "Epistemology" refers to the study of knowledge. The word *episteme* is Greek for "knowledge."

14. See Aristotle, *Nicomachean Ethics*.

15. See, e.g., Friedrich Nietzsche, *Beyond Good and Evil: Prelude to a Philosophy of the Future*, trans. Walter Kaufmann (New York: Vintage Books/Random House, 1966).

16. For an illuminating discussion of "transcultural virtues" in the context of the Olympics, see Mike McNamee, "Olympism, Eurocentrism, and Transcultural Virtues," *Journal of the Philosophy of Sport* 33 (2006): 174–187. I am indebted to McNamee's paper.

17. See Plato, "Euthyphro," in Steven M. Cahn and Maureen Eckert, eds., *Philosophical Horizons: Introductory Readings* (Belmont, CA: Thomson/Wadsworth, 2006), 22–31.

18. See note 4 above.

19. R. Scott Kretchmar argues that there are particular excellences connected with winning. See Kretchmar, "In Defense of Winning," in Jan Boxill, ed., *Sports Ethics: An Anthology* (Malden, MA: Blackwell Publishing, 2003), 130–135.

20. See Robert L. Simon, *Fair Play: The Ethics of Sport*, 2nd ed. (Boulder, CO: Westview Press, 2004), especially chap. 2, "Competition, a Mutual Quest for Excellence," 17–39. Simon argues that contestants can "meet the challenge set by an opponent" (36) without winning.

21. See Barry Wilner and Ken Rappoport, *Miracles, Shockers, and Long Shots: The Greatest Sports Upsets of All Time* (Lanham, MD: Taylor Trade Publishing, 2006), chap. 11, "Billy Mills, the Lakota Legend," 127–133.

22. See Matthew Syed, "Top 50 greatest Olympic Games moments," Times Online, http://www.timesonline.co.uk/tol/sport/olympics/article4316031.ece (accessed May 15, 2009).

23. Apparently Zátopek was an outstanding mensch off the track as well. For a heart-warming account of how he later gave his gold medal for the 10,000 meter in the 1952 Olympics to Australian runner Ron Clarke, see Christopher McDougall, *Born to Run: A Hidden Tribe, Superathletes, and the Greatest Race the World Has Never Seen* (New York: Alfred A. Knopf, 2009), 94–98. Clarke reportedly said of Zátopek: "There is not, and never will be, a greater man than Emil Zátopek" (McDougall, 98).

24. "Norwegian awarded for Olympic sportsmanship," Cbcsports.ca, http://www.cbc.ca/sports/story/2006/04/05/syrup-skicoach060405.html (accessed May 15, 2009).

25. Speaking of appreciation, I would like to thank Elizabeth N. Agnew for her helpful comments on this paper.

**Part 4**

# ETHICAL ISSUES

*Stephen Kershnar*

# THE OLYMPICS AND STEROIDS

In this chapter, I discuss whether the International Olympic Committee (IOC) may, and perhaps should, permit athletes to use performance-enhancing drugs (PEDs). I begin by discussing the concept of a PED and then briefly review the Olympic rules prohibiting their use. I then discuss the three main arguments against PEDs, specifically that permitting their use endangers the athletes who use them, harms competitors, or makes the competition unfair. I conclude that these arguments fail and that the ban on PEDs, if justified, rests on utilitarian considerations (for example, audience preferences or protecting children).

## Performance-Enhancing Drugs

PEDs are not well defined. In general, PEDs are drugs that are taken with the intention of improving athletic performance. They differ from therapeutic drugs, which are taken to treat injury or disease. The difference is not a sharp one, in part because some drugs have both effects and in part because helping someone to recover from injury is one way of improving performance. In addition, in the Olympics athletes can be disqualified for taking a PED even if they did not take it with the intention of improving performance. For example, a sprinter might not have known what she was taking and merely did so because she was told to by her trainer.

Some PEDs pose a health risk to the user, but this is not an essential part of its definition. One type of PED is an anabolic steroid, and one type of anabolic steroid is a synthetic hormone related to testosterone that is taken in order to increase strength and muscle mass, and speed recovery from injury. Little is known about the lifetime medical and psychiatric risks of these drugs, although they are suspected to pose significant risk.[1] Another type is human growth hormone (HGH), which is used to make persons grow taller and build them up. Outside of the athletic context, physicians regularly use anabolic steroids and HGH to treat an array of medical ailments. A third type of PED enhances performance by increasing the blood's oxygen-transporting capacity, which in turn increases the athlete's aerobic capacity and endurance. Increasing oxygen transporting can also be done via synthetic compounds, or by a process known as blood doping, whereby blood is removed from an athlete, frozen, and then injected back into him before a competition. This increases the athlete's blood volume and oxygen-carrying blood cells (erythrocytes) beyond the natural range. Synthetic compounds and blood doping have similar effects to high-altitude conditioning.

## Olympic Doping Scandals

The Olympics have had many PED-related scandals. In the 1988 Olympics in Seoul, Canadian sprinter Ben Johnson won the 100-meter dash and set a new world record in so doing. He tested positive for the steroid stanozolol and was stripped of his gold medal. It was then awarded to the runner-up, Carl Lewis, who had tested positive for banned substances prior to the Olympics. In the 2000 Olympics in Sydney, track-and-field star Marion Jones won or was part of the winning team in three events (100 meters, 200 meters, and 4-by-400-meter relay team) and got the bronze in two others (long jump and 4-by-100-meter relay). She was later stripped of her medals after admitting that she used steroids. She is currently facing a six-month prison sentence in part because she perjured herself in a federal investigation of her steroid use during the Olympics. In 1990, after the fall of the Berlin Wall, documents were discovered that indicated that East German coaches and trainers administered anabolic steroids and other drugs to female athletes without their or their parents' consent.

In fact, disqualifications in the Olympics have been common over the past quarter-century. The accompanying table offers a summary of the disqualifications at the Olympics over this period. (It should be noted

## Olympic disqualifications

| Year | Location | Number of athletes disqualified (number of stripped medals) |
|------|----------|-----------------------------------------------------------|
| 1984 | Los Angeles | 12 (2) |
| 1988 | Seoul | 10 (4) |
| 1992 | Barcelona | 5 (0) |
| 1996 | Atlanta | 2 (0) |
| 2000 | Sidney | 12 (12) |
| 2004 | Athens | 27 (8) |
| 2008 | Beijing | 12 (4) |

that six of the violations in the past two Olympics, in 2004 and 2008, were for doping horses in equestrian competitions.)

## Olympic Rules on Doping

In 1999, in an IOC-led movement, the World Anti-Doping Agency was formed. The 2007 Olympic Charter clearly bans PEDs. Rule 44 asserts that the World Anti-Doping Code is mandatory for the whole Olympic movement. The introduction to the World Anti-Doping Code asserts that the purpose of the code is: "To protect the *Athletes*' fundamental right to participate in doping-free sport and thus promote health, fairness, and equality for *athletes* worldwide. . . . Doping is fundamentally contrary to the spirit of sport." In Article 1, "doping" is defined as "the occurrence of one or more of the doping rule violations [set forth in other parts of the Code]."

Article 4.3 sets out the criteria for inclusion in the code, which is that a drug must meet two of the following three criteria: there is evidence that it has the potential to enhance or enhances sport performance; there is evidence that it poses a potential or actual risk to the athlete; or the drug use or its method of use violates the spirit of sport. It violates the spirit of sport if it conflicts with the value of excellence in performance, ethics, fair play, honesty, dedication and commitment, and so on. A drug or method can also be banned if it masks or has the potential to mask the use of a prohibited drug. Article 4.4 allows athletes with documented evidence of medical conditions that require the use of a prohibited drug to use it for therapeutic purposes as long as certain evidentiary conditions are met.

## An Argument for Permitting Performance-Enhancing Drugs

My strategy in exploring PEDs is to look at the strongest arguments for prohibiting them. If these arguments fail, and I argue they do, then there probably is no good reason to prohibit them. Before proceeding to the three best arguments for prohibition, it is worth briefly considering a few unconvincing or incomplete arguments.

One reason that might be given for prohibiting PEDs is that their use conflicts with the rules. As a result, they are a form of cheating and are wrong. Of course, what is at issue is whether there should be rules banning PEDs, so citing the current rules does not address this issue any more than citing the current laws against gay marriage tells us whether these laws should be rescinded.

Other arguments focus on potentially valuable results that prohibition of PEDs might bring about, such as increasing audience size and interest, or providing drug-free role models for children. These arguments depend on empirical claims about the effects of PED prohibition. In the absence of a discussion of the costs and benefits of the different rules, these arguments are highly speculative. For example, without polling results or the use of data from professional sports that allow PED use, it is hard to know whether an audience would prefer watching juiced or clean athletes. Similarly, we would need to know whether driving PEDs underground results in less use of them among children. Even if prohibition does make the world better, this is decisive only if utilitarian considerations should guide athletic policy. This is not the view of the World Anti-Doping Agency, as can be seen in their reasons for banning doping.

Another argument for PED prohibition is that drug-free competition is more aesthetically appealing when compared to watching competition between pharmaceutically enhanced freaks. This is analogous to the argument that Major League Baseball should continue to disallow aluminum bats because of the unsatisfying "ping" sound they make when a batter hits the ball. Until this argument is connected to a moral consideration (for example, increasing audience enjoyment), this does not provide a moral reason for the ban.

## Argument 1: Harm to Self

One argument for prohibiting PEDs is that they endanger the health of PED users and that the IOC should protect Olympic athletes against themselves. Here is a general version of this argument.

> *Premise 1:* If PEDs pose an unreasonable risk to athletes' health, then it should be prohibited.
>
> *Premise 2:* PEDs pose an unreasonable risk to the athletes' health.
>
> *Conclusion:* Hence, PEDs should be prohibited.

The first premise rests on the notion that sports authorities should protect athletes from harming themselves, whether in training or competition, at least when the risks are unreasonable. The second rests on the notion that when the risks are taken into account, PED use is unreasonable.

One problem with this argument is that some types of PED (for example, blood doping) pose at most a minor risk to athletes' health. For other PEDs, it is not known whether they pose a significant risk of harm. For example, Drake Bennett, writing for the *Boston Globe*, points out that some athletes take testosterone in amounts that doctors ordinarily prescribe for a man who needed to replace testosterone lost as the result of testicular cancer.[2] The prescription of anabolic steroids within this range has been done for over seventy years. Also, researchers trying to summarize the scientific findings on the dangers of anabolic and androgenic steroid use concede that the long-term effects are poorly understood.

Second, prohibiting PEDs drives them into the shadows. Some athletes will still use PEDs even after their prohibition. Because they are banned, medical experts are less likely to monitor their usage, and the drugs are more likely to be of lower quality and incorrectly labeled. If our interest is in lessening the danger to athletes, we have to balance the benefits to those induced not to use them against the costs to those who will continue to use them. The balance of costs and benefits is unclear.

Third, a criterion is needed to distinguish reasonable versus unreasonable risks. As Bennett points out, sports authorities already allow athletes to take significant risks with their health. For example, one study found that playing in the NFL for more than three years results in an 80 to 90 percent chance of permanent disability.[3] Concussions in ex-NFL players are thought to put them at risk for dementia and depression, and the weight of linemen puts them at risk for heart disease, heart attack, and damaged joints.[4] Boxing also endangers athletes. An argument is needed why these risks are considered reasonable while PED risks are not.

Even the notion of a "reasonable" risk depends on the expected costs and benefits to the particular athlete, and this in turn likely depends on an individual athlete's goals and values. Some athletes, perhaps even a majority, likely think it worthwhile to risk their health for a chance to compete at the elite level. The balance might tip even more in favor of risk-taking when success brings fame, money, a better spouse, and so on. It might be thought that even if athletes were willing to take such risks, the risks are unnecessary. We then need a criterion to distinguish necessary and unnecessary risks, and it is hard to see what that might be.

Fourth, people who don't like paternalism might wonder whether we should allow athletes to decide for themselves what risks to take. After all, most athletes will be informed about the risks, and the ones who are not are likely uninformed because they choose not to be. From an antipaternalist perspective, protecting athletes against themselves treats them as children.

The "harm to self" argument fails because not all PEDs pose a significant risk to athletes' health. Even if they do, it is not clear that banning them lessens the overall risk. Even if they do pose a risk to health and even if banning them lessens the overall risk, it is not clear that the risks are unreasonable, and even if they are we normally let persons decide for themselves what risks to take.

## Argument 2: Harm to Others

The idea behind the second argument against PEDs is that via their use, athletes harm their competitors. In short:

*Premise 1:* If PED users harm their competitors, then PED use should be prohibited.

*Premise 2:* PED users harm their competitors.

*Conclusion:* Hence, PED use should be prohibited.

Premise 1 rests on the notion that a sport's rules should prevent harm to others. Premise 2 rests on the notion that competitors are pressured into taking risky PEDs and as a result they are harmed.

Let's leave aside concerns about the safety of PEDs. If by "harm" we mean a setback to an interest, then athletes harm each other all the time. Athletes have an interest in winning, feeling good about themselves, getting the advertising dollars of a champion, and so forth. When an athlete loses, her competitor has set back that athlete's interests. If "harm" refers to a wrongful setback to an interest, then this argument begs the question by assuming, in Premise 2, that the pressure is wrongful. The training habits and natural abilities of some athletes put enormous pressure on their competitors to increase their conditioning, strength, speed, and technique. Some of these training methods (for example, weight training) might risk the health of some athletes. If there is something that distinguishes these pressures from the pressure to take PEDs, there must be an important difference. We need to know what it is; as far as I can tell, there is no plausible difference.

One could say that athletes would all be better off if no one used risky PEDs, but it is in the self-interest of any one athlete to use risky PEDs.[5] Consider an athlete, Al, who is trying to decide whether to use steroids. Either his competitor, Bob, is using them or he is not. If Bob is, then Al needs to use them to stay competitive. If Bob is not, then Al gains an advantage by using them. If every athlete reasons in a similar fashion, then a collectively irrational result occurs: namely, everyone uses risky PEDs. The same might be true with regard to other burdens, such as training on Sundays. A ban on PEDs and Sunday training allows athletes to arrive at the collectively rational solution. However, the people who own athletic leagues are not obligated to enforce collectively rational solutions; hence, the argument never gets off the ground. In addition, there might be parties who benefit from PED use (for example, the audience and athletes whose bodies respond better to PEDs), in which case the assumption underlying this argument, that prohibition benefits everyone, is likely false.

## Argument 3: Unfairness

The third argument is the notion that PED use is wrong because it involves an athlete's taking an unfair advantage relative to his competitors. Thus:

*Premise 1:* If PED use is unfair, then it should be prohibited.

*Premise 2:* PED use is unfair.

*Conclusion:* Hence, PED use should be prohibited.

The first premise rests on the notion that unfair means of competition should be prohibited; the second rests on the notion that PED use is unfair. In this context, "fair" has to refer to something other than what is permitted by the rules, because what is at issue is what the rules should permit. There are several plausible accounts of fairness; let's examine whether one might justify the prohibition of PEDs.

On one account, a competition is fair if everyone has an equal opportunity to compete. The analogy here is a race: a race is fair only if everyone begins the race at the same starting line. The reason this might be thought to support a prohibition on PEDs is that not every competitor has equal access to them and, even if they did, not every competitor's body responds to them in the same way.

The difficulty here is that competitors also differ in their access to coaching and training conditions. Athletes from richer countries often have better coaches and trainers. In addition, athletes from countries with a tradition in a particular sport often begin training earlier and have better training partners. This might be thought to be a good thing, in that it is the competition in coaching and training techniques that leads to improvements in performance. This is similar to the way in which competition in electronics leads to the production and sale of better and cheaper cameras, televisions, iPods, and the like. In addition, athletes do not have equal natural abilities, so even if the training conditions were equal, some athletes have natural advantages over others. Some might say that PEDs make things worse by adding yet another source of inequality to already unequal starting lines. Again, it is not clear why this inequality is distinct from other advantages (for example, differences in psychological preparation or biomechanical feedback) that the IOC and other sport authorities permit.

On a second account, a competition is fair if the ranking of competitors (whether via wins, points, times, distances, or whatever) tracks the competitors' relative abilities. Because PED use improves performance, at least in the short run, it is not clear how this objection relates to PED prohibition. For example, the ability of a sprinter is his disposition to run fast under race-like conditions. If PED use in a sprinter—for example, Ben Johnson—makes him disposed to run faster than he otherwise would, it increases his ability and thus may affect race outcome.

On a third account, a competition is fair if the ranking of the competitors (points or wins) tracks competitors' merit or desert. An individual's merit is the degree to which her ranking tracks her relative performance within the rules of a competition. This does not tell us what rules should be in place and hence does not justify the prohibition. Desert is a moral notion. What constitutes desert is a controversial matter. On a common account, a person deserves something when he is responsible for doing an act and that act makes it desirable that he receive that good. There are different theories about what feature of an act makes it desirable that a person receive something. On various accounts, it rests on a person's contribution, hard work, or sacrifice. For example, on some accounts, a construction worker deserves his wages because he contributed to the construction company's profits, worked hard toward its goals, or sacrificed his time and energy for its benefit. Also, on similar accounts, a student deserves a good grade in physics because she worked hard in trying to learn it or sacrificed much in order to learn it.

This account of fairness is likely false. Imagine that we discover that academic success is largely a function of genetics.[6] For example, persons who score highest on the medical school and law school entrance exams do so largely because of their genes and not because of hard work or success. This does not make admission-based board scores unfair. In fact, if they are the best predictor of who will be the best doctor or lawyer, then this is probably the fairest way to rank candidates.[7] If the competition to get into medical and law school need not track desert in order to be fair, the same is likely true for Olympic competition. Even if this account of fairness is true, PED users sacrifice by taking health-related risks. Hence, they are arguably more deserving, although sacrifice-based desert will have to be weighed against other bases of desert.

On a fourth account, a competition is fair if it is guided by rules that are rational. On one version of this account, seen in the work of Harvard philosopher John Rawls, a competition is fair if it is guided by a set of rules that would be chosen by free and equal persons under fair choosing conditions.[8] To decide what these rules would be, imagine a group of people who have to choose a set of rules to guide competitions. These people are rational, and they know some general facts about athletic competition, health concerns, audience preferences, and so on. In addition, they know nothing about themselves as individuals—in particular, they do not know their moral beliefs, so that their choices yield a rational set of rules rather than an application of their current moral beliefs. Would persons in such a situation choose to prohibit PEDs? It is hard to tell. They might reason that a system that allows some technological advantages (for example, Lasik eye surgery, high-tech poles for pole vaulting, low-resistance swim suits, and complex computer-aided biomechanical feedback) but not others (for example, steroids and amphetamines) is arbitrary and thus to be avoided. They might be even more likely to reach this conclusion given that they are likely to permit therapeutic drugs (for example, Prozac, antibiotics, and insulin) and some nutritional supplements (for example, creatine, amino acids, and vitamins) and want to avoid arbitrary distinctions.

## Conclusion

The best arguments for prohibiting PEDs are the harm-to-self, harm-to-others, and unfairness arguments; they all fail. The table on the opposite page offers a summary of the arguments and why they fail. The utilitarian arguments (that is, arguments about maximizing audience enjoyment and protecting children) rest on a utilitarian framework that is controversial and depend on empirical claims that need support. Given these shortcomings, the IOC probably does not have a good moral reason to prohibit PEDs.

## Notes

1. For example, consider Gen Kanayama et al., "Long-Term Psychiatric and Medical Consequences of Anabolic-Androgenic Steroid Abuse: A Looming Public Health Concern?" *Drug and Alcohol Dependence* 98 (2008): 1–12.
2. Drake Bennett, "Are Steroids as Bad as We Think They Are?" *Boston Globe*, December 12, 2004, http://www.boston.com/sports/other_sports/articles/2004/12/12/are_steroids-as_bad_as-we-think_they_are/
3. For the notion that playing in the NFL for three years or more risks an ex-

# Arguments for prohibiting PEDs

| Argument | Why prohibit PED use | Problems with the argument |
|---|---|---|
| Rules | It violates the rules. | Argument begs the question |
| Utilitarian | It makes the world worse | Argument assumes utilitarianism. Argument needs empirical support. |
| Harm to self | Users harm themselves. | Some PEDs are not hamrful. Prohibition will likely increase harm. Argument should focus on unreasonable harm, and for many athletes PED harm is reasonable. Argument assumes paternalism. |
| Harm to others | Users harm competitors. | Argument should focus on wrongs, not harms. |
| Unfairness | It is unfair. | PED use does not prevent athletic success from tracking ability, merit, or desert. Fairness depends on rationality, and it is rational to permit PED use. |

tremely high rate of permanent disability (80 to 90 percent in one study), see Rick Collins, "Steroids and Sports: A Provocative Interview with Norm Fost, M.D.," *SteroidLaw. com*, http://www.steroidlaw.com/steroid-law-45.html (accessed February 8, 2012).

4. For the claim about concussions, see Alan Swarz, "Concussions Tied to Depression in Ex-NFL Players," *New York Times,* May 31, 2007; "Report: Signs of Damage Linked to Dementia in Strzelczyk's Brain," ESPN.com, June 15, 2007, http:// sports.espn.go.com/nfl/news/story?id=2905142&campaign=rss&source=ESPNHead lines. For the claim about size, see E. J. Mundell, "Supersized in the NFL," *Health News* 2004, http://www.lifeclinic.com/fullpage.aspx?prid=524269&type=1.

5. This is a type of Prisoner's Dilemma in which individuals acting rationally in their own self-interest arrive at a collectively irrational outcome (that is, one that is worse for everyone).

6. That genetics plays a significant role in explaining who drops out and how far people go in education, see Richard Herrnstein and Charles Murray, *The Bell Curve* (New York: Basic Books, 1994), chap. 6. For example, for whites the IQ of the average high school graduate is 106, the average college graduate is 116, and the average graduate of professional school is 126. Ibid., 152.

7. For the claim that LSATs are strongest predictors of who passed the bar examination, see Linda Wrightman, "The Threat to Diversity in Legal Education: An Empirical Analysis of the Consequences of Abandoning Race as a Factor in Law School Admission Decisions," *New York University Law Review* 72 (1997): 1–53.

8. This account was famously set out in John Rawls, *A Theory of Justice* (Cambridge, MA: The Belknap Press of Harvard University Press, 1971).

*Joseph D. Lewandowski*

# OLYMPIC BOXING
## A Not So Sweet Science

> A boxer's victory is gained in blood.
> —Ancient Greek inscription (100 BCE)

At one level, Olympic athletes are simply individuals who compete for a prize.[1] Of course, the kind of competition athletes engage in is not arbitrary or haphazard. Rather, in Olympic sports, as in all competitive sports, athletes vie with one another within the context of jointly shared constraints that enable and limit their actions in various ways. Without the 3-point line in basketball, for example, there can be no 3-point shots and no creativity or excellence in 3-point shooting. In everyday conversation we call such soft constraints "rules," and action in adherence to a set of rules constitutes for us a game or event, such as basketball or the pole vault.[2] Basketball players and pole vaulters are in this regard merely individuals who have chosen to compete for a prize by adhering to the soft constraints, or rules, that create the very possibility of basketball games and pole-vaulting events.[3] To be sure, what makes an individual a better or worse Olympic athlete is the extent to which he or she excels in particular competitions made possible by certain constraints. Indeed, it would not be an exaggeration to claim that one of the defining goals of Olympic competition is for individuals to try to maximize their creativity and skill levels—and, in so doing, surpass other athletes and win prizes— *within* their chosen set of constitutive rules.

All that is to say that the relationship between rules and Olympic athletics is of profound practical importance and philosophical interest. For in competitive sport, rules do not merely guide or regulate athletic endeavors; they also, and more fundamentally, define and constitute those endeavors as such.[4] In fact, the various constitutive rules that define and enable Olympic games and events are in no small way decisive for the levels of skill and quality of competition athletes can be expected to achieve and spectators can hope to enjoy.[5] One might even go so far as to assert that Olympic athletic performances, regardless of individual training or talent or willpower, can in one sense only be as good as the rules that constrain them. To put the matter simply: while rules create the condition of possibility of Olympic games and events, not any set of rules will suffice. *What is needed is the right kind of rules.*

What makes rules the right kind? As it turns out, the answer to that question is more complicated than one might expect. For optimizing the constraints of Olympic athletics—making them neither too tight nor too loose—entails a nuanced understanding of Olympic sports and the complex ways in which constitutive rules function to enable and limit human choices and actions within those sports. In an attempt to contribute to such an understanding, in this chapter I analyze boxing. I hope to show that boxing is paradigmatic of the importance—and elusiveness—of achieving an optimal tightness of constitutive rules in an Olympic event. Specifically, using Jon Elster's "constraint theory," which is designed to explain how individuals maximize their choices and skills and realize their goals within constraints, I attempt to clarify how and why the rules of Olympic boxing do not work, as well as offer some preliminary suggestions about how to improve the sport.[6]

Despite their various and often divergent points of view, fight fans who have followed the ups and downs of Olympic boxing in the past decade or so are likely to agree that the sport's rules are a mess. More so than any other Olympic sport, it is in boxing, which first appeared in the modern games in 1904, that debates about unfair judging, physical danger, and the ostensible immorality of an Olympic "blood sport" have contributed to increasing and tightening the event's rules. Given the violence and distinct bodily risks inherent in boxing, as well as the many prominent stereotypes surrounding the sport, this is perhaps not surprising. It is also not without historical precedent. In fact, the most recent clamor over the boxing competitions at the past few Olympic Games is really part of a long and checkered legacy of suboptimal constraints in Olympic boxing matches. Indeed, the history of Olympic boxing is in many ways the history of suboptimal constraints.

To see this we need look no farther than a well-known dramatic scene in ancient Greek boxing (known as the *pyx*), which took place at the Nemean Games.[7] Two nude and heavily oiled men, Kreugas of Epidamnos and Damoxenos of Syracuse, square off in a kind of shallow pit, or *skamma* (literally, "dug-up place"). With the apparent exception of prohibitions on biting or kicking an opponent, or striking him when he is down, no constitutive rules constrain the boxers' actions.[8] Instead, an almost "anything goes" atmosphere prevails.[9]

There are no weight classes and no rounds or time limits, though rest breaks are allowed if mutually agreed upon by both combatants. The fighters wear no headgear or mouth guards. In place of padded gloves each man wears what amounts to oxhide handwraps (known in Greek as *himantes*), leaving their fingers free to grab and clench.[10] A match is won when a boxer signals with a finger that he cannot go on or is beaten into unconsciousness.

On this particular day the fight has been long and hard. As dusk falls the historian Pausanias recounts what happened next:

> While they were boxing evening came on, and they agreed in front of witnesses that each would allow the other in turn to land a punch. Now at that time boxers did not yet wear the hard *himas* on the wrist of each hand, but boxed with the soft *himantes,* which were bound in the hollow of the hand so that the fingers were left bare. . . . Now Kreugas aimed his punch at Damoxenos's head. Then Damoxenos told Kreugas to lift his arm, and when Kreugas had done so, Damoxenos struck him under the ribs with his fingers straight out. The combination of his sharp fingernails and the force of the blow drove his hand into Kreugas's guts. He grabbed Kreugas's intestines and tore them out. Kreugas died on the spot.[11]

Certainly there is some reason to doubt the likelihood of a man disemboweling another simply by the force of a single open-handed blow, regardless of how sharp his fingernails may be. Yet Pausanias's account of one of ancient Greece's most famous "ring deaths" makes evident that what is wrong with Olympic boxing is what has always been wrong with Olympic boxing: the rules that constitute the sport do not sufficiently enable skilled, creative, and competitive athletic performances. In the case of ancient boxing matches especially, what prevail are unconstrained confrontations crudely intended to do physical injury.[12]

Yet the historical reservoir of ancient Greek culture and literature does contain an object lesson in how the right kind of constraints can actually maximize creative outcomes and minimize physical risks. That lesson, which Elster makes the leitmotif of his work on the interconnection between constraints and actions, is found in the labors of the mythological hero Odysseus. For Elster, Odysseus is heroic precisely because of the ways in which he manages to achieve an optimal tightness of bounds in his undertakings. To grasp the core of Elster's argument we need only recall the encounter with the Sirens, wherein Odysseus deliberately has himself constrained by his crew and manages to listen to the Sirens' call unharmed. In this labor, as in many others, Odysseus's own creative choice of constraint actually frees him to act in ways that otherwise would not have been possible. Odysseus's *choice of constraint* (lashing himself to the mast and stopping the ears of his crew) enables a unique *action within that constraint* (listening to the call of the Sirens without perishing).

In fact, what makes Odysseus exemplary here is that his initial choice of constraint was optimal—tight enough to keep him safe, yet loose enough to enable him to maximize his efforts and realize his goal. From an Elsterian point of view, in other words, Odysseus's actions are a model of *constrained maximization*.[13] Modern Olympic boxers, by contrast, do not manage anything near a similar degree of bounded rational choice and embedded creative action, for they do not have the option of choosing or creating their own constraints. Instead, as Olympic athletes, they must simply adhere to the constitutive rules that define their sport.

Now what began in ancient Greek boxing as the problem of too few constitutive constraints conversely has emerged in the contemporary Olympics as the problem of too many—and *the wrong kind*—of constraints. To see this we need only contrast the near absence of constraints in ancient Greek boxing—illustrated above by the fact that Kreugas and Damoxenos felt the need to improvise their own constraints in the course of their competition—with the tight constitutive constraints that currently choke contemporary Olympic boxing. Those constraints include:

- Bouts consist of four rounds, two minutes per round, with one minute's rest between rounds.

- Certain headgear (introduced in 1984) is mandatory.

- Bouts are won by knockout or on total number of points scored.

- Points are awarded only when a blow with the marked part of the glove lands on an opponent's head (front or side) or body (above belt).

- There are five judges, who use computerized scoring (introduced in 1992).

- Judges use two buttons (one for each fighter) and must immediately press the appropriate button when they see a boxer score a legal blow.

- Points are scored only when three (or more) judges depress the button for the same boxer within one second of each other.

- In heated exchanges of blows, when no obvious punches are landing, judges delay scoring until the exchange ends, at which time they press the button for the boxer whom they believe was most successful during the exchange.

- In cases of a tie in the number of points scored, judges must decide the winner based on aggression and style.

- Blows to the arms and blows landed without force are not to be counted as points.

- A boxer is considered down if, as a result of being hit by a legal blow, he touches the canvas with any part of his body except his feet.

- When a boxer is down, the referee must initiate a count of ten. Though the count is timed electronically, with an audible beep, the referee has final discretion.

- Knockdowns earn neither an additional point for the boxer who floors his opponent nor a point deduction for the boxer who is floored.

- If a boxer remains down after ten seconds the opponent wins by a knockout.

- If a boxer regains his footing after being knocked down, he must be given an eight count, after which the referee may command him to "box" or deem him unable to continue and award the victory to his opponent.

- When a boxer receives three counts in one round or four counts over the duration of the bout the referee must stop the competition and award victory to his opponent.

Of course not all of these rules are problematic. In light of the current discussion of the difficulty of achieving constrained maximization in Olympic boxing, however, three constraints in particular stand out as decidedly suboptimal. These are: round and bout length, mandatory headgear, and computerized scoring. Let me briefly highlight the shortcomings of each.

First, the length of the rounds and the bouts in Olympic boxing is simply too short. Compressing the time frame in which athletes can fight fosters a kind of "more is more" approach among Olympic boxers and their competitions. Rather than display the controlled violence and pugilistic style that makes boxing a "sweet science," Olympic boxers inevitably—and quite rationally, given the existing time constraints—merely opt to "keep busy" by throwing hurried punches in an effort to impress the judges and register points. Thus it is no accident that Olympic boxers, whose characteristically superb conditioning would easily enable them to endure longer rounds and longer fights, often throw many more punches than their professional counterparts. Indeed, one of the telltale signs of a contemporary Olympic boxing match is the preponderance of quick but meaningless flurries, known as "pitty-pat" or "shoeshine" punches, and a decided lack of athletic complexity and creativity.

Second, the "more is more" approach adopted by Olympic boxers as a result of the suboptimal constraints of round and bout length is exacerbated by the wearing of mandatory headgear. Introduced as a safety precaution in 1984, the presence of headgear enlarges the size of the target, emboldens boxers to lower their guard and rush their opponents (thereby abandoning complex defensive techniques), and dramatically increases the number of punches aimed at the head. The result in Olympic boxing is typically eight minutes' worth of wild punches targeting an opponent's headgear. In this way, the suboptimal constraint of mandatory headgear actually encourages attempts at point-scoring headshots and discourages the creativity and skill needed to produce elaborate punch combinations while moving skillfully about the ring. Combined with the suboptimal time constraints, therefore, the presence of headgear undermines the cultivation and demonstration of a crucial and multifaceted component of boxing. That component is *ring generalship,* whereby boxers maneuver themselves and their opponents around the ring in a fluid but calculating fashion that controls the action as well as the space in which that action takes place.

Here we should also underscore what all experienced amateur boxers already know, namely, that headgear is mostly "for show." That is to say, headgear primarily protects boxers from cuts and accidental and intentional clashes of heads. Consequently, while Olympic boxers are not often cut, they almost always take many more repeated blows to the head per minute than their non-headgear-wearing professional counterparts. Hence the introduction of mandatory headgear in Olympic boxing in 1984 appears to have had effects directly contrary to the ones sought by headgear proponents. Headgear gives a dangerously false sense of protection against the kind of long-term brain injuries that result from repeated concussive blows to the head—as, for example, it has done in ice hockey and American football, where an increasing number of retired athletes demonstrate a variety of diminished cognitive faculties, including memory loss and speech problems, at a surprisingly early age.

Third, along with round and bout length and the wearing of headgear, computerized point scoring has, at least from the perspective of optimizing the constitutive constraints of Olympic boxing, proven to be a disaster. Introduced in an attempt to reduce subjectivity in judging, the current computerized system tends to transform Olympic boxers into characters in a rather predictable video game, with judges as their gamers. With computerized scoring, boxers have the incentive, as suggested above, to throw as many punches as possible given the shortness of the rounds and bouts and the need to earn the judges' click of a button. And so the punches fly. But as far as the computer is concerned, those punches only land when three of the five judges/gamers click their respective buttons within one second of one another.

The problems with computerized scoring are myriad. Judges watch individual punches, rather than the fight as a whole. Style and ring generalship—what, in essence, make boxing *boxing* and not fencing or wrestling—play absolutely no role in the judges' scoring. Three of the five judges must agree that the marked part of the glove has landed appropriately for a point to count. When only two judges concur no point is scored, despite an obvious blow landing. In addition, no correction of a mistaken—or overenthusiastic—push of a judge's button is possible: the computerized tally is instantaneous and without review. And the landing of a strong blow, such as one that produces a knockdown, garners the same single point as a pitty-pat blow—assuming, that is, that three of the five judges actually see the blow land and manage to click the correct button within one second of one another.[14]

It should by now be apparent how and why the short rounds and bouts, mandatory headgear, and computerized scoring hamper contemporary Olympic boxing. Instead of creating optimal conditions of possibility for constrained maximization, in Olympic boxing what we repeatedly see is athletes literally trapped in and by poorly designed constitutive rules. Clearly, an increase in the round length to three minutes, and a corresponding increase in bout length to, say, five rounds, would begin to optimize the sport's constitutive time constraints. So, too, would a return to the pre-1984 days of no headgear, which would enable Olympic boxers to develop and exhibit better defensive and counterpunching skills, as well as help to reduce the overall number of punches directed at the head.

But the more serious—and more challenging—problem comes in how to redefine the constraints that inform the scoring of a boxing match. This is the case for several reasons. The first, and most obvious, is that victory in boxing, as the Greeks rightly recognized, is characteristically "gained in blood." That is to say, violence, however constrained, is constitutive of the sport—"They call it fightin' for a reason," as one hears often in a boxing gym. Thus the rules of the sport must be tight enough to ensure the maximum level of safety for the boxers and yet still enable a robust fight to occur.

Second, that "robust fight," however violent, must also be constrained in ways that enable and reward points for individual style, technique, and athletic complexity. Boxing may indeed be a combat sport. But judging it is a holistic enterprise—an enterprise that, however counterintuitive, shares more with judging figure skating (where competitors are evaluated on various dimensions of their performance) than it does with another combat sport, such as fencing (where the mere electronic tally of touches determines victory). Hence the sport requires a less restrictive and more flexible set of scoring constraints that enable and effectively take into account a broader range of athletic elements—especially ring generalship and style—and does not overly emphasize the landing of individual blows to score points.

Third, unlike nearly all other Olympic sports, boxing is unique insofar as it contains what is perhaps best characterized as a "lottery moment." In tennis, for example, a competitor down two sets to nil and one point from elimination in a third set faces an arduous, and extremely improbable, comeback effort. The rules of tennis do not make it possible for a player to go from imminent defeat to decisive victory *with a single stroke* of the racquet. But in boxing an athlete, no matter how far behind in points, can in fact win the match with a single blow. This possibility is part of what makes the sport a compelling drama of overcoming—and thus of particular interest and resonance for spectators and participants alike. The constitutive rules of boxing must consequently be loose enough to allow for the drama of a come-from-behind knockout, yet not so loose that they encourage or reward a style of fighting that relies more or less exclusively on such a "one-punch" strategy at the risk of injury to the boxers or boredom for the event's spectators.

Thus, while remedying the time constraints in Olympic boxing is rather straightforward, how to reconstitute the constraints that enable safe, competitive, highly skilled, and reasonably judged bouts is rather less obvious. Nevertheless, there are precedents to be found in the constraints of professional boxing and, as suggested briefly above, even in an Olympic sport such as figure skating (or diving or gymnastics, for that matter).

To begin, rather than having five judges engaged in computerized scoring, there should be three judges who score the bout without the aid of computers and two individuals—call them "safety monitors"—who use a computerized device simply to tally the number of headshots landed on each boxer. Safety monitor A, for example, would be assigned to the boxer in the red corner, while safety monitor B would observe the boxer in the blue corner. These safety monitors would be allowed to make no judgments about the effectiveness of the punches or the competitiveness of the fight; rather, they would simply click a button every time the boxer assigned to them is struck cleanly on the head. A pre-established rule would place an upper limit on the number of clean headshots landed in any given round, as well as over the course of the five-round bouts.[15] In cases where this number was exceeded, the referee would be informed. He would then have the discretion to stop the fight and award the victory to the boxer who landed the excessive number of clean blows to his opponent's head.

Using a modified version of the "ten-point must" system found in professional boxing, three judges should score Olympic boxing *by rounds.* And they should do such scoring in two general categories, each with very different criteria and unique features. In the first category—call it the "punch category"—a maximum of five points per round is awarded to the boxer who lands the greatest number of clean (unblocked) and effective (solid) punches. Thus, as in professional boxing, individual punches would not score points per se; instead, judges would take a more holistic approach to scoring the boxers' overall success in landing punches, awarding a mandatory five points to the fighter who wins the round with his punching and four points to the fighter who loses the round. Unlike professional boxing, a knockdown would earn one mandatory additional point for the boxer who downed his opponent. So, for example, a highly competitive round in which both boxers landed many clean and effective punches but one of them knocked his opponent to the ground twice would result in a score of 7–5 in favor of the boxer who scored the two knockdowns.

In the second category—call it the "style category"—a similar round-based five-point must system would prevail. But these points would be awarded based exclusively on technique, style, and ring generalship. The boxer who exhibits the greatest mastery in technique, style, and ring generalship would earn five points for the round, while his opponent would earn four points. Moreover, in this category a single mandatory point would be deducted for each flagrant foul—low blow, hitting behind the head, intentional head-butt, and so on—identified by the referee. No additional points beyond the maximum of five could be earned. So, for example, a superb exhibition of ring generalship by one boxer and two fouls by his opponent would result in a score of 5–3.

At the end of each round, each judge would thus produce two sets of scores on his scorecard: one in the punch category and one in the style category. These would then be added together to produce a round score. To take the examples presented above, let us imagine that the boxer who scored the two knockdowns was also the superior stylist, and that his opponent, while managing to land many clean blows, also threw two low blows called by the referee. In this case the total round score would be 12 (7 + 5) to 8 (5 + 3). These round scores would then be totaled at the end of five rounds on each judge's scorecard. As is the case in professional boxing, the scoring decision by the judges would decide who wins and who loses the match. Victories awarded by unanimous, majority, and split decisions on the judges' scorecards would be possible.

In the event of a tie (either in identical point scores awarded by all three judges or in decisions where one judge's scorecard awards the highest score to the red corner, another judge's scorecard awards the highest score to the blue corner, and the third judge's scorecard has the score even), the boxer who earned the most mandatory knockdown points would win. In the event of a tie in the number of mandatory knockdown points earned—or when no knockdown punches have been scored—the boxer with the least number of mandatory point deductions for fouls would be declared the winner.

## Conclusion

Let me close by anticipating some likely objections to my analysis and admittedly provisional suggestions about how to reconstitute the soft constraints of Olympic boxing. Most obviously, it might be argued that the elimination of headgear and the introduction of safety monitors to track blows to the head merely reintroduces the problem it sought to avoid, that is, the risk of head injuries. Surely once Olympic boxers know that a surefire way to win a bout is to land $x$ number of headshots, they will, or so one might argue, simply look to land that magic number. In this way one could object that the soft constraint on an upper limit of blows to the head actually incentivizes the throwing of punches to an opponent's head.

While this objection seems intuitively plausible, it can be countered from two angles. In the first instance, the requirement that these punches be clean (unblocked) and of a fairly high number would make the incentive to strike an opponent's head no greater than it otherwise would be in a fight without safety monitors. Scoring blows to the head, after all, is a common and often effective way to win a boxing match. In the second instance, the fact that a boxer who receives too many headshots in a round or bout loses the match should actually encourage him to be more mindful of his defensive strategies and thus protect his head more than he otherwise would.

Such counterarguments aside, however, here we return to one of the central themes of this chapter, namely, the persistent difficulty in creating the conditions of possibility for skilled, competitive, and safe Olympic boxing events. As emphasized in the foregoing analysis, constituting the rules that define boxing inevitably entails striking a delicate balance between making the constraints loose enough to enable a robust fight to occur—even when one boxer is losing rather badly—and yet tight enough to ensure the safety of those engaged in that fight. Regardless of the details of the alternative set of rules presented here, it is fair to say that something like the computerized monitoring of blows to the head is a better way to minimize head injuries than the illusion of safety and engendering of suboptimal skill levels created by mandatory headgear.

Of course one might also object that the introduction of holistic round scoring based on fuzzy criteria—such as "clean" and "effective" punches, "style," "athletic complexity," "technique," and "ring generalship"—only invites the kind of subjectivity in judging that has historically plagued Olympic boxing, and many other events as well. Yet the attempt in Olympic boxing to eliminate subjectivity in judges' scoring and replace that element of human judgment with computerized tallies based on the push of a button is, as we have seen above, deeply flawed. The challenge in judging Olympic boxing does not lie in how to eliminate its subjective elements. On the contrary, boxing judges must be charged with *judging the full picture*—and not merely electronically recording the individual details—of what they see in a boxing match.

Olympic boxing judges, to put the matter in the vocabulary used here, must be allowed to *evaluate* the skill levels, style, and relative success of individual endeavors in constrained maximization. Achieving adequate judging in boxing—or in other Olympic sports where skill and style are inseparable, such as figure skating—is not so much about eliminating individual bias as it is about properly *delimiting* it. What is needed is to create the conditions under which good evaluative judgments of skill and style are most likely to occur. In this regard concerns about subjectivity in judging Olympic boxing are too often focused on the egregious scoring of particular bouts at the expense of examining the constitutive rules that inform and disable, as we have seen, those judges' evaluative efforts. Good judges, like good athletes, require the right sets of constraints to excel. In a sport where athletes and their evaluators are perennially marred by bad rules, there is thus reason to anticipate that optimizing the constraints that define Olympic boxing will generate not only better boxers and more competitive bouts but also better judges and more adequate scoring decisions.

## Notes

1. As the etymology of the English word *athlete*—from the Greek *athletes*, meaning "one who competes for a prize"—makes clear.

2. For the purpose of clarifying this definition, we can contrast the "soft" constraints of rules with "hard" constraints of gravity or limits on time travel.

3. Basketball players and pole vaulters, in other words, are those individuals who elect to adopt a "lusory attitude," as Suits (1995) so elegantly describes it.

4. See Searle (1995) on regulative and constitutive rules; Suits (1995) makes a similar set of arguments.

5. Clearly there is also a distinct class of rules designed to create the conditions of possibility of the *fairness* of sporting games and events, such as rules against the use of performance-enhancing drugs. This explicitly moral function of constraints is certainly not unimportant, but nevertheless is beyond the scope of the present inquiry, which is concerned with the ontological features of constitutive rules rather than the moral functions of such rules.

6. The studies of primary interest here are Elster's *Ulysses and the Sirens* (1984) and *Ulysses Unbound* (2000). For a related but more expansive attempt to apply Elster's work in the philosophy of sport, see Lewandowski (2007).

7. The Nemean Games was one of four competitions, along with those held at Delphi, Isthmia, and Olympia, which contain the historical origins of what is today known simply as "the Olympics."

8. Miller (2004).

9. Though referees stand by, forked rods in hand, and periodically flog competitors for what is deemed a "foul."

10. For a fascinating history of boxing gloves, see Murray (2008), on whose work I draw here.

11. Excerpted from Miller (2004). But see also Sweet (1987).

12. The Romans, for example, used a glove with sharpened metal inserts, known as *caesti* (Murray 2008).

13. For a more thorough discussion of sport as constrained maximization, see Lewandowski (2007).

14. However improbable, it is in fact possible in the current computerized system for a knockdown to score no points.

15. Clearly the exact threshold number would need to be set by a task force devoted to Olympic boxing, and would need to include medical specialists, judges, referees, and former Olympic boxers. Regarding the boxers, it would be interesting to know what constitutive rules former competitors in the sport would want to retain, modify, or newly create.

# References

Elster, J. 1984. *Ulysses and the Sirens.* Cambridge: Cambridge University Press.
———. 2000. *Ulysses Unbound: Studies in Rationality, Precommitment, and Constraints.* Cambridge: Cambridge University Press.
Lewandowski, J. 2007. "Boxing: The Sweet Science of Constraints." *Journal of the Philosophy of Sport* 34: 26–38.
Miller, S. 2004. *Ancient Greek Athletics.* New Haven, CT: Yale University Press.
Murray, S. 2008. "Boxing Gloves of the Ancient World." *Journal of Combative Sport.* http://www.ejmas.com/jcs/2010jcs/jcsart_murray_1007.html.
Searle, J. 1995. *The Construction of Social Reality.* New York: Free Press.
Suits, B. 1995. "The Elements of Sport." In *Philosophic Inquiry in Sport,* ed. W. J. Morgan and K. V. Meider, pp. 8–15. Champaign, IL: Human Kinetics.
Sweet, W. E. 1987. *Sport and Recreation in Ancient Greece.* Oxford: Oxford University Press.

*Regan Reitsma*

# SHOULD THE OLYMPICS BE THE VERY BEST?
## A Plea on Behalf of the Second-Rate

The Olympic motto "Faster, Higher, Stronger" evokes vivid images of athletic striving.[1] A champion sprinter straining to shave off another hundredth of a second from his own world-record time; a world-class high jumper contorting her body to scale a yet greater height; a weight lifter—veins bulging, cheeks puffed—exerting every ounce of his being to squat as much as the reigning gold medalist he is competing against. This wonderfully redolent triad's use of comparatives—fast*er*, high*er*, strong*er*—seems at one and the same time to describe the intensity and internal drive of Olympic athletes and to urge these very same competitors to ever greater achievements.

Does this motto, in all of three words, mean to suggest even more: namely, that modern Olympians are the very best athletes in the world?[2] That they not only have a burning passion to outdo their Olympic rivals—and their past selves—but that they run faster, jump higher, and display greater strength than the athletes at any other sporting competition in the world?

If so, the motto is mistaken, at least with respect to some Olympic sports. Take the men's Olympic football (soccer) tournament. It doesn't draw the world's best footballers with any consistency. And the quality of play in the Olympics is widely recognized to be considerably lower than in the World Cup, the European Championships, and the Champion's League. The Olympic men's football tournament is not the premier event on the international football calendar. It isn't even a "top-shelf" tournament, among the several best in the world.

What should the International Olympic Committee (IOC) do about this? If the men's football tournament isn't, and isn't likely to become, a top-shelf event, should the IOC's executive board drop the sport from its schedule?

The idea has been suggested. For instance, Bob Harig, a golf writer for ESPN.com, proposes the following "litmus test" for an Olympic event: he says that "to determine whether a sport is of Olympic caliber," we should ask, "Does winning a gold medal trump anything else an athlete can do?"[3] Harig clearly associates the Olympics with the very highest quality in competition; an Olympic gold medal constitutes the pinnacle of achievement in an athlete's career in such sports as track and field, weight lifting, gymnastics, swimming, and speed skating.[4] But most world-class footballers dream of World Cup or Champion's League glory, not an Olympic medal.[5] According to Harig's reasoning, the Olympic men's football tournament should be abolished.

I disagree with Harig's proposal. As a culture, we have a tendency to speak in the highest, most admiring terms about striving to be "simply the best." But Harig's mentality—his uncompromising commitment to excellence, along with his overly atomistic thinking—would do serious harm to the Olympics and to some of its most important goals. When it comes to men's football, the IOC should settle for less than the best, a second-rate tournament.

## An Everyday Debate Leads to a Philosophical Question

The question "Which sports truly belong in the Olympics?" makes for boisterous pub debate. You can imagine how these conversations go. Chump blathers, "Trampoline? Seriously, why do I have to watch bouncing people instead of good old American football?" As always, Grump has his own, better idea: "The modern Olympic movement would most certainly broaden its significant appeal if only it were to include intellectual competitions such as chess." Opinions are spouted. Disagreements arise. In the midst of this, an argumentative move, at its heart philosophical, is often made: someone proposes criteria. Consider a few examples from the blogosphere. There are bawling, clamorous advocates for the policy that any sport named "synchronized"—synchronized swimming, synchronized diving—should be tossed out of the Olympics.[6]

And a member of the editorial board of a newspaper, the *Fresno (California) Bee,* has suggested, more broadly, "It's not a sport if there's no ball."[7] As the Olympics is indeed a sporting event, so much, I guess, for synchronized swimming, as well as trampoline and chess. Such proposals in turn prompt equally boisterous objections and more debate.

The IOC confronts the same basic question as Chump and Grump. Every four years or so, it reviews its roster of sports. In 2005, the IOC decided to exclude men's baseball and women's softball from the 2012 games in London. In 2010, it rejected formal appeals to reinstate these sports in 2016. Despite the prevalence of Harig-style protests, golf has been added to the roster in 2016, along with rugby sevens, but not karate, squash, or roller sports, which were also considered.

As with the barstool deliberations, the IOC's roster decisions raise a philosophical question about the proper criteria for a sport's inclusion. *On what grounds* should such decisions be made? The IOC has one, and only one, formal criterion: a sport must have an international governing organization recognized by the IOC, such as the Federation Internationale de Basketball (FIBA) for basketball, and the Federation Internationale de Football Association (FIFA) for football. But clearly the IOC should consider other factors, such as a sport's Olympic tradition, the parity and general quality of play of its Olympic tournaments, whether the sport has global appeal, whether it has an intractable doping problem, and whether a new sport, if added, would create a more egalitarian balance of men's and women's sports. We should probably throw a bone, too, to the howling Trumps of the world, who want the IOC to continue to consider past and prospective ticket sales for a sport's events and the level of interest of corporate sponsors. Because the construction of "the world's greatest sporting stage" is an expensive project, it makes perfect sense to give the free market a voice—though not, sensible people should insist, a bully pulpit.

The difficult question is how to balance all of these relevant factors. Even if we agree that tradition, parity, ubiquity, equality, popularity, and marketability should be given consideration, it wouldn't be immediately clear how much weight, relative to each other, they should each be accorded. A brief discussion of dressage, an equestrian competition, illustrates this basic point.

## A Hard Case

Dressage, in the modern Olympics since its onset in 1896, has tradition on its side. But its modern detractors ask how much respect this tradition should be given when the world has passed by the cultural institutions that once made sense of the sport. A nation no longer needs an elite warrior class with exquisitely precise equestrian skills to reveal its prowess. I don't think this antitraditionalist argument works, though. Given the advent of modern weaponry, similar things could be said about the bow and arrow, but no serious thinker has put a target on archery's back.

The following argument against dressage is, perhaps, more thought-provoking. Much of the athleticism in dressage, mocked by its detractors as "nothing but dancing horses," is displayed by the animal, not the human rider. If a supporter of the event parries with the argument that the dressage specialist is an athlete because in order to exert her will upon the horse she has to have a remarkable ability to concentrate and years of training with the horse, he would be hard-pressed to argue that chess doesn't belong at the Olympics. Intellectual competitions also take profound focus, and chess masters presumably spend as much time with their knights and pawns as dressage riders do with their horses. If the best defense of dressage opens the Olympic door this wide to chess, how good could the argument be?

Permit me to enter a sketchy proposal into the fray. At the risk of being guilty of my own reckless fit of boisterous clamoring, I'm given to the idea that chess—no doubt an excellent game—lacks a feature essential to Olympic competition, namely, athleticism.[8] An Olympic sport should have, at its heart, a physical challenge. (What else holds together hockey and cycling and basketball and slalom skiing?) Yes, chess players physically move pawns with their hands, and their brows and palms sweat.[9] But chess is essentially an intellectual, not a physical, challenge, and so—in my view—it doesn't belong at the Olympics. As its riders do confront physical challenges, the case against dressage isn't as strong as the case against chess. Accordingly, I would argue that whether dressage belongs on the Olympic roster turns, at least in part, on whether it presents a sufficient physical challenge to its riders to be in the Olympic tournament alongside physically demanding sports such as hockey and cycling. (Uh, anyone suddenly feel inclined to talk about the case for de-rostering curling?)

Whatever you happen to think of my sketchy proposal, the more important question is how, broadly speaking, the IOC should approach roster decisions, some of which raise difficult, philosophical questions. It's easy to bandy about opinions—to bawl, clamor, and cook up half-baked arguments. But the IOC really ought to try to think its way to sensible roster conclusions. How, though?

## Algorithms, Casuistry, and Practical Wisdom

One suggestion is that the IOC could attempt to construct a systematic decision procedure, such as an algorithm. It could assign points for a sport's level of tradition, its level of parity, its marketability, and so on, and include only those sports whose Olympic tournaments score sufficiently high on this "Olympic calculus."

Some moral philosophers have attempted, similarly, to construct a moral calculus. For instance, classic utilitarians such as Jeremy Bentham (1748–1832) and John Stuart Mill (1806–1873) claim that there is only one *fundamental* moral value, the promotion of pleasure, which they call "the maximization of utility." According to Bentham, to discover what morality requires you to do, you need to figure out which action, of those available to you, would create the most pleasure, impartially considered. The utility-maximizing action, the action with the highest utility score, is the right thing to do, all things considered.

Some moral philosophers, myself included, have been skeptical of the utilitarian's claim that the promotion of pleasure is the only *fundamental* moral value. It seems to us that morality is complex; many different moral considerations deserve fundamental respect—not only the promotion of human welfare, but also (among other considerations) respect for moral rights, fairness, and desert. In other words, we think Bentham's algorithm oversimplifies moral decision making.[10] I also think there are instances in which a person ought morally to do what is, say, fair even if doing what's fair isn't utility-maximizing. In short, I'm skeptical of the accuracy of Bentham's moral calculus.

Likewise, when it comes to thinking about the Olympic roster, there is, as I've already mentioned, a wide range of factors that deserve consideration; and such issues as tradition, parity, and marketability don't seem "commensurate"—that is, comparable along a single metric. (Exactly how much tradition would a sport need, for example, to make up for a lack of parity?) I suspect that if the IOC were to construct an algorithm, not only would this algorithm fail to capture the underlying complexity of at least some Olympic roster decisions, there would also sometimes be strong reasons to doubt its results, its accuracy.

Whatever the prospective value of an Olympic calculus, the IOC hasn't pursued one. Instead, its executive board appears to employ a decision-making process moral philosophers call "casuistry," a careful evaluation of particular cases. In the practice of casuistry, it's a good idea to seek out and to employ helpful general principles, but important decisions are made on a case-by-case basis, with special sensitivity to the particular details of the case in question. Casuistry has a disadvantage. It can breed suspicion in observers. People have speculated (I'm not sure how plausibly) that the IOC dropped women's softball not because of a lack of parity—its stated argument—but out of anti-American sentiment. (The U.S. team has been dominant.) Without a predetermined calculus or algorithm, it's harder to ensure that decision makers have been objective and fairminded. But despite this general disadvantage, casuistry has the virtue of taking very seriously the complexity of Olympic roster decisions.

As moral philosophers have remarked, when we lack a good systematic decision procedure and so must practice casuistry, we very much need to develop experience and good judgment, "practical wisdom." When it comes to Olympic roster decisions, is there such a thing as "practical wisdom"? I think so. Good, hard thinking about the Olympic roster isn't futile. Alongside hard roster decisions, there are also, just as clearly, sound arguments.

Here are three. First, the case against American football is exceedingly strong. This sport doesn't meet the IOC's single, formal criterion: there isn't an international governing body for American football. But more to the heart of things, there is little participation in American football, as its name suggests, outside of the United States; it's not a sufficiently global sport. Accordingly, its Olympic gridiron tournament would lack parity—both in the short term and the long, as a zeal for the pigskin isn't spreading across the globe. Sorry, Chump; "good old American football" doesn't deserve to make the Olympic cut. Second, the "No ball, no Olympics" policy is a demonstrably bad policy. It would rule out—sensibly, in my view—hopscotch and chess. But with its fetish for ball sports, it would also exclude, far less sensibly, sports such as gymnastics, running, and swimming from the Summer Games and—given that hockey has a puck, not a ball—the entire roster of the Winter Games. (Wipe your fevered brows, prospective Olympic hockey players; there's no reason to suffer ball envy.) Third, the *Fresno Bee*'s "No synchronized in the title" policy is superficial. The IOC could meet this policy's demand without making a substantive roster change, simply by changing the names of synchronized sports.

I certainly don't want to seem humorless. Many proposals in blog and bar are made in jest, and some score very high taken as spicy provocations. But taken as serious proposals, the arguments of Chump, Grump, and the goodly editor of the *Fresno Bee* fail: the IOC shouldn't adopt them. Myself, I don't intend to propose an Olympic calculus; my aspirations are considerably lower. (Less than Olympian?) I'll argue merely that the IOC should not adopt Harig's "Simply the best" policy. Please keep an open mind to the possibility that, similar to the argument against "No ball, no Olympics," Harig's proposal is also a demonstrably bad policy.

## What Does Harig's Policy Actually Require?

This much is clear. According to Harig's "Simply the best" policy, the IOC should hold a tournament in a particular sport *only* if winning the tournament would be, for the relevant athletes, the pinnacle of achievement in their athletic careers. This policy doesn't imply that other considerations such as tradition and parity are unimportant. But it does accord a special type of authority to quality: the absence of top quality "defeats" all other considerations. It requires that a sport's second-rate tournament should be excluded from the Olympics *even if* it scores (very) high on other metrics: even if, say, it creates a more egalitarian roster of sports, is chock full of parity, and is beloved by fans and wealthy sponsors alike.

What's not immediately clear is how rigorously Harig would apply the term *best*. Would he require that the Olympic golf tournament be the *single* best golf tournament in the world? (John Antonini, another golf writer, seems to; if an Olympic tournament isn't, as he puts it, "the ultimate competition, a special world championship," it should be abolished.[11]) Or would it be satisfactory, in Harig's view, if an Olympic golf tournament were *as good as* the four major PGA events?

As I suggested earlier, Harig's policy could also be interpreted as saying, even less rigorously, that an Olympic tournament must be at least "top-shelf." To be top-shelf, a tournament must be very closely comparable in terms of quality to the very best tournaments. At present, the quality of the football in the English Premier League is better than in Italy's Serie A. From top to bottom, the level of talent in the Premiership is higher. But the two leagues are closely comparable, both "top-shelf." Both have world-class players and coaches; both have teams that have won the Champion's League in recent years. By contrast, the level of play in the top flight in Holland, the Eredivisie, is very good—it fosters excellent young talent—but a very significant step down from both England and Italy. It's good, but not absolute "top-shelf."

Here's what I propose. Since I don't know Harig's own preferences, let's construe his proposal, charitably, in its least demanding way. And let's also append a sensible proviso to it. Hindsight reveals that a straightforward, unqualified "Simply the best" policy, had it been implemented thirty years ago, would have had regrettable results. At the time, the basketball being played in the NBA was, by leaps and bounces, better than anywhere else in the world. Its talent level was higher than collegiate basketball, and the best American college players were often able to dominate other Olympic teams. The Olympic tournament, not even in shooting range of the NBA, wouldn't have met the demands of Harig's policy—even on its top-shelf interpretation. But in recent years, the quality of Olympic men's basketball has had a strikingly positive trajectory. Winning the NBA title remains a much grander achievement than winning an Olympic gold medal, but the Olympics has steadily grown in quality (and so in parity as well). Accordingly, I will read Harig's proposal in this way: if an Olympic tournament is not, *and is not likely to become,* a top-shelf event, then it should be abolished.

## Two Kinds of "Simply the Best" Argument

Harig-style arguments come in at least two forms. Here is a representative example of one type. Keith Kropp, a journalist, argues that the Olympic men's and women's tennis tournaments should be abolished because they are "redundant." Many of the same tennis players who participate in the four Grand Slam tournaments also compete against each other in the Olympics. Tennis players, after an eleven-month calendar, are fatigued by the time the Olympics arrives. If Nicolas Massu of Chile won the gold medal in singles in 2004 at Athens, and not Roger Federer, was Federer able to give it his level best? A weary fan base, too, shows little enthusiasm or esteem for the Olympic title: "Massu . . . most likely would have achieved greater recognition in tennis," Kropp says, "had he won the French Open."[12]

Harig makes the same type of argument against men's golf. Even if the best players do choose to travel to the Olympics (a prediction about which Harig is skeptical), he says, "at least for now, it remains hard to fathom a player's coveting Olympic gold over major-championship hardware. You can bet that [the] Claret Jug [the trophy earned by the winner of the British Open] will mean more than a medal ever would."[13] According to these arguments, second-rate tennis and golf tournaments with first-rate, but tired and poorly motivated, athletes don't belong in the Olympics.

If applied to men's football, Harig's policy would also require its exclusion, but for a notably different reason. Since men's Olympic football is a qualified under-23 tournament—all but three players on each team have to be twenty-three years of age or younger—its tournament isn't a heavy-legged carbon copy of the World Cup. It generally has an almost entirely different roster of players and a significantly different roster of nations. The objection to the quality of the Olympic men's football tournament is that it simply doesn't get the best talent, well rested or not.[14]

There are exceptions to the rule that the world's best footballers don't participate. A few Olympic teams at the 2008 games included a world-class star or three: Sergio Aguero, Lionel Messi, and Javier Mascherano played for Argentina; Ronaldhino and Diego for Brazil. But otherwise the Argentine and Brazilian rosters were populated by good, but not (yet) excellent, players. None were, at the time, consistent first-choice members of the "senior" national team. Holland made an uncharacteristically aggressive move to put together a capable team; it kept together the core of the very successful under-21 team that won qualification to the Olympics and attempted to add quality veterans who would complement its young talent. Even so, its "over-age" players were Gerald Sibon and Kew Jaliens, journeyman players in the Dutch Eredivisie with little national team experience, and Roy Makaay, a formerly world-class forward on the downside of his career. The Dutch roster didn't include the far more talented Wesley Schneider, Arjen Robben, Robin van Persie, or Rafael van der Vaart. As for Brazil, Kaka showed interest, but in the end didn't travel to China.

It's also true that some of the very best football players haven't played in a World Cup. The brilliant George Weah was from Liberia, which has never qualified. And occasionally a world-class player withdraws for reasons other than injury: recall, as poor Holland can't forget, Johan Cruyff and Ruud Gullit (in 1978 and 1990, respectively). But the numbers strongly disfavor the Olympics. A significant percentage of world-class players would and do choose to participate in the World Cup, but would not and do not in the Olympics.

To finish up this Harig-inspired argument: it's fairly hard to imagine that the weaker talent level at the Olympics doesn't translate into a lower quality of play than one sees at the World Cup. No doubt, by any sensible standard, the quality of Olympic men's football is high. Argentina and Brazil have at their disposal considerable pools of talent, and so the very young teams they brought in 2008 were very good. On paper, Holland looked formidable, though it didn't manage to shine. Many African nations took the Olympics very seriously. The Asian teams, predictably, ran their hearts out. Even so, the talent level in 2008, which was comparatively a good year for men's Olympic football, was simply not up to Harig's uncompromising standards. It was good, but not absolute top-shelf.

What about the sensible proviso? Is Olympic men's football, similar to men's basketball, arguably on its way to being top quality? No. The under-23 format is a serious obstacle, as the best players in the world are often at their very best in their late twenties, when the accumulated benefits of training and match experience optimally converge with high levels of strength and endurance. But the main obstacle is that FIFA doesn't intend to compel professional clubs to release players for "Olympic duty."

Here's the context. Similar to tennis, the football calendar is long and packed. The world's best players, even those from Africa and South America, belong to European clubs. In most European leagues, the club season runs from late August through May, more than nine months of the year. And an elite club participates not only in its national league, but also in either the Champions or Europa League, as well as in season-long national cup tournaments. Thus, world-class footballers are stretched thin. This prompts clubs, who pay considerable sums for a player's rights and salary, to "protect" their fatigued stars. FIFA has stepped in, as it should, to provide rules about when a club is required to release a player to his national team. It essentially compels clubs to cooperate for World, European, and African Nations Cup qualification, and for select international "friendly" dates. But FIFA has given only limited support to footballers who want to go to the Olympics against the wishes of their clubs. In fact, Olympic teams find it difficult to pry even the very best under-23 talent from nervous managers, as the club seasons are just getting going when the Olympic tournament begins in August.[15]

To sum up, Olympic men's football is unlikely to rival the World Cup in terms of talent and quality. Simple logic tells us that anyone who thinks—as I do—that men's football belongs at the Olympics must dispute the wisdom of Harig's uncompromising commitment to excellence.[16]

## Why Should the IOC Reject Harig's Policy?

Harig's policy would have highly undesirable consequences. To begin with, the death of men's Olympic football would be unfortunate. The arguments against including trampoline, chess, dressage, American football, and women's softball simply don't apply to men's football. Football is a physically demanding ball sport that requires a high level of athleticism. It has, without any doubt, global appeal. Though South American and eastern European teams have a notable history of success in the Olympic tournament, there is generally a significant degree of parity. Men's football also has Olympic tradition on its side; since the second Olympic Games in 1900 it's been a part of all but one Olympiad (1932 in Los Angeles). Football doesn't raise a special concern about gender equality; the women's tournament, in fact, is top-shelf. The men's tournament does very well by market standards. It sells tickets: the attendance at the Beijing Olympics was 1.4 million, an average of almost 44,000 fans per match. The men's tournament has also evoked affection from several important footballers. Messi's strong desire to represent Argentina was touching. And Juergen Klinnsman, who won a World Cup victory with West Germany in 1990, is reported to have said, "The moment I received the bronze medal in the Olympics in Seoul 1988 . . . it was my number one outstanding emotion." In brief, making the absence of top quality a disqualifier would force the IOC to abolish an otherwise highly successful tournament.

Far more seriously, Harig's "uncompromising commitment to excellence," if applied across the board, would compel the IOC to de-roster many of its current sports. The Olympics would include gymnastics, but not cycling; swimming, but not boxing; table tennis, but not hockey. The sketchy story I've told about the complex negotiations and compromises between the IOC and FIFA could be told about other Olympic sports, too. If the IOC were unwilling to accept less than top-shelf quality of competition, the Olympics, already a somewhat strange brew, would make for an even stranger concoction of sports.

As the Olympics gave up its characteristic breadth, it would not only lose its grip on the title "the world's biggest sporting stage," it would also lose a peculiar power it currently has. Bright and articulate, Klinsmann is unlikely to think that the quality of the football at the 1988 Olympics was up to the standards of the 1990 World Cup. What makes sense of Klinsi's strong, pro-Olympic sentiment is that the Olympics' top-quality events, as well as its global character, add significance to its second-rate tournaments. These second-rate tournaments matter so much because the Olympics as a whole matter so much. Why should the IOC give up this power to create extra value? Earlier, I accused Harig's thinking of being "atomistic." His policy asks the IOC to evaluate its sports one by one, rejecting each tournament that is not, by itself, up to the highest standards in terms of quality. But this atomistic focus on the quality of tournaments, taken individually, would make the Olympics as a whole less valuable.

Consider also the following argument, which is directed at the "gospel of excellence" mentality behind Harig's proposal. Harig-style thinking would seem to demand that FIFA "fix" the World Cup, because it is not, if you really think about it, optimally excellent in terms of quality. There are, after all, fairly weak teams in the World Cup: in 2006, Germany beat Saudi Arabia 8–0 in the first round. Top to bottom, the quality of the teams in the European Championships is actually higher: it's hard to imagine any of the sixteen teams in the 2008 "Euros" giving up eight goals to another. Of course, unlike the Euros, the World Cup generally includes two of the strongest footballing nations: Argentina and Brazil. But it also includes the North Koreas, Costa Ricas, and Saudi Arabias of the world. Were FIFA to include only the very best, say, sixteen national teams, most of the teams would be from Europe. South America would generally be represented by Argentina and Brazil, and sometimes by another team or two. The field wouldn't include any teams from the Middle East, Asia, or Central America (except occasionally Mexico). And probably the United States would not often make the cut. The tournament just might include an African team—though probably not, as the international records of African squads at major tournaments have been relatively poor. No African team has ever made it to the World Cup semifinals, and only two have ever gone to the quarterfinals. In short, the World Cup is currently set up to be a world sporting event. If it were to treat top quality as a requirement, it would be a less global—and, I think, a much less meaningful—tournament.

In summary, quality, however important, isn't important enough to make such changes to the World Cup. And Harig's "Simply the best" policy, which gives top quality defeater status, similarly threatens the global nature of the Olympics.[17]

## Don't Get Me Wrong

Perhaps my arguments are anathema to a true believer in the gospel of excellence and high achievement. I'm not sure. But let's be clear: my plea on behalf of the second-rate doesn't imply a love of the mediocre. The Olympics has a strong and unobjectionable incentive to be a high-quality sporting event and should require its men's football tournament to meet a high standard—just not as high as Harig's policy suggests.

Also, if it were to follow my advice, the IOC wouldn't have to give up its wonderfully redolent triad "Faster, Higher, Stronger." There is a different strategy for striving to be "the best" than Harig's cut-throat policy promotes. The IOC could choose to exemplify the internal drive and intensity of an excellent athlete by aiming to elevate its football tournament as high as it possibly can, consistent with its other goals. Treating "being the best" as an ideal toward which a competitor strives is certainly consistent with ending up with a silver instead of a gold medal. There's really no dishonor in second place—especially if, in making a Herculean effort, one has exemplified or preserved other important values.

What values? At the heart of this discussion is a question about what the Olympics should ultimately be about. The IOC claims that it aims, among other things, to build a better and more peaceful world through sport. Of course, this claim could be nothing more than cynical advertising, a veneer of high-minded moralizing covering a steely, money-making machine. But the IOC could make good on its declared mission in several ways: for instance, by carefully policing its own officials to ensure that they are not taking kickbacks from would-be Olympic site hosts; by making decisions that prevent corporate sponsors from dictating its roster decisions; and, as I suggest here, by self-consciously preserving its global character, which would require it to ignore the call—short-sighted, in my view—to abolish each Olympic tournament that isn't, or isn't soon to be, absolutely top shelf.

Whether there should be Jamaican bobsledders at the Olympics I haven't said. But go ahead, IOC. Give us a world-class football star or two, a world-class football star or fifteen in the making, and some eager young footballers who are not, perhaps, destined for greatness. If it is necessary to endure football that is of lesser, though still high, quality for the sake of a broad and legitimately global sporting tournament that, as the Olympic Charter puts it, "blends sport with culture and education" and encourages cultural exchange, so be it.[18]

# Notes

1. Pierre de Coubertin, the founder of the modern Olympic movement, proposed the Latin triad (or hendriatus) *"Citius, Altius, Fortius"* in 1894. It was introduced as the official motto of the Olympics in 1924 at the Paris Games.

2. Evidence that the International Olympic Committee does believe this: on the home page of its official website, www.olympic.org, a visitor is able to click on the link "Best Athletes in the World," which provides the number of athletes that competed in the 2008 summer games in Beijing.

3. Fact or Fiction, ESPN.com: Golf, August 6, 2008.

4. Bob Harig, "Olympic Golf Not All Smooth Sailing," ESPN.com: Golf, October 9, 2009.

5. As we will see, the world-class German forward Juergen Klinsmann dissents.

6. For one such example, see http://msgnet.org/2008/08/top-five-summer-olympic-sports-that-dont-belong/.

7. See http://fresnobeehive.com/opinion/2008/08/which_olympic_sports_shouldnt.html.

8. For a strikingly well-defended account of what a game is, as well as a very clever attempt to refute Wittgenstein's famous skepticism about the pursuit of an analytic definition of "game," see Bernard Suit's much-neglected book, *The Grasshopper: Games, Life, and Utopia*, with an introduction by Thomas Hurka (Peterborough, Ontario: Broadview, 2005).

9. It's also true, of course, that most sports require strategy and so include intellectual challenges. My argument doesn't deny this.

10. In his book *Utilitarianism* (1863), Mill attempts to address this objection to Bentham's theory. Mill admits that moral decision making is more complex than Bentham believes, but tries to preserve the central tenets of utilitarianism.

11. Fact or Fiction, ESPN.com: Golf, August 6, 2008.

12. "Tennis Shouldn't Be in the Olympics," *Ventura County (California) Star*, August 7, 2008.

13. Harig, "Olympic Golf Not All Smooth Sailing."

14. At the "Access World Forum" website, in the garbled prose of a sloppy poster, a person named Paul Dohert makes this Harig-style argument: "Its a joke—the age restrictions etc. Either do it properly—or not at all. Its a perfect example of a sport that shouldn't be in the olympics—ie its nowhere near the pinnacle of the sports career. And the Olympics should be." (Please enter "sics" throughout.) See http://www.access-programmers.co.uk/forums/showthread.php?t=153135.

15. The Olympics isn't even, perhaps, the best international *youth* tournament. The footballing world is highly professional, and young talent is being sought earlier and earlier. Hence, the World Championships for under-17 and under-20, run by FIFA, are considered the real hotbed for emerging players. Most of the best players in an under-23 tournament are already relatively well known. So if the IOC were to attempt to sell the men's tournament as the place to "see the stars of the future," it could be accused of false advertising. One idea would be to make the Olympic tournament into an under-20 World Cup. But, at present, the Olympics is lost in this sea of "youth" football tournaments.

16. You'll notice, I hope, that I don't mean to argue against all "defeaters." My own sketchy proposal treats a competition's lack of physicality as a defeater: if a competition is not, at heart, a physical challenge, this would be reason enough, whatever its other merits as an Olympic tournament, to abolish it. I am merely arguing against Harig's suggested defeater.

17. Here's a thought experiment. Given that most of the world's premier male sprinters are from the Caribbean and North America, and given that, accordingly, the Pan-Am games often have, from top to bottom, the best quality, would Harig's policy demand that the Olympics drop the 100-meter race? If so, doesn't this count as an objection to his proposed policy?

18. The Olympic Charter, at http://www.olympic.org/Documents/olympic_charter_en.pdf.

Part 5

# RACE AND GENDER ISSUES

# THE STRONG MEN KEEP A COMIN' ON

## African American Sports Participation and the Discourse of Public Dissent

> Walk togedder, chillen,
> Dontcha git weary. . . .
> The strong men keep a comin' on
> The strong men git stronger.
> —Sterling Brown

For African Americans, 1968 was one hell of a year. On February 17 the Black Panther Party's Huey P. Newton was arrested after a gun battle in West Oakland, California, which resulted in the death of a white police officer, John Frey. On April 4 the Reverend Dr. Martin Luther King Jr. was assassinated by James Earl Ray at the Lorraine Motel in Memphis, Tennessee. And on October 16 at the Olympic Games in Mexico City, American sprinters Tommie Smith and John Carlos shook up the world when they used their victories in the 200-meter dash as a platform to lead black athletes in a protest against the United States and its policies on human rights issues related to African Americans in particular and oppressed people in general.

Indeed, as Smith and Carlos stood atop the victory stand awaiting the playing of America's national anthem, "The Star-Spangled Banner," all that they had trained for in preparation for the 1968 Olympic Games and the attention they would receive should they win came rushing forth as a torrent of focused, uncompromised emotion.[1] Clad in their USA track warm-up suits, wearing black socks without shoes to symbolize poverty and black leather gloves (Smith wearing the right and Carlos wearing the left of the same pair) to symbolize black power and unity, they lifted their clenched fists in protest as the anthem played. Their silent gesture was a sign of the times, booming thunderously across the globe as a defiant symbol against the hypocrisy of an American style of democracy that had traditionally devalued blacks and systematically denied the Race full access to basic human rights, economic opportunities, and the promise of a future filled with unlimited possibilities.[2]

The aim of this chapter is to examine the history of African American resistance to systematic oppression, including the development of black male sports participation as a critical vehicle in the liberation of blacks from social, economic, and political inequality in the United States. Specifically, I theorize that the actions of Tommie Smith and John Carlos in Mexico City were in line with the paradigm shift taking place in the 1960s. Framed by slavery and its twentieth-century derivation of Jim Crow segregation, black athletes like Smith and Carlos maintained a connection to other African Americans based on their collective memories of degradation, dehumanization, and abuse, as well as memories of past successes and victories over their oppression, all of which assisted in the development of an oppositional consciousness. These thick memories bound African Americans together as a community, providing the impetus needed to inspire particular individuals to act bravely in the face of uncertainty, knowing that they were working to change the circumstances affecting their community.

This understanding advanced a philosophy of resistance that allowed individuals and communities to adjust to the changes taking place in American society. This philosophy was easily communicated from one generation to the next through demonstrations of public and private dissent, whereby resistance was identified as a social good and individuals were recognized for their positive impact on their fellow community members. In areas of public life considered mundane and trivial, African Americans in general and black men in particular were more aware of the necessity to effectively model forms of resistance that could serve to inspire black communities to continue to pursue freedom as an achievable reality.

Finally, in viewing Smith's and Carlos's actions at the 1968 Olympic Games through the lenses of resentment, social justice, and prophetic pragmatism, concepts explored by philosophers Friedrich Nietzsche and

Cornel West, I seek to represent the importance of sports participation as a critical vehicle of liberation for African Americans as a whole. Moreover, through Smith and Carlos, I seek to advance the discourse of public dissent as a significant factor in the success of marquee social actors in their fight for human rights.

## An Oppositional Consciousness: Foundation for Dissent

The 1968 Mexico City Games, similar to every Olympic Games before it and since, was a politically charged spectacle. Nations such as the United States, Mexico, the Soviet Union, and the People's Republic of China all vied to assert and boast their country's values, mores, and ideals based on the outcomes of particular events. The success of individual athletes would be cumulatively added to the overall medal count of their countries, which in turn would serve to validate and affirm the countries' global position as either superior or inferior. However, for black athletes such as Tommie Smith and John Carlos, the Mexico City Games presented an opportune time and place to expose the plight of African Americans who were suffering under American policies that supported racial inequality, police brutality, and the abject poverty experienced by a majority of blacks.

Similar to the 1936 Berlin Games, where African American sprinter Jesse Owens's gold medal performances in the 100 and 200 meters, the long jump, and the 4-by-100-meter relay were recognized to have symbolically unraveled Adolf Hitler's ideology of the Aryan superman, the 1968 Summer Olympic Games proved to be an exercise in domestic and foreign policy for black athletes, who boldly broke with the American Olympic Committee's demands for obedience and acquiescence. What is more, through their explicit representation of displeasure and disgust with American race relations, Smith and Carlos would in fact argue that a majority of African Americans did not buy into the imagined sense of community promoted by the United States under the guise of friendly international sports competition.[3]

Nevertheless, by the 1960s the political importance of black athletes as radical advocates of social change had evolved significantly from the stoic models of manhood and citizenship that Joe Louis and Jesse Owens represented during the 1930s, or the self-sacrificing martyrdom demonstrated by Jackie Robinson during the 1940s and '50s, to explicit displays of resentment, disgust, and rage. Moreover, unlike their ancestors, the 1960s generation of African Americans had few illusions that they might achieve the so-called American dream, without simultaneously acknowledging—and protesting out loud—the reality of living in an American society that had never valued blacks as human beings. For Smith and Carlos, the overtly political atmosphere of the Mexico City Olympic Games juxtaposed against their victories in the 200-meter dash became the ideal backdrop to address the social, political, and economic realities that a majority of African Americans faced daily.

Oppressed groups have sought throughout history to free themselves from the hegemonic power structures that have conspired to limit their opportunities and so overcome their subaltern status. Those designated as subordinate and/or socially inferior recognized the need of naming their oppression and identifying its mechanisms of operation as a way to begin the process of challenging the power of the dominant group within a discourse of dissent. In other words, from their position in the margins, these groups developed an oppositional consciousness that sought to (1) understand the conditions of their institutionally prescribed positioning; (2) challenge the rights of their oppressor to designate them as inferior; (3) develop methods whereby they might resist the internalization of their external status; and (4) break free from their subjugated designation in an effort to become visible as human beings with all the benefits and privileges that status entitles.

According to German philosopher Friedrich Nietzsche, the denial of one's economic, social, and political opportunities in general and the negotiation of one's morality in particular creates the desire to resist and revolt against the system that dictates the rules and regulates one's life chances.[4] Nietzsche's notion of resentment represents a rejection of a dominant ideology by the oppressed and marginalized, who detest their subject status as unacceptable. The oppressed respond in various ways to the limitations placed on their ability to pursue lives free from degradation and moral compromise. These individuals, as a result of their oppression, are deprived of the opportunity to respond properly to external events and are coerced into negotiating their convictions, values, and morality as a means of survival. Forced to make compromises, they lie to protect themselves, their families, and their communities.

Those who are marginalized, be it through individual actions or through collective forms of agency based on traditions, devise creative ways to compensate for, and refute and deny, ideas associated with their so-called inferiority. These traditions, some of which are simple, nonthreatening gestures and others overt acts of rebellion, are layered within complex meanings and interpretations. In other words, for those seeking justice, Nietzschean resentment can be manifested in covert forms of deception, which redirect anger into constructive ways of responding to the external circumstances. However, for African Americans during segregation, overt manifestations of resentment, such as protests, riots, and isolated acts of violence against white power, were constant reminders of the contentious nature of American life. Nietzsche recognizes the necessity of such rituals: "For every sufferer instinctively looks for a cause of his distress; more exactly, for the culprit, even more precisely for a guilty culprit who is receptive to distress—in short, for a living being upon whom he can release his emotions, actually or in effigy, on some pretext or other: because the release of emotions is the greatest attempt of relief, or should I say, at anaesthetizing on the part of the sufferer, his involuntary longed-for narcotic against pain of any kind."[5]

According to Nietzsche, men of moral power will rebel against the slavish morality of the oppressors. And while he never endorses moral compromises, he does understand the need of the sufferer to release pent-up rage. This expression of frustration, caused primarily by the act of being marginalized, oppressed, and labeled as inferior, is central to understanding the development of an oppositional consciousness.

In seeking to realize the possibilities associated with the altering of their social position, the oppressed and marginalized support the development of a parallel world that allows them to create and advance a philosophy of resistance with the intention of claiming the collective humanity of the oppressed while simultaneously ending domination by the oppressor. What is more, this philosophical construction serves to fashion a more complete sense of the self, thereby creating social actors within a particular community capable of delivering his or her oppressed group from the grip of oppression through their recognition, acceptance, and performance of a purpose-driven state of being.

In the case of the 1968 Olympic Games, Tommie Smith and John Carlos became effective social actors who were able to elevate the plight of African Americans on the world stage, thereby challenging the power of the dominant group to limit access to the truth about their nation's internal affairs. What is more, the realization of their greater purpose demanded that they act in a way that acknowledged and promoted the humanity of their oppressed group, which in turn would accelerate the unraveling of the status quo. Inspired by Smith and Carlos, whose initial response to systemic oppression and domination was informed by their understanding of what was both just and morally right, individuals looking to their examples would free themselves from the socially prescribed practices of degradation, humiliation, and objectification by formulating an array of responses to various external challenges.

Indeed, creating or initiating additional responses to systemic oppression serves to psychologically insulate the oppressed from the demoralizing and debasing effects of racial subjectivity. As a result of the actions of Smith and Carlos, a new identity—a counterhegemonic construction of the previously maintained subject status—developed, along with the necessary rituals and methods of production needed to assist in the creation and sustainability of a strategic form of resistance. The wearing of black socks, as well as the iconic symbol of a clenched black fist, has come to represent resistance from overt forms of oppression.

However, without an understanding of the history associated with these symbols and gestures, as well as of the traditions used to develop and nurture individuals' connectedness to their community (most of which are based on the thick memories associated with the past), individual social actors who take the initiative to liberate themselves and their communities from oppressive forces and circumstances would be few and far between. In other words, in order to achieve an understanding of one's role in a community that seeks to be free from oppression, individuals have to be connected to the larger communal memory. Without a connectedness to the community narrative, individuals are less likely to initiate challenges to the system that denies full access to rights and privileges guaranteed by the laws of the land.

These critical factors advance the development of an oppositional consciousness that transforms and elevates while redefining one's purpose, actions, and importance for community members and other athletes. Moreover, this differential consciousness articulates a "new subject position . . . [that] permits a functioning within, yet beyond, the demands of a dominant ideology."[6] Indeed, this theoretical construction of the function of black athletes in African American culture accounts for the numerous individuals who were unwilling to submit to the immoral nature of segregation and the ability of human beings to abuse other human beings.[7] As a consequence, oppressed individuals took the initiative to lead protests and revolts throughout American society, and eventually in Mexico City at the 1968 Olympic Games.

African Americans were well aware of the circumstances that dictated their position in society during segregation. It makes obvious sense that in seeking freedom from social injustice and moral degradation, black men and women utilized multiple forms of public and private dissent to disprove the claims made against their humanity that justified their systemic abuse.

African American philosopher Cornel West notes that human struggle "is a form of tragic thought in that it confronts candidly individual and collective experiences of evil in individuals and institutions, with little expectations of ridding the world of all evil."[8] However, through various alternative artistic and political uprisings, we are able to confront both the institutions and their advocates, recognizing that in the end each of us shares the same fate. This understanding of our existential plight is what separates the philosopher West from his contemporaries, whose romantic pursuit of social, economic, and political justice seeks solutions to complex problems associated with intersecting identity constructions based on a historically relative set of circumstances. What is lost is the idea that human beings are constantly seeking justice from other human beings who are asserting their power and ability to dominate. It is this sense of justice that frames Smith and Carlos's example of resistance.

Even still, West's prophetic pragmatism is interconnected with that of tradition and progress in that all human struggles or forms of resistance are guided by the tenets of integrity, fairness, compassion, and a sense of morality. What is more, those seeking liberation for their oppressed community are persistent in their criticism of the dominant ideology, even as they consistently work to inspire heroic acts of bravery in the self-reflective identity-building process. For Tommie Smith and John Carlos to struggle against dominant forces calls upon those traditions of rebellion and resistance from which an oppositional consciousness draws its sustenance and strength. And yet even these traditions become diluted over time and need to be redefined for those seeking deliverance from a contemporary set of oppressive circumstances that continues to deny one's individual and collective claims to humanity. For African Americans, the 1968 Olympic Games became an important event by which they might resist and rebel against notions of second-class citizenship based on institutional racism, while insisting that black athletes were more than capable social actors who had the ability to impact the future of America.

## Resistance and the Performativity of Public and Private Dissent

At the beginning of slavery in the Americas, European nations developed and reaped the benefits of a brutal system that generated incremental wealth for landowners and investors based on the "free" labor provided by those designated as slaves. Regarded as defective types to be used as brutes and beasts of burden, people of African descent rebelled against the institution that dehumanized, degraded, and abused them. Relegated to the fields, factories, and plantations as cultivators, harvesters, and processors of sugar cane, tobacco, cotton, coffee, and other valuable commodities, blacks fought against the institution of slavery and the evolving social construction of race, which established blackness as an identifiable marker of inferiority. What is more, the social hierarchy promoting white dominance and black subordination, created by European-American lawmakers, religious leaders, and a neo-patriotism established to justify the treatment of men and women of African descent for the sake of profitability, advanced a new world economy that depended upon the fiction of race.

In America, slavery reduced human beings of African descent, with thousands of years of history, various cultural practices, and grounded traditions, to that of an obtuse underclass considered unworthy of compassion or respect. These black men, women, and children were forced to work from dawn until dusk, performing various tasks under the constant threat of violence and degradation. What is more, they did this with very few chances to achieve the freedom that a majority of whites enjoyed unchallenged. Marriages between enslaved black men and women were not honored or even recognized as valid unions by white slave owners. In fact, under the gaze and guidance of their masters, black women were raped, conceiving and producing children that would increase the value of their owner's estate. As economic assets, both adults and children were relegated to working on farms, plantations, and factories, or designated as market goods to be sold to the highest bidder. To be sure, slavery was an evil enterprise that created monsters out of men whose insatiable desires for wealth and power robbed them of their humanity, and people of African descent of their dignity.

Although hundreds of thousands of black people suffered and perished under the mantle of slavery and its devices, the institution could not cool the desires for justice or passion for freedom that burned in the hearts of the men and women who survived. Moreover, from the ranks of those considered the wretched of the earth, the debased circumstances served as a location for the creation of heroes and martyrs, whose examples of courage and bravery advanced a philosophical position that the race would come to depend upon as black people sought to realize their freedom.

Utilizing various methods of resistance, people of African descent chanced to free themselves from a most brutal existence: one that exploited their bodies but could not claim their minds. Indeed, when we examine the history of resistance among the enslaved black populations in North America and the Caribbean alongside the development of the institution of slavery, we find numerous examples of blacks challenging the rights of men to own other men. Black men such as Toussaint Louverture, Nat Turner, and Frederick Douglass used various forms of resistance, including public dissent and violence, to claim freedom from the jaws of slavery not only for themselves, but for blacks as a whole.

In order to inspire an entire community to continue to seek liberty, African Americans had to be inspired from within by individuals (like Louverture, Turner, and Douglass) who felt the pull of freedom the greatest and could articulate through their actions the best way to proceed. What is clear is that each understood the ennobling strength in speaking truth to power by asserting their claims to humanity, manhood, and eventually full citizenship. Indeed, each of their performances inspired multitudes of enslaved and free black men and women to act in a more heroic fashion. Moreover, their collective example of public and private dissent represents a tradition of resistance handed down and across generations, with the specific intention of serving as a springboard for revolutionary thought and action that black people have cherished in their quest for freedom and equality. To be sure, Tommie Smith and John Carlos, in the tradition of Frederick Douglass, chose to stand up for themselves and all African Americans to claim what had rightfully been theirs: their humanity and full citizenship.

## The Seeds of Revolt in a History of Rebellion

In 1966, after earning his doctoral degree in sociology from Cornell University, Harry Edwards returned to the campus where he had been a member of the San Jose State football, basketball, and track and field teams. At San Jose State, Edwards experienced firsthand the contradictory nature of being an African American student-athlete on a college campus where the fact of his blackness limited his ability to participate as a full-fledged member of the student body. What is more, with the consent of the athletic department, and under the guise of the university administration's acting to ensure the comfort of white students by maintaining a separate and unequal environment, Edwards as well as other black athletes encountered various forms of surveillance intended to regulate their abilities to move freely. This tension between their rights as students and the expectations that the university maintained for them as commodities performing a service drove Edwards and a number of his colleagues to pursue social justice through the discourse of public dissent. In other words, black athletes recognized that they were being used as non-beings and treated unfairly based on the social construction of race, and responded by choosing to speak out publicly against the systematic denial of human rights and privileges afforded to their white counterparts.

In response to the repudiation of basic campus housing and the regulation of educational pursuits beyond the approved fields of "physical education or criminology," Edwards challenged the system in terms indicative of the advancement of the philosophy of resistance borne out of slavery and Jim Crow. In his book *The Revolt of the Black Athlete* (1969), Edwards recalls vividly the series of events that led to his vision of a unified resistance against the social, political, and economic situation that African Americans in general and black athletes in particular found themselves involved in. Edwards writes:

[I]n the fall of 1967, two events occurred that brought all the talk and discussion to a head. First Tommie Smith, in Tokyo for the World University Games casually commented that some black athletes would perhaps boycott the 1968 Olympics. He merely gave a simple answer to an equally simple inquiry. A Japanese sports reporter had asked, "Do I understand correctly that there is talk in America about the possibility that black American athletes may boycott the 1968 Olympic games at Mexico?" Smith answered, "Yes, this is true. Some athletes have been discussing the possibility of boycotting the games to protest racial injustice in America."[9]

Clearly, Smith's provocative commentary, alluding to the possibility of black athletes boycotting the 1968 Olympic Games as a protest against the continued oppression of blacks in America, set the stage for the black liberation movement to resonate south of the border in Mexico City. However, the lack of a concrete plan or unified decision among the potential participating black athletes to see a protest through motivated Edwards to pursue a plan of action that would dovetail with Smith's statement and concerns. As Edwards recalls:

The whole plan for the revolt originated from a discussion between me and Kenneth Noel, then a master's degree candidate at San Jose State. He, like most of the black males on the campus, was a former athlete. Most of the Afro-American males on San Jose State College's campus were former athletes who no longer had any eligibility left but who had not yet graduated. . . . Ken was one of the three who had graduated after a six-year term as an undergraduate and then continued on for a Master of Arts degree. Our rather casual conversation centered around the old and the new aspects of life at San Jose State for black students. After talking for about an hour, it suddenly dawned on us that the same social and racial injustices and discriminations that had dogged our footsteps as freshmen at San Jose were still rampant on campus—racism in the fraternities and sororities, racism in housing, racism and out and out mistreatment in athletics, and a general lack of understanding of the problems of Afro-Americans by the college administration.[10]

Edwards and Noel were both well aware of the tensions present on college campuses across the United States and the increased number of conflicts between black student-athletes, coaches, and university administrations. Both Edwards and Noel believed it was the perfect time to advance a program of public dissent that strategically used the upcoming Olympic Games and the overall dependency of the U.S. teams on the success of black athletes as a backdrop to protest the social, economic, and political disparities found in America.

In the media, Edwards asked of what "value is it to a black man to win a medal if he returns to be relegated to the hell of Harlem?"[11] As a trained sociologist and scholar of African American life and history, Edwards recognized that the traditional struggles for full citizenship that blacks had been engulfed in since the founding of America were inextricably linked to their noble pursuit of visibility as human beings. Therefore, a protest centered on exposing the human rights violations and atrocities perpetrated against African Americans through the refusal of black athletes to participate in the Olympics fell within the civil rights discourse of nonviolent disobedience. Simultaneously, such a demonstration of strength and resilience would advance the tradition of resistance that blacks continuously revisited in their ongoing quest for equal access to the rights and privileges enjoyed by white Americans and human beings within a civil society. The organization that Edwards founded in 1967, the Olympic Committee for Human Rights (OCHR), later the Olympic Project for Human Rights (OPHR), provided the opportunity for black athletes to effect change in American society while perpetuating the civil rights movement defined by sit-ins, marches, and freedom rides.[12]

In *The Revolt of the Black Athlete,* Edwards recalls the lives of the African American boxer Joe Louis, the men of the Negro Baseball Leagues, and the heroic Jackie Robinson, and how sports had proved to be the most effective avenue whereby black men could claim not only their manhood and citizenship, but also the humanity of their communities. Edwards's historical accounting of the importance of black athletes to the liberation process of African Americans as a whole is significant, though it requires explanation. In other words, there is a need to revisit the time period that informs the development of the oppositional consciousness African Americans utilized in their quest for social justice through sports participation. This recognition was important for Edwards and his colleagues, who were well aware of the implications of boycotting the 1968 Olympics. Nevertheless, the aim of the OCHR was to inspire participants, black athletes in particular, who qualified for the Mexico City Games to commit themselves to the mission of telling the world about the plight of African Americans in the United States.

From 1964 to 1967, Edwards and several black athletes at San Jose State University met frequently to discuss issues related to their recognition of themselves as two people on the university campus: black athletes and American citizens. These athletes understood the need to use their knowledge of their "twoness" as a position to speak out against societal racism. However (and this was to be expected), the scholarship athletes were fearful of losing their financial support if the administration got wind of their efforts to change the culture of the campus. Fortunately for Edwards, Smith and his teammate, the world class sprinter Lee Evans, were two of more than a dozen potential Olympians who had been primed to act on behalf of African Americans as a result of their exposure to the black liberation movement and its goals and objectives. Moreover, Malcolm X's evocative speeches, the Reverend Dr. Martin Luther King Jr.'s philosophy of nonviolent disobedience, and the Black Panther Party's aggressive ten-point program to change the lives of African Americans all appealed to Smith and Evans's desires for black progress.[13]

Transplants from northern California's rural farming community, Smith and Evans maintained an active connection to the thick memories of slavery and Jim Crow because of their families' histories and connections to the South. Recognizing the ability of African Americans to overcome their subjectivity within the context of a racist society, Smith and Evans freely participated in the open discussions hosted by Edwards and Noel. Through their unified concerns, collective strategic planning efforts, and overall disillusionment that the American dream could be accomplished through sports participation, the OCHR was founded.[14]

By October 1967, while seeking to attract other like-minded individuals to join in the movement, Edwards had become well aware of the potential implications of this unified *revolt* of college athletes protesting against the exploitation of their muscle but the denial of their humanity and citizenship on the world's stage. On Thanksgiving Day in Los Angeles, near UCLA's campus, more than two hundred black athletes and activists, including Dr. Martin Luther King Jr., attended the workshop led by Edwards. During the workshop, Lew Alcindor (who would later embrace the religion of Islam and change his name to Kareem Abdul-Jabbar) articulated his feelings about being valued as an athletic commodity and relegated to the margins of society as black.

I'm the big basketball star, the weekend hero, everybody's all-American. Well, last summer I was almost killed by a racist cop shooting at a black cat in Harlem. He was shooting on the street—where masses of black people were standing around or just taking a walk. But he didn't care. After all we were just niggers. I found out last summer that we don't catch hell because we aren't basketball stars or because we don't have money. We catch hell because we are black. Somewhere each of us has got to make a stand against this kind of thing. This is how I take my stand—using what I have. And I take my stand here.[15]

Alcindor's impromptu speech was an indicator of the growing number of African American athletes' acknowledging their "twoness," as well as their willingness to speak truth to power on behalf of their communities in an effort to improve the lives of the millions of blacks living in poverty and uncertainty. Similar to Smith, Alcindor used his position as a "big basketball star, the weekend hero, [and] everybody's all-American" to take a stand against the continued racism affecting African Americans. At the Los Angeles meeting, Smith, the world's leading 200- and 400-meter sprinter, said, "I can't tell another black athlete that it is his duty to forget a goal that he has sought for himself. In fact, I hope a boycott won't be needed to bring about the necessary changes in our country. But if a boycott is deemed appropriate, then I believe most black athletes will act in unison."[16] Smith's hopeful disposition and attitude was challenged by African American athletes such as Ralph Boston, an Olympic champion and world record holder in the broad jump, who felt that the Games should not be used as a political tool.[17] Not to be excluded from the criticism of the upstarts, former Olympians Bob Hayes, Rafer Johnson, and Jesse Owens refused to support the decision of the young lions challenging the status quo. The most famous of the naysayers, Owens was against the proposed boycott because he believed that sports were not the place for politics and that the Olympics represented the perfect place for "Negroes" to claim their citizenship through their patriotic act of participation.

However, former Major League Baseball player Jackie Robinson, NBA great Bill Russell, and Dr. King recognized and embraced the efforts of the young black men and women, whose position was recognizably similar to—and just as important as—those who participated in the lunch counter sit-ins, bus boycotts, and marches that had been taking place across the United States. Robinson recognized that the effort being made by Edwards and the collective of African American athletes was important to the liberation process of all black people. Regarding the OPHR, Robinson would say, "I feel we've got to use whatever means, except violence, we can to get our rights in this country. When, for 300 years, Negroes have been denied equal opportunity some attention must be focused on it."[18] Robinson's commentary validated the OPHR movement as an important contribution to the discourse on civil rights.

By the spring of 1968, Smith, along with Edwards, Noel, Evans, and Carlos, had become synonymous with the Olympic Project for Human Rights, and the debate surrounding the role of black athletes was seen as important to the outcome of the Olympic Games for the United States, as well as to the civil rights movement. In what would become a classic Edwards provocation, he challenged black athletes to "stand up as men and women and refuse to be utilized as performing animals for a little extra dog food."[19] Moreover, Edwards boldly confronted the ideological foundation of the United States within the discourse of public dissent by challenging Washington, D.C., to make good on its promises of equality for all, or be embarrassed on the world stage by those who held the keys to success. In the months leading up to the Mexico City Games, a number of significant events occurred that would make Tommie Smith's and John Carlos's demonstration on the winner's podium in Mexico City even more significant.

First, on April 4 the Reverend Dr. Martin Luther King Jr. was assassinated by James Earl Ray at the Lorraine Motel in Memphis, Tennessee, the day after he gave his prophetic "I've Been to the Mountaintop" speech to a crowd of supporters of the city's striking garbage workers. Second, after winning the California presidential primary, U.S. senator, civil rights supporter, and activist Robert F. Kennedy was murdered on June 5 in Los Angeles, California, by Sirhan Sirhan, a Palestinian immigrant. Third, in response to the number of incidents involving African American athletes and the question of participation in the coming Olympic Games, *Sports Illustrated* began a five-part series of articles on July 1 under the title "The Black Athlete—A Shameful Story," exposing the fallacy of African American athletic success as a vehicle to social acceptance and equality.

Then, after months of preparation in anticipation of the opening of the Olympic Games in their country's capital city, on October 2 Mexican students led a protest against the Mexican government, demanding democratic reforms, better jobs, and opportunities for the Mexican people. The Mexican government responded with unmitigated violence, resulting in the deaths of several hundred men, women, and children, most of which were union workers, students, professors, and innocent bystanders. With this as the intersecting social and political backdrop, American sprinters Tommie Smith, Lee Evans, and John Carlos entered the Olympic Village at Mexico City determined to do something. But what exactly was still to be resolved.

On October 16 Smith, Evans, and Carlos understood that in Mexico City they, not Harry Edwards, were now at the center of the Olympic Project for Human Rights and that action, if any, would be determined by them. In other words, the OPHR would be a success only if they took charge and stood up in the face of adversity by making a significant statement that would inspire others to follow their example. Indeed, after qualifying in the preliminaries for the 200-meter finals, Smith and Carlos prepared for the race of their lives.

Immersed in the energy and excitement of the Olympics and in the race that would determine the success or failure of the OPHR, Smith and Carlos nervously gathered their thoughts and focused on the desired outcome of victory. In their respective lanes they waited until the announcer commanded the field to ready itself. As the crowd watched the athletes bend and stretch and finally crouch down and gather themselves into their starting blocks in preparation for the starter's signal, all that Smith and his colleagues and teammates had endured over the preceding eighteen months had come down to a twenty-second block of time.

In his autobiography *Silent Gesture* (2007), Smith recalls the moment right before the beginning of the race: "They gave the get-set signal, and I thought, 'The time is nigh.' Everything was culminating in the moment: all the things that had happened because of the proposed boycott, and the years that I trained, not only in school training with a coach, but also in the summer when I worked in the fields with my father, in what we'd call the Bottom, that wide area in central California where my family and I had moved from Texas when I was little."[20] In a split second, Smith recalls the multiple connections tied to his presence in Mexico City and the overall importance of his performance at the Olympic Games. He realized that with a victory he would be in a position to speak loudly to the concerns of the millions of impoverished and disenfranchised African

Americans in the United States seeking deliverance from an oppression that had been a feature of black life for generations.

As the starting pistol sounded, Smith and teammate Carlos exploded out of their compacted stances, pushing against the blocks to propel themselves forward. From the beginning of the race Carlos took the lead, but Smith was not far behind. Finding the will to accelerate past his teammate, Smith captured the lead and claimed first place with the record time of 19.83 seconds. Australian Peter Norman edged out John Carlos to claim second place. With the hard part over, Smith and Carlos prepared to present their argument to the world. In his gym bag, Smith had placed a pair of black leather gloves to be used as props in his individual protest. Being that he and Carlos would be on the stand, he offered the left glove to his willing teammate, who followed his lead.

After receiving their medals from Lord Killanin of Ireland, the vice-president of the IOC, Smith and Carlos (along with Norman, who supported their efforts by wearing an Olympic Project for Human Rights badge) stood atop the victory stand waiting for the playing of America's national anthem. As the anthem played they lifted their clenched fists and bowed their heads in protest of America's continued oppression of African Americans.

This bodacious exercise in defiance and public dissent instantly sent a shock wave throughout the Olympic Games that was felt around the world, especially in the United States. Responding immediately to the silent gesture, the president of the International Olympic Committee, Avery Brundage, and the U.S. Olympic Committee on his suggestion suspended Smith and Carlos from the Olympic team, giving them forty-eight hours to "get out of Mexico."[21] However, not to be denied the opportunity to exploit the event and the circumstances leading up to the protest, the international media broke into a frenzy of activity, descending upon Smith and Carlos as they made their way to the Olympic village to collect their belongings. The next day, Thursday, October 17, ABC (American Broadcasting System) sports reporter Howard Cosell interviewed Smith at ABC's Olympic studios, giving Smith the perfect opportunity for him to explain to the world what his and Carlos's actions meant. Smith said, "My raised right hand stood for the power in black America. Carlos's left hand stood for unity of black America. Together, they formed an arch of unity and power. The black scarf around my neck stood for black pride. The black socks with no shoes stood for black poverty in racist America. The totality of our effort was the regaining of black dignity."[22]

The symbolism embedded in Smith and Carlos's protest, so eloquently described by Smith, was a brilliant example of thoughtfulness and bravery in the face of adversity, what Cornel West suggests is the result of prophetic pragmatism. Not surprisingly, the Olympic committee members, who saw their overtly political gesture as an embarrassment to the games and an affront to the United States, did not share the black medal winners' ideas. Some even suggested that their medals be taken away from them.

In the end, Smith and Carlos lost opportunities to advance their careers beyond the Olympic Games and even received death threats from whites who felt the two had embarrassed the United States to fulfill some personal need for attention. To be sure, Smith and Carlos understood the necessity of sacrificing themselves in this way to bring attention to the challenges and consequences of being black in America. Clearly, within the tradition of their ancestorial fathers—Louverture, Turner, Douglass, Johnson, Louis, Robinson, Malcolm X, and King—Tommie Smith and John Carlos used the Olympic Games as a world stage for public dissent. They took advantage of the opportunity to advance the social and political progress of their marginalized group by boldly challenging the continued abuse of blacks in America.

## Between Thick and Thin: African Americans and the Quest for Freedom and Equality

During slavery, people of African descent shared a common history of oppression based on the social construction of race devised by whites to exploit the black body as a form of free labor. By the 1960s, African Americans mobilized their collective understanding of the origins of racial segregation, the past related to slavery, and an imagined homeland of Africa, all with the intent of overcoming their subjectivity as second-class citizens.[23] Indeed, by acknowledging a past filled with narratives of survival, heroics, and victories over white oppression, African Americans were able to galvanize their communities around the common goals of freedom and equality.

What is more, in the process of "self-making" and community building, African Americans promoted various acts of resistance as necessary to individual and group identity development. Indeed, community members recognized that rebellion in some format was an important and significant social good.[24] To rebel or defy the wishes of those responsible for one's oppression, although potentially detrimental to one's individual comfort, was necessary in influencing how a community remembered its history and maintained its desires for freedom. By adopting a philosophy of resistance that both refuted and denied institutionalized notions of subjectivity, African Americans created and advanced methodological tools by which to challenge the dominant group's influence on the social reality faced by those restricted to the margins.

The civil rights movement of the 1960s maintained the struggle for freedom from the grips of white supremacy through various acts of defiance while using the vehicles of social mobility, such as education, politics, the arts, science, and sports participation, as a means for blacks to achieve visibility and equality as human beings. Still, the thick memories associated with slavery and the ability of the African American community to overcome their subjectivity during segregation remained central to the liberation movement advanced during the civil rights era. In order to break free from the binding nature of race as a category used to define their social positioning and therefore "knowability," African Americans developed both overt and covert methods to speak truth to power in an effort to claim not only their humanity but their right to the privileges that being born in America and contributing to the growth of the nation provided its citizens.

Within the context of the late twentieth century, African American athletes came to embody the spirit of those freedom fighters, who during slavery used every means at their disposal to fight and/or claim their and their community's humanity. Plainly, in championing the cause of liberation and freedom for blacks as well as other oppressed people, Tommie Smith and John Carlos endowed themselves with certain characteristics that recalled the traditions of the past, while simultaneously generating an understanding of the need to have and maintain an oppositional consciousness in future generations as long as oppression exists.

Moreover, by maintaining the thick and thin memories of the past, African Americans are able to recall the origins of the production of counternarratives to the "biases, distortions, and omissions" prevalent in mainstream historical texts and media, which are maintained by the majority community.[25] In the end, Tommie Smith's and John Carlos's participation within the context of the 1968 Mexico City Olympic Games represents the continuation of the liberation process that had begun during slavery.

## Notes

The epigraph is from the poem "Strong Men," in *The Collected Poems of Sterling Brown,* ed. Michael Harper (Evanston: Northwestern University Press, 1980), 56.

1. Australian sprinter Peter Norman, who finished second in the 200-meter dash, supported Smith and Carlos's effort to draw attention to the plight of black people in America by wearing an Olympic Project for Human Rights button on his warm-up suit. Norman paid dearly for his decision back in Australia: he was ostracized by the media for embarrassing the nation and was reprimanded by the Australian Olympic authorities for his participation in the overtly political gesture.

2. The capital R here is intended to establish people of African descent as a group of individuals who share a cultural background, as well as an overall juxtaposition against whites, who are identified in this essay as the dominant group.

3. The Olympic Games were supposed to promote peace among nations through athletic competition. In addition, they aimed to foster respect for the peoples of those nations with varying creeds, religions, and races.

4. My original reading of Nietzsche's philosophical musings appeared in "We're American Too: The Negro Leagues and the Philosophy of Resistance" in *Baseball and Philosophy: Thinking Outside the Batter's Box,* ed. Eric Bronson (Chicago: Open Court Publishing, 2004). As I pointed out in that essay, Nietzsche's seminal works have been at times unfairly recognized as an inspiration or justification for the world's nihilists and doomsayers, and even for the creation of the Third Reich in Nazi Germany. This chapter does not explore Nietzsche's political ramifications. Reference to Nietzsche throughout this chapter will be to one of his concepts that I take the liberty to contextualize within the theoretical construct of an oppositional consciousness developed during slavery and advanced through the civil rights era of the 1960s, and the performances of Tommie Smith and John Carlos at the 1968 Olympic Games.

5. Nietzsche, *On the Genealogy of Morality,* ed. Keith Ansell-Pearcon and Carol Diethe (Cambridge: Cambridge University Press, 1994), 99.

6. Chela Sandoval, *Methodology of the Oppressed* (Minneapolis: University of Minnesota Press, 2000), 43.

7. In his essay "Oppression and Slavery" in *Between Slavery and Freedom* (Bloomington: Indiana University Press, 1992), Bill Lawson establishes the fact that the ability of one human being to own another was the establishing factor that allowed for blacks to be marked as a group that could in fact be oppressed.

8. Cornel West, *The Cornel West Reader* (New York: Basic Books, 1994), 166–168.

9. Harry Edwards, *The Revolt of the Black Athlete* (New York: Free Press, 1969), 41–42.

10. Ibid., 42–43.

11. Cited in Douglass Hartman's *Race, Culture, and the Revolt of the Black Athlete* (Chicago: University of Chicago Press, 2003), 93.

12. Ibid., 38.

13. Huey Newton, Bobby Seale, Elbert Howard, Sherman Forte, Reggie Forte, and Bobby Hutton founded the Black Panther Party for the purpose of protecting the black community from the violence meted out by white law enforcement. Eventually, the party included in its mission and goals the objective of gaining freedom, full employment, decent housing, and a decent education for blacks.

14. Edwards generalizes the experiences of all black athletes as a knowable phenomenon, as he concludes that no one black athlete can truly become successful and autonomous as long as African Americans suffer as a whole.

15. Quoted in Edwards, *Revolt*, 53.

16. Quoted in Jonathan Rodgers, "A Step to An Olympic Boycott," *Sports Illustrated*, December 4, 1967, 31.

17. *Track and Field News*, December 1967, 15–16.

18. *New York Times*, December 14, 1967.

19. Quoted in Rodgers, "A Step," 30.

20. Tommie Smith, *Silent Gesture: The Autobiography of Tommie Smith* (Philadelphia: Temple University Press, 2007), 31.

21. Edwards, *Revolt*, 104.

22. Smith, *Silent Gesture*, 173.

23. In *The Ethics of Memory* (Cambridge, MA: Harvard University Press, 2002), Avishai Margalit argues that within communities there are two types of human relations: thick ones and thin ones. According to Margalit, "Thick relations are grounded in attributes such as parent, friend, lover, fellow-countryman. Thick relations are anchored in a shared past or moored in shared memory. Thin relations, on the other hand, are backed by the attribute of being human. Thin relations rely on some aspects of being human, such as being a woman or being sick. Thick relations are in general our relations to the near and dear. Thin relations are in general our relations to the stranger and the remote (7).

24. West, *Cornel West Reader*, 107.

25. Thad Sitton, "Black History from the Community: The Strategies of Fieldwork," *The Journal of Negro History* 50:2 (Spring 1981): 176.

*Kutte Jönsson*

# OLYMPIC AMAZONS AND THE COLD WAR
## The Rise and Fall of Gender Radicalism

During the Cold War, athletic performances were also political statements. But that was then. For every year that passes since the fall of the
Berlin Wall in 1989, the memories from that time seem to become more
and more blurred. Of course, there are those who simply do not want to
remember, who just want to forget and even erase that period from the
collective memory.

If we agree that Cold War sports were political in their essence, we
may also interpret this fact from different angles. The most obvious interpretation is to say that Cold War sports manifested the conflict between
two economic and political systems—that is, state socialism versus capi-
talism, or communism versus liberal democracy. This is the most obvious
interpretation. But it was also a war between different kinds of gender
constructions of the female athlete, and the Olympic Games were the
most important stage on which this war took place.

From a Western perspective the female athletes of the Eastern Bloc
were controversial, especially the East German "wonder girls" of the
1970s and 1980s. During these decades athletes such as Marita Koch,
Katrin Krabbe, Heike Drechsler, and Kornelia Ender dominated the
Olympics. Their physical appearance was controversial. Many commentators reduced them to mere doping cheaters manufactured in state-
controlled laboratories. In fact, this description is a rather common one.
But what does it mean to describe them in this way? Well, for one thing
it means that they must have challenged—and potentially undermined—
the Olympic spirit and Olympic values because they presumably were

neither "natural" nor "clean" athletes. In short, they were bad for the Olympic ideal.

Of course, this is just one way of understanding the Eastern Bloc sports phenomenon. Another perspective is to say that these athletes—and what they stand for symbolically—made important and valuable contributions to the gender debate in sport. More precisely, they showed, through their mere existence, a different way of being a female athlete in a heavily gendered and masculine sports world.

The Eastern Bloc athletes were often outstanding, and it is not a secret that their bodies were partly built by powerful performance-enhancing drugs. They also transcended narrow gender boundaries, partly because of the heavy use of such drugs. In doing so they also transcended the traditional conception of modern sport as a males-only arena. In this chapter I discuss some of the essential arguments concerning the rise and fall of gender radicalism. Gender radicalism, as I define it here, can be manifested by athletes who act at the edge of gender boundaries, sometimes transcending these boundaries. In order to make my argument as clear as possible I focus on the polarization between Eastern Bloc sports culture (as it appears to us through the common story of Olympic sports) and Western sports culture. I hope to show how the mere existence of the Eastern Bloc challenged commonly accepted conservative gender norms, and this challenge resulted in an overall improvement in the status of female sports. Another way of putting this is to say that the fall of the Berlin Wall also became the fall of the (last?) serious attempt at being gender radical at the Olympics and led to the return of traditional and reactionary gender values.

## The Gender Issue in Sport: A Question of Masculinity

It is a well-known fact that modern sport is founded on masculine ideals and norms. The ongoing (re)production of gender has always been strongly manifested in sports. The Olympic Games is no exception.

Historically, female participation at the Olympics has often been a controversial issue. The founders of the modern Olympic Games were against the idea of female competitors, at least on equal terms. Or, as Pierre de Coubertin once wrote, "Personally, I do not approve of women's participation in public competitions, which does not mean that they should not engage in a great many sports, merely that they should not become the focus of a spectacle."[1] But thanks to the women's movement and other progressive political forces, women slowly became part of the Olympic family. Hardly anyone would question women's participation nowadays. However, this does not mean that there are no remaining obstacles to gender equality. The world of sports in general, and the Olympic sports world in particular, is still an arena where traditional gender structures are constantly reproduced in favor of traditional masculinity.

Many people have strong opinions about gender differences. For example, people commonly claim that it is a biological and physiological fact that men are stronger than women and therefore also "better" at sports. Some people go on to argue that because of this, gender inequality is not a serious problem in sports. Others, however, claim that it is—and not only when it comes to sports on the basic level, such as children's sports, but also when it comes to elite sports.

## English's Proposal

In one of the most famous essays on this topic, "Sex Equality in Sports," feminist sport philosopher Jane English argues that if we believe in equality, we should seek to implement it at all levels of sport, including elite sport. If we think this is a compelling premise, and I believe it is, then we must ask how we should reduce or even eliminate the inequalities that persist. English has a suggestion. She constructs a theory of distributive justice, for which she proposes a model of distribution where "proportional attainments for the major social groups" emerge.[2]

English applies a traditional principle of equality of opportunity to sports in much the same way as the principle is supposed to work as an instrument of favoring socially disadvantaged groups of society in other areas. In a sports context, it means that a society is just only if the percentage of athletes from each "major social group" corresponds to the population as a whole, which means that it is unjust if fewer than half of the professional athletes are women. English identifies some obstacles for implementing such a proposal. For example, the fact that many sports are based on male-specific physiological traits limits opportunities for women to excel. She claims that there are some *permanent* biological differences that no political ideology can change.[3]

English's argument is problematic. "Biological" arguments are commonly used to legitimate the gender hierarchy—for example, by seeing women's gender roles as something that is natural.[4] English falls into that pitfall when she refers to "permanent biological differences" between men and women. Her approach to this issue is certainly the most common one. Gender inequality issues usually come down to the issue of unfair or unequal distribution of resources, under the assumption that bodily differences between men and women are static and therefore unchangeable.

## The Masculine World of Sport

In the gender equality and sport debates, some have proposed more radical suggestions than redistributing resources. One suggestion is that there should be gender integrated or gender neutral competitions, where men and women compete against each other on equal terms.[5] Many may find this proposal absurd. But why think this? Is not gender segregation an example of gender conservatism? And in what way does gender conservatism serve women's status in sports? Is not fully accepted gender segregation only a tool for securing the dichotomy between male and female athletes? And is not that in turn a way of favoring male athletes?

Of course, one can argue that since boys and men are encouraged to do certain sports whereas girls and women are not to the same extent, it would be unfair to female athletes if they were forced to compete with male athletes. The reason is not that females are biologically or physiologically inferior, but rather that they are treated as socially inferior. So even if women had formal equal opportunities to be professional athletes, this would not automatically challenge the conservative norms of sport, for the simple reason that the dichotomy between men and women in sports would still exist. In other words, it may very well be the case that the core problem of inequality of sports is embedded in the existence of the gender dichotomy.

Even when female athletes have beaten their male competitors, voices have been raised that male athletes are still "better" than female athletes. Consider China's Zhang Shan, winner of the skeet shooting competition in the 1992 Olympic Games in Barcelona. Zhang was the only female participant in that competition. And as it turned out, her presence was also a problem for some. Nonetheless, she won the competition fair and square. What was wrong with that? Well, it was wrong, at least according to the International Olympic Committee. Her beating the male shooters seemed to be embarrassing to them. So what to do?

The IOC found a solution. At the next Olympic Games, in Atlanta, female athletes were not allowed to participate in skeet shooting. All of a sudden, skeet shooting had become an exclusively male Olympic sport. However, in the subsequent Games, held in Athens, female athletes were welcomed back—but in a women's class. Without doubt, Zhang Shan challenged the male-defined sports world. She was not the first to do so, and she will most certainly not be the last.

The most famous example is the so-called "battle of the sexes" in 1973, where feminist tennis player Billie Jean King challenged and won over the male "sexist" Bobby Riggs; another, more recent example is when Swedish golf player Annika Sörenstam played in a "males only" tournament organized by the Professional Golf Association of America in 2003. At the Olympics, however, there have never been such challenges. Nonetheless, there are plenty of examples where female athletes have challenged conservative gender norms—often by entering the Olympic arena with "gender ambiguous" bodies, that is, bodies that cannot easily be categorized as "male" or "female."

Stella Walsh was a Polish American runner and gold medalist in the women's 100 meters at the 1932 Olympic Games in Los Angeles. In 1980 she was killed by robbers in Cleveland, Ohio. The autopsy of her body indicated that she had both male and female genitals.[6] Some claimed, though, that she "mostly" had male genitals and should therefore be biologically categorized as a man. In the aftermath of this incident it has been debated whether Walsh cheated her way to athletic success. This argument contains some problems. First, it is not clear how to distinguish between biological circumstances and socially defined circumstances.[7] Second, it seems obvious that Walsh's gender identity was as a woman. This is an interesting point when it comes to sport. If we agree with the common statement that men have an advantage in sport (either because of genetics or social circumstances), this implies that Walsh had a disadvantage for the sole reason that she defined herself as a woman. Hence, it would have been unfair to force her to compete with men.

Stella Walsh is not the only athlete accused of "gender cheating." A more recent example is Jarmila Kratochvílová, a runner from Czechoslovakia (now the Czech Republic) who in 1983 broke the world record for the women's 800 meters. She is still the world record holder, but was constantly suspected of using illegal performance-enhancing drugs. In the media she was referred to as belonging to "the third sex." Both Walsh and Kratochvílová diverged from traditional gender norms.

More people could be added to this list. My point is that these examples suffer from very narrow concepts of what constitutes the categories "male" and "female." Whether athletes are defined as male or female, they all have to relate to the fact that modern sport is built upon "masculine" traditions. But what do we mean by masculinity (as opposed to femininity), and how can we come to the conclusion that sport is built upon masculinity? Historically, one can easily see how masculinity has been attached not only to men but also to certain qualities that are *defined* as masculine ( as opposed to feminine). Two such qualities are muscular strength and toughness.

Even if the world has changed over the decades, masculine ideals have persisted. Gender theorist R. W. Connell, for example, argues that "sport has become the leading definer of masculinity in mass culture."[8] Every man and woman has to relate to these ideals, and Connell also argues that these norms tend to exclude women from sport. From a feminist standpoint, Connell argues that "men's greater sporting prowess has become a theme of backlash against feminism. It serves as symbolic proof of men's superiority and right to rule."[9]

In the light of Connell's argument it seems reasonable to be concerned about the current state of sports with respect to gender equality. Even if sports history is full of "strong women," they always have had to compete on traditionally male terms. One can argue that there are no female sports, but only women in male sports. One can even, as the Swedish philosopher Torbjörn Tännsjö does, say that many sports are competitions in masculinity for both men and women.[10]

From a feminist point of view we have good reasons to complain about how the sports culture and the sports world are constructed. Some theorists go so far as to say that sport is a patriarchal project.[11] This goes for the Olympic sports culture as well. For example, consider the founder of the modern Olympic Games, Baron Pierre de Coubertin, who claimed that the Olympic Games were not appropriate for women.[12] Of course, most would disagree with this today. But that does not mean that there are no obstacles when it comes to women in sport. Masculine norms are one such obstacle. But obstacles can also lay before those women who in fact fulfill the masculine ideals and norms, but in a "wrong" way. In other words, women are welcomed to the world of sports. But when they enter the sports arena, they have to obey the narrow gender norms that are embedded within the sports culture.

In fact, throughout history there have been different strategies for making women the exception in sports. One such example was when the IOC introduced gender verification tests in 1968 in order to prevent cheating and unfair competition. These tests were called "femininity tests" for the simple reason that only women were forced to undergo them. Before the 2000 Olympic Games, after complaints from female athletes who found the tests to be insulting, these tests were abandoned.[13] Obviously, the tests violated the privacy and integrity of the female athletes. But an even more interesting point is this: Why did the IOC think such tests were needed?

Many researchers have stated that there is a great deal of ambiguity when it comes to defining a person's gender. Many have questioned the possibility of making clear distinctions between the biological and the social aspects of gender. In fact, it is difficult to be certain which factors are most relevant to a person's "biological" sex. Is it the chromosomes or the genitalia? Furthermore, what is a person's sex if the person's chromosomes do not correspond to his or her gender identity? These questions need to be answered before we can make claims regarding a particular person's status as a man or woman. But perhaps we do not need such determinations in the world of sport. Maybe it does not matter if an athlete is defined as a man or a woman. Masculinity will still be the ruling ideology of sport that every athlete needs to relate to, albeit in different ways.

## The Rise of Gender Radicalism and the East German "Amazons"

Should we consider Stella Walsh to be gender radical? Should we consider Jarmila Kratochvílová to be gender radical? Or, for that matter, the swimming and track and field teams of East Germany (GDR)? I think we should.

As said before, these athletes entered and conquered the Olympic world with "masculine" bodies. They were thereby placing gender issues on the map, but by operating from *within* the masculine sports world. In fact, their performances showed the sports world that women do not have to be "feminine" in a classical sense of the word in order to be successful in (sports) life. From a gender egalitarian point of view this must be seen as a positive consequence, but not one without objections, of course.

One obvious objection would be to say that the masculine ideology of sport in general was not really challenged by the GDR "wonder girls." Even if the female Olympians of the GDR challenged the masculine ideology, they also confirmed that ideology by using the tools of the ideology in order to be successful athletes. This gives us reason to doubt the force of the challenge. Still, in some aspect they were challenging the masculine norms by breaking the link between masculinity and maleness. They were masculine, but they were also challenging masculinity with their female bodies. Therefore it would be accurate to describe them as Amazons of the sport world. Sometimes this term has been seen negatively. But from a gender radical feminist point of view, we can revalue the concept and make it positive.

Amazons, according to Greek mythology—from which the concept derives—were female warriors; and even if they (biologically) were defined as women, they acted "like men." The East German "wonder girls" were warriors too, not only for the sake of the East German communist regime but also (unintentionally) for the sake of gender radicalism and women's right to compete on masculine terms.

Many have been upset by the Eastern Bloc Amazons. In fact, some commentators argue that the records they set should be eliminated and forgotten. I think this would be bad for sports, simply because it would narrow the concept of gender even further. There are more arguments one can add to this, especially from queer theory.

One of the most famous queer theorists, Judith Butler, argues that ideals are not static; they can be changed. She also claims that women's sports can play an important role in rearticulating gender ideals.[14] If we now return to the 1970s and 1980s, we may claim—in the spirit of Butler's argument—that the female athletes of the Eastern Bloc were changing gender ideals, even if the change was "helped" by the use of steroids

and other performance-enhancing drugs. And even if they used such technologies, this does not imply that their performances should not count as
"real" and valid. Now, some may disagree, arguing that their results
should not count as real, because of the well-documented fact that these
women used performance-enhancing drugs. But the fact is that they were
never caught cheating. In fact, they were a part of a sports culture where
the use of performance-enhancing drugs was widely accepted. Besides,
performance-enhancing drugs have always been a part of sports culture,
whether we call the use of the drugs "cheating" or not. It was no worse
that female athletes from the East used, say, steroids for the sake of winning than male athletes from the West used them for the same reasons. In
fact, one may say that the female athletes' use of performance-enhancing
drugs was politically progressive in that the drugs were changing their
bodies in ways that contradicted the norms of how female athletes are
supposed to look.

## The Fall of Gender Radicalism and the Return of "Woman"

The Eastern Bloc female athletes may not have been revolutionary, but
they certainly were changing the perception of female sport. In that particular way they *were* gender radical, and an example of what I like to
call the rise of gender radicalism. They were not "women" in a traditional sense; they were, first and foremost, athletes!

The fall of the Berlin Wall in 1989 soon became the fall of the entire
Eastern Bloc. And the fall of the Eastern Bloc also became the fall of a
specific sports culture. It was also the end of the Cold War sports era.
Some even called it the end of history, saying that the West had won.[15]

One may ask if this meant that the Eastern Bloc athletes became
"normalized," that is, subject to the Western paradigm of commercialized and market-based sport. The obvious answer is, of course, yes. They
were no longer helped and sheltered by a strong state. Instead they became players on the sport market, where the Olympic Games are the
most "expensive" brand. A whole sports culture seemingly vanished
from the face of the earth. It was not enough to be an excellent athlete, it
was also crucial to be able to sell yourself on the market. The signs had
been there before the fall of the Iron Curtain, but after 1989 it became
reality.

At the 1988 Olympics in Seoul we saw the American runner Florence Griffith-Joyner, "Flo Jo," win the gold medal in the 100 meters. Later athletes, such as the Americans Gail Devers and Marion Jones, followed in Flo Jo's footsteps. But Flo Jo was accused of using steroids and other performance-enhancing drugs. Whether that is true or not is not important for this particular discussion. Instead, let us focus on how she was perceived in contrast to her colleagues from the Eastern Bloc. Flo Jo, among other Western athletes, never really challenged gender norms (as we know them in a Western context). On the contrary, she can be seen as the main symbol of the complexity of how to read gender ascriptions.

Flo Jo wore makeup and painted fingernails, she smiled at the cameras, and she flirted with the public. She lived up to the gender stereotypes. She was, without doubt, a "woman."

Of course, first and foremost she was a brilliant athlete—that is, if we can separate her athletic performance from how she appeared before the public. It is not easy, however, to make such a distinction. On the one hand, to some extent it is possible to distinguish between appearance and performance. It is possible to focus only on the result and nothing more. On the other hand, especially in sports, it is extremely difficult if not impossible to see beyond the appearances. This, I believe, has an impact on how one looks at a sport performance. We all are influenced by cultural, political, and moral values, values that we bring into the sports stadium. Now suppose we find ourselves standing before two equally good runners, one from the West and one from the East. And let us say that we find one of them more appealing, simply based on stronger preferences for, say, the West. In this case there are cultural layers, containing political implications, between us as spectators and the athletes we watch. We cheer for one of them, and all of a sudden the performance in itself becomes political; the competition becomes a political statement or action. But it is not just that. The performance in itself becomes a political language, the running "speaks" to us in words we all can understand. And— one may add—gender issues are always political.

With this in mind, consider again the polarization I have observed between Flo Jo and, say, Marita Koch. Both of them were clearly excellent runners. They had different running styles, but no one could say that they were not good runners. One of them, Flo Jo, did not challenge gender norms; she was never described as a monster, based on the simple fact that she attracted commercial interests and spectators due to the ways in which she played on her femininity. Marita Koch, however, challenged gender norms. From a strict and narrow Western perspective it is not difficult to see that Flo Jo was easier to like than Koch. In other words, we as spectators were heavily influenced by the cultural norms of how to view a certain performance. A performance is not a static matter of fact; as stated earlier, interpretations of it are formed by the cultural and social norms in which the performance comes to life. Moreover, ever since the fall of the Berlin Wall and the diminishing of the Eastern Bloc there is only one ideology at work: the liberal democratic, capitalistic ideology. There is nothing beyond this ideology; there is no "outside" of this ideology. From this one can draw many political conclusions, and one of them is that the accepted gender constructions have become even narrower than they were before. In what way does this support widened gender autonomy among athletes—especially female athletes? The sad and simple answer is: it does not. But perhaps we should not paint the future in such dark colors. Perhaps there are pockets of wider autonomy within the current market system of Olympic sport.

## A Defense of Gender Radicalism (in a New Dress)

In this chapter I have suggested that the gender norms at work in the Olympics have changed since the fall of the Berlin Wall. Also, I have claimed that these changes have been bad (in general) for women's sports. I know that for some this may be difficult to digest.

But do we have any reason to think that the world of sport has been going backward since the fall of the Berlin Wall? No, not necessarily. In fact, many female sports have been better, at least when it comes to the actual results. This is a rather uncontroversial statement.

A perhaps more interesting aspect related to the development of sport since 1989 is linked to the *conception* of Olympic sports. In a competition the swimmers of today would easily defeat the swimmers from the GDR. Training knowledge and techniques have grown, as have the technologies surrounding the sport. But—and this is a major "but"—this does not mean that there have been advances in gender equality. In fact, we have good reasons for thinking that the gender norms of the commercialized sport world have hardened. There is little resistance to these norms. In other words, there is a shrieking lack of alternative perspectives when it comes to gender norms in the context of sport. Resistance to these norms does exist, but my sad suspicion is that this resistance has already become a part of the power structure, and has therefore lost its potential to foster a revolution in gender norms.

## Postscript: Berlin 2009

Twenty years after the fall of the Berlin Wall, the city of Berlin was once again the place for an ethical and political controversy regarding sport and gender. In an outstanding performance the eighteen-year-old South African runner Caster Semenya won the gold medal for the women's 800 meters. Soon after her winning the gold, however, the International Association of Athletics Federation (the IAAF) announced that they suspected that biologically, Semenya was a man, not a woman. Based on that suspicion they forced her to take a degrading gender test. In a second the whole world knew about Semenya.

So what was "wrong" with her? Well, evidently she was too strong, too fast, and too masculine to be a female athlete. Rumors said she had ten times higher levels of the so-called male hormone testosterone compared to "average women." This cannot be acceptable, the IAAF thought, and suggested a treatment that would make her weaker simply by lowering her testosterone levels, a treatment that would take about six months to implement. In short, the IAAF treated Semenya as if she had taken steroids. She was a "natural-born cheater."

Evidently, according to the IAAF, Semenya's body was wrong. And for the sake of *fairness*, they believed she had to undergo medical treatment in order to be "normal." This would result in her not having an "unfair advantage" over her fellow competitors. But what is "normal" when it comes to elite athletes? Elite athletes are never normal in a general sense. For instance, who could say that the Jamaican sprint runner Usain Bolt is normal? During the championships in Berlin he broke the world record at 100 meters and 200 meters for men. Just like Semenya, Bolt was superior. But no one questioned Bolt for being just that. No one forced him to take degrading tests (besides the doping tests). And no one suggested that he was too strong or too fast compared to his fellow competitors. Why? Because Bolt was considered to be normal, at least within the range of normality for male athletes. The fact that he was superior was not an issue. It is usually not. Athletes are allowed to be superior. Sports history is full of superior athletes. Normally, no one holds the superior athlete responsible for being superior. And no one held Bolt responsible for his victories during the championships. But then he did not challenge, threaten, or transcend gender norms. Semenya did. And that was a problem for the IAAF, who immediately started an investigation in order to clarify her gender.

On July 6, 2010, the investigation was finished. After eleven months the IAAF finally decided to allow Semenya to continue competing as a woman.

The Caster Semenya case showed, once again, that the world of sports still is a place where gender norms not only are solid to the ground, but also tend to harden as soon as someone (usually some female athlete) challenges or transcends these norms.

## Notes

1. Pierre de Coubertin, *Olympism: Selected Writings,* ed. Norbert Müller (Lausanne: International Olympic Committee, 2000), 583.

2. Jane English, "Sex Equality in Sports," in *Philosophic Inquiry in Sport* (Champaign, IL: Human Kinetics, 1995), 284–285.

3. Ibid.

4. Susan Moller Okin, *Women in Western Political Thought* (Princeton: Princeton University Press, 1979), 106.

5. See, for example, Torbjörn Tännsjö, "Against Sexual Discrimination in Sports," in *Values in Sport,* ed. Torbjörn Tännsjö and Claudio Tamburrini (New York: E & FN Spon, 2000); Claudio Tamburrini, *The "Hand of God"* (Göteborg: Acta Universitatis Gothenburgensis, 2000); Kutte Jönsson, "Who's Afraid of Stella Walsh?" *Sport, Ethics and Philosophy* 1:1 (2007): 239–262.

6. Berit Skirstad, "Gender Verification in Competitive Sport: Turning from Research to Action," in *Values in Sport,* ed. Tännsjö and Tamburrini.

7. See, for example, Anne-Fausto-Sterling, *Myths of Gender* (New York: Basic Books, 1985).

8. R. W. Connell, *Masculinities* (Berkeley: University of California Press, 1995), 54.

9. Ibid.

10. Tännsjö, "Against Sexual Discrimination," 109.

11. Tara Magdalinski and Karen Brooks, "Bride of Frankenstein: Technology

and the Consumption of the Female Athlete," in *Sport Technology*, ed. Andy Miah and Simon B. Eassom (London: Elsevier Science, 2002), 209.

12. Angela J. Schneider, "On the Definition of 'Woman' in the Sport Context," in *Values in Sport*, ed. Tännsjö and Tamburrini, 123.

13. Skirstad, "Gender Verification."

14. Judith Butler, "Athletic Genders: Hyperbolic Instance and/or the Overcoming of Sexual Binarism," *Stanford Humanities Review* 6:2 (1998), http://www.stanford.edu/group/SHR/6-2/html/butler.html (addessed January 24, 2012).

15. See, for example, Francis Fukuyama, *The End of History and the Last Man* (New York: Free Press, 1992).

*Charlene Weaving*

# BUNS OF GOLD, SILVER, BRONZE
## The State of Olympic Women's Beach Volleyball

Significant media hype surrounded the uniform regulations inflicted upon beach volleyball players at the 2000 Sydney Olympics, and the discussions were variously critical, supportive, and, in some instances, mocking in nature. Over a decade later, it is worthy to examine the issue in further detail to analyze the lasting negative implications that the uniform rule created.

The main purpose of this chapter is to examine women's positioning within the modern Olympic movement in the twenty-first century. I argue that in attempting to cling to both the spirit of just peace and Olympism and the goal of constant improvement described in the Olympic motto, *Citius, altius, fortius,* women athletes have become distanced from Olympic ideals through persistent sexualization. The founder of the modern Olympic Movement, the Baron Pierre de Coubertin, described the value of the Olympics in the following manner: "The irreplaceable value of the Olympic Games consists in that they are peculiar celebrations during which people of all religions, all tribes, all nations and all ranks can be unified with the others and during which it is revealed to them the deep sense of community above every kind of difference and border. It is necessary and advantageous to regard and cultivate the Olympic Games as a great celebration of the whole of mankind, because in this way it promotes mankind."[1] Coubertin's vision of the modern Olympic Games clearly articulates the international unification goal of the Games and seems to discourage any type of discrimination. I hope in this chapter to demonstrate that the uniform rule in beach volleyball is contrary to the values that the Olympics supposedly celebrates.

Drawing on an interpretation of liberal feminism based on Joy De-Sensi's discussion of feminism in sport, and arguing from a North American liberal feminist philosophical perspective, I believe we should be concerned with the rules mandating that women players must wear bikini bottoms in competition. The general claim of liberal feminism is that women's oppression is caused by a lack of equal civil rights and educational opportunities due to prejudices related to sex, race, and age.[2] Liberal feminism demands reform in order to extend political, legal, and educational opportunities for women. I argue that the uniform rule not only contradicts the main underpinnings of Olympism, it also leaves little room to celebrate humanity and ultimately hinders a universal conception of women's participation at the Olympics. Additionally, such a rule creates a negative legacy by impacting female volleyball players participating at the university and high school levels. "Short-shorts" have become the norm on the indoor courts, and there seems to be heightened emphasis placed on how female volleyball players believe they ought to look and dress.

## Brief Historical Observation

Historically, women's relationship with the Olympic movement has been an uneasy one. For example, some researchers note that if women were caught trying to sneak into the Ancient Games site to view the spectacle, they would be tossed off a cliff to their death.[3] This example illustrates the fact that women have had to fight not only to participate at the Games but also simply to be a part of the festival. Even today the relationship between women athletes and the Olympic movement remains controversial. For instance, when Coubertin ignited the modern Olympic movement, the debate regarding women's positioning in the Games continued, and members of the International Olympic Committee (IOC) and the general public struggled with what women's role should be within the Olympics. Women were barred from participating in the inaugural modern Olympic Games, but were eventually "allowed" to participate in the early 1900s in selected events. It was considered more appropriate for women to participate in so-called "feminine appropriate" activities like gymnastics and figure skating than activities like long-distance running and rowing. Coubertin believed that women's glory should not come through athletic records, but rather they should excel in encouraging their sons to seek records.[4]

In the mid-1900s, IOC leaders tried to constrict women's participation, arguing that female athletes were better suited to the roles of ornamental figures and dancers in the opening ceremonies rather than competitors in the Games.[5] For instance, at the 1928 Summer Olympics, members of the Canadian women's track and field team, who went on to win several gold medals, were required to take an oath promising not to embarrass the country with unladylike behavior prior to the beginning of the Games in Amsterdam.[6] This example emphasizes the struggle women faced between upholding appropriate feminine ideals and competing as legitimate Olympians.

In examining the contemporary status of women's participation (eighty-two years later) in the 2010 Winter Olympics, held in Vancouver, we would find that women competed in most of the same events that the men did. However, some limitations and differences exist in the distances that men and women raced: for example, in cross-country skiing and long-track speed skating, men ski and skate longer distances than women. In the bobsled event, women were "able" to compete for the first time at the 2002 Salt Lake City Winter Games. Despite the significant progress that has been made, some inconsistency and inequality in the Olympics still exist. For example, women are not yet allowed to fly and soar in ski jumping. Some of the reasons given for the exclusion surround the notion of the potential harm that women's bodies could sustain from such a high jump.[7] The harm argument and the supposed concern for women's health are myths that women athletes have struggled with since the Victorian period, and one could argue that sexist undertones and inequality still exist within the Olympic Games. Another relevant example involves women's ice hockey. In the women's ice hockey tournament, the third back-up goalie does not receive a medal, but in the men's event, the third-string goalie does. Additionally, in women's ice hockey, women do not body check. It seems that women do not check because of traditional paternalism and the belief that women could potentially harm themselves via the added contact. Clearly, inequality can and does occur in the Olympics.

It is important to acknowledge that women have advanced significantly since the genesis of the Olympic movement. Despite these advances, however, areas of concern remain. Furthermore, the persistent sexualization and trivialization of women athletes have emerged as a moral dilemma in sport within the past ten years. If systemic sexist oppression and lack of equal opportunity did not exist at the Olympics and within the Olympic movement, the sexualization and trivialization of women athletes might not occur or be of concern; but, given the unequal relationship, there are grounds for further investigation.

## Clarifying Sexualization

It is important to explain how I interpret sexualization within the sporting context. I base my definition and interpretation on Paul Davis's work. In "Sexualization and Sexuality in Sport," he examines the differences between sexuality and sexualization and claims that sport is "unfit"[8] to be nonsexual.[9] Davis acknowledges that the difference between the two terms occurs in diverse mediums, with one grounded in sport performance and the other outside of sport performance. He argues that athletes are sexual beings, and their sexuality should not be denied; however, he claims that it is morally objectionable to sexualize athletes outside the performance-specific action.[10] Davis describes the performance-specific species of sexualization as the sexualized images of athletic performances that frequently appear in newspaper and television coverage of sport (for example, a picture of a female figure skater that focuses on her buttocks or crotch areas during her skating routine). He notes three ways in which an athlete is typically sexualized:

1. Deliberate focus on particular, sexually significant body parts for the purpose of titillation.

2. Freezing or emphasis on body postures for titillation purposes.

3. With respect to photographs, accompanied by a punned caption—sexualized comic relief.[11]

To explain why sexualization is objectionable, Davis maintains that it is important to examine the nature of sport and sexual response from a historical perspective.[12] He also approaches the concept of sexualization from a phenomenological perspective and describes what it means to be a person. With respect to sport, Davis claims that, similar to sexual desires, the embodiment of the person is the object of our interest. He maintains that we are not interested in bodies or immaterial souls, but rather enjoy sexual responses. The person as a body-subject intrigues us. He further notes that sport is a celebration of the body-subject whereby the athlete ultimately seeks the unity of the self and the body.[13] I argue that the beach volleyball rule leads us to focus attention primarily on the bodies of the athletes rather than the "whole athletic package" and, as a result, the athletes' excellent volleyball skills are not valued as much as how the participants look in their uniforms.

Davis argues that sexuality is good, but sexualization is wrong because it objectifies the subject by artificially focusing on sexually significant body parts. This focus, he claims, detaches the body from its key bodily agency.[14] When the sexualization of an athlete decontextualizes the body and subject, a bifurcation between sexualization and sexuality occurs. In other words, sex/sexuality is good because one is attracted to the person as subject, whereas sexualization is wrong because one primarily views the person as an object and the subject is removed. Davis's theories provide a very relevant argument—that sport should not be considered as nonsexual, and neither should athletes; but it is morally objectionable to sexualize athletes. We can draw similar conclusions about the process of sexualization as we can about sexual objectification. In other words, "sexualization" and "objectification" can be used interchangeably.

It is important to acknowledge that viewing someone as a sexual object is not necessarily problematic. For example, philosophers Robert Baker, Martha Nussbaum, and Sandra Bartky argue that there are some instances in which it is acceptable to view another person primarily as a sexual object.[15] A popular example of such an instance occurs when two people are in a mutually respectful relationship. At the same time, Baker, Nussbaum, and Bartky argue that consistent sexualization can become problematic when it is extended to one's being and identity. A good example of this notion is the beach volleyball uniform regulation, which I address below. In the case of beach volleyball and the imposed rule, persistent sexualization occurs within the context of the game as well as outside of the performance.

Sexualizing women athletes is contradictory to Olympic ideals. The Olympic movement is concerned with promoting values of peace, equality, and the true essence of the human spirit, not the persistent sexualization of women athletes. If we focus only on women athletes as sexual objects and consequently take away their subjectivity and trivialize their athletic ability, it becomes more difficult to focus on the human spirit and the celebration of universal humanity.[16]

## Beach Volleyball and Sexualization

The most striking example of sexualization at the Olympics occurs in the popular sport of beach volleyball. In this Summer Games event, women competitors must adhere to the following uniform regulations: "The top must fit closely to the body and the design must be with deep cutaway armholes on the back, upper chest and stomach. The briefs should be . . . a close fit and be cut out on an upward angle (15 degrees) towards the top of the leg. The side width must be a maximum of 7 centimeters."[17] Male beach volleyball players do not have any such specific rules regarding the cut or angle of their shorts. Typically, male players choose to wear long, surfboard-style shorts and T-shirts or tank tops. According to the Federation Internationale de Beach Volleyball (FIVB), the uniform rules for male competitors state: "The tank top must fit closely to the body and the design must be with open arms, respecting the space for the required placements of the manufacturer trademark, player number, country flag and country code, also respecting the place for the player's name. The shorts must be in accordance with the enclosed diagram and not be baggy. For all players the bottom of the shorts must be a minimum of 15cm above the top of the knee cap."[18] Despite the fact that the rules state that the shorts should "not be baggy," there seems to be a loose interpretation of the term "baggy"; male volleyball players routinely wear baggy bottoms (they are not skin-tight spandex material like the women's bottoms, nor are they as baggy as the basketball shorts typically worn in the National Basketball Association, the NBA). Given the attire of the male players, it is not reasonable to suggest that the women's bikini bottoms help in the biomechanical aspect of the game of beach volleyball, since the male competitors' longer shorts do not appear to affect their play. It may be fair to say that this particular event, beach volleyball, includes a style component (suggesting as it does a beach party, with sun, surf, and fun); but the women competitors do not get a choice with respect to their style of uniform because their uniforms are a regulated rule created by the FIVB in 1999.[19] I believe that the goal of such a rule is to sell the sex appeal of the female beach volleyball players. I further argue that the rule has roots in the feminine apologetic (that women athletes should apologize and/or compensate for being athletes) and the supposed stigma of lesbianism. I suspect that there still remains great fear of women's appearing too manly or unfeminine. So, in order to ensure the heterosexuality and marketability of beach volleyball, perhaps officials figured tiny, sexy uniforms would be a sure bet.

This rule has become the media's dream. During the 2000 Sydney Olympic Games, for example, the *Toronto Sun* displayed a woman beach volleyball player bent over, with the camera angle focused on her backside and genital area. Below the photograph the caption read, "God Bless Bondi Beach." In the accompanying article, the journalist discussed how much he enjoyed covering the women's beach volleyball event at the Olympic Games because of the "beer and babes" at the venue.[20] This is a good example of Davis's definition of a sexualized image as well as his third point (when a photo caption trivializes athletic ability and/or skill). Many examples of Davis's criteria for sexualization can be found throughout media coverage of beach volleyball during the Olympics. Media coverage of women's beach volleyball seems to possess the same inherent message—one of sexualization and trivialization. There are countless examples of questionable photographs of women beach volleyballers, with such captions as "Buns of Gold, Silver, and Bronze," and "Athens 2002: Tradition Meets T & A."[21]

Some might argue that there are different uniform rules for male and female beach volleyball players because of our preconceived ideals of what society has determined to be "sexy" for males and females. As stated earlier, I approach this issue from a North American perspective, and I realize that different cultures and countries view sexuality in different ways. In North America, it is not considered desirable to see male beach volleyball players play in a Speedo. Moreover, I do not believe that socially constructed ideals should play a factor in determining what is best for promoting athletes. One member of the FIVB suggested that the rule is not intended to promote nudity but rather to regulate what competitors wear:

> At an indoor volleyball world championships event last year, the Cuban men were wearing obscenely short shorts. It was gross; the most distasteful thing you've ever seen. They were wearing spandex and when it got wet they might as well have been wearing nothing. At the outdoor events, the

women from the Latin countries thought six centimeters of fabric [over the hip] was too much. And the Brazilian women were scrunching up their bikinis like G-strings. Athletes have the most toned bodies and the best figures. I don't think you should hide that. But it needs to be done in a classy way.[22]

Unfortunately, one individual's notion of "classy" is another individual's notion of "offensive." Moreover, we need to question the double standard of what's appropriate for uniform bottoms for males versus females in the sport. Furthermore, who has the authority to determine what is considered "classy"? One can understand why women players may wish to wear their bottoms like G-strings because, unfortunately, a woman with a good set of buns in a G-string who bends over during Olympic competition will get more endorsement offers and media fame than her athletic ability alone would foster. However, my concern lies in the fact that an official rule was created to promote women's sexuality and *requires* female athletes to show a certain amount of skin. The lack of rights the athletes have and the lack of choice and freedom to decide what type of bottoms they wish to wear are troubling. One needs to question whether the athletes are celebrated or exploited in the new modern Olympic movement. I maintain that the Olympics have become an example of extreme commercialization; however, I am hesitant to agree that it is ethical to sell the sexuality of its participants.

The message sent out via the uniform rule perpetuates the belief that women's beach volleyball only attracts viewers and a fan base by promoting the sexualization of the women athletes. It also promotes the notion that women's sport is not a good enough product to sell on its own, and that women athletes are not talented enough to attract viewership—that we need to market them as sexualized, "sexy" women rather than strong, powerful, athletic women. I see this as a step backward for women's participation and positioning in the Olympics, as well as their overall perception in society.

At the summer Olympics in 2004 in Athens, Greece, some argued that beach volleyball took a new turn for the worse and reached an ultimate low by including cheerleaders at the beach volleyball venue. Some beach volleyball competitors thought that the bikini-clad dancing cheerleaders at the venue were disrespectful to the sport; as one commentator described the scene: "To start with, there are cheerleading Brazilian beauties, flown in to gyrate on the touchline before, during, and after every match. Then there is the music. While Coubertin favored massed bands and national anthems, beach volleyball pipes in crowd favorites, such as KC and The Sunshine Band grunting "That's the way . . . uh-uh . . . I like it."[23]

It could be argued that the dancing bikini girls are merely an extension of beach volleyball's image as a hypersexual sport. However, I believe that there is something wrong and inappropriate with such a display at the Olympics, and other organizations and individuals have criticized the uniform rule. For instance, the Women's Sport Foundation petitioned the FIVB to change the rule regarding the uniform regulations, but their petition was denied. Individual players have also spoken out against the rule and have been told that they don't have to play the game.[24] Some women volleyballers believe the rule is good for their sport. They maintain that they have not lost their autonomy in choosing to wear the uniforms, and they enjoy the way the media covers their sport, believing that they are in control of their own exploitation. This train of thought is concerning because it seems that both men and women have bought into the idea that women athletes should be sexualized and that sexualization has become so normalized it is as if it is actually part of their training program. Still, one might ask: Why not show off a strong bronzed body in a G-string? I maintain the question that really needs to be asked is: How much control should a sport organizing body have over an athlete? Not only should we be concerned with the extent of control the organizers possess over the athlete; we should be equally concerned with the officials' ability to suggest that it is the athletes who choose to wear the revealing uniforms, rather than the fact that the rules are what control the athletes' appearance. In addition, the sexualization and exploitation create a false sense of empowerment: the media attention is short lived and doesn't focus on the athletes' skills and abilities but instead focuses on the backsides and genital region of women's bodies. Much ethical discussion surrounds athletes' rights regarding doping during the Olympics; athletes' right to compete without being sexualized, however, is not viewed as a major ethical concern. On the contrary, it appears as though the sexualization of women athletes has become so normalized that the issue is not given a second glance. Returning to Davis's argument, we cannot forget that there is something wrong with the persistent sexualization of women athletes and how it is indeed problematic and worthy of discussion. By constantly presenting women athletes as sexualized beings, we remove subjectivity and trivialize their athletic abilities and accomplishments.

## Where Do We Go from Here?

I believe that we should revisit the uniform rule for women's volleyball and address the potential harm it espouses. As I see it, there are four main types of harm associated with the uniform rule. The first is physical, in that there are some risks associated with diving and rolling around in sand while wearing only a small bit of fabric covering sensitive genitalia. Second, a less concrete, but no less important, harm is that associated with the persistent sexualization of women athletes. One only needs to refer to the *Report of the Task Force on the Sexualization of Girls*, published in 2007 by the American Psychological Association, for evidence. Researchers found that continued sexualization negatively affects girls both cognitively and in their physical functioning, causing them to experience increased body dissatisfaction and appearance anxiety and to form negative sexual beliefs and practices.[25]

Third, observers are concerned with the importance of Olympians as role models, and Olympic women volleyballers are no exception. I refer to this as the "trickle-down effect." Most universities in Canada, for example, have a women's indoor volleyball program. I was quite shocked to see the size of the shorts that the players from my own institution voted to wear for their season: their shorts were very short (resting just below the buttocks). The players spent their season hiking down their shorts and feeling uncomfortable. The next season they decided to go with a longer version of spandex shorts, yet still had to deal with "wedgies." High school girls now see short-shorts as an integral part of the game of volleyball. It seems that if girls do not wear short-shorts, some agonize that they will come across as sexual prudes and not be accepted by their peers. I find it troubling that many teenage girls worry about how they look while participating in sports. In response to appearing prudish, of course one can object to short-shorts and still enjoy sexual activity. One does not negate the other.

Another trickle-down effect of the culture of Olympic beach volleyball involves the Xbox video game Extreme Beach. Players can choose from a pool of characters, all of whom sport barely-there bikinis, and can even enter a secret code in order to maneuver the characters to strip down and play naked. One could argue that as a result of the uniform rule in women's volleyball, strong, powerful athletes and the sport itself have become trivialized and ridiculed.

Another concern with the small, skin-showing uniforms involves Islamic women's participation in beach volleyball. It is difficult to imagine given the current rule how an Islamic woman would ever be able to compete in beach volleyball at the Olympics. For instance, Sania Marzia, an Indian tennis star, received death threats for wearing a T-shirt and a tennis skirt.[26] I believe that more consideration must be given to the universal component of the Olympics and the idea of opportunity for all when formulating rules such as uniform regulations at the Olympics. As Islamic women continue to increase in numbers at the Olympics, modifications to uniforms have been allowed and embraced. For example, track and field Islamic uniforms (a full one-piece garment that is made from advanced technological fabric) and the burkini (a bathing suit designed for practical use that complies with religious regulations) allow Islamic athletes to participate in sports in attire that respects their beliefs and traditions. It is devastating that a rule is in place that prevents some women from competing in elite beach volleyball competitions in the Olympic Games. It is ironic that an organization as powerful and universal as the IOC chooses to continue to incorporate such a constricting rule while at the same time promoting its messages of freedom, diversity, and humanity.

In short, we ought to be concerned with the path beach volleyball has taken and the added stress it has placed on many women athletes. For example, sport sociologist Christine Brooks has reported that some elite beach volleyball players have had their breasts enlarged and overtrained their stomach muscles in order to obtain a "washboard" abdominal look—because they desire to fit the expected ideal beach volleyball image (and they want to feel confident wearing such little clothing).[27] This strikes me as contradictory to the Olympic experience. Furthermore, I do not consider a rule that limits participation based on willingness to expose the body a way to enhance humanity in Olympic sport.

Even though the status of women at the Olympics has increased—for example, women Olympians now receive significantly more media coverage than they did in the early 1900s, and they are able to participate in more events that were previously denied to them (e.g., soccer, martial arts)—it is important to recognize the tension that still exists between being a woman and being an Olympian.[28]

In advance of the 2012 Olympics, in May 2011 the Badminton World Federation (BFW) proposed a new dress code for women players: to "create a more attractive presentation," the regulations now sanctioned women to wear skirts or dresses instead of shorts during competition. The rule change was described as a damaging attempt to "sex up" the sport, according to the UK Sports Minister, Hugh Robertson.[29] The American Deputy President of the BFW, Paisan Rangsikitpho, denied that the proposed changes were an attempt to "sex up" women's badminton; he said, "We just want them to look feminine and have a nice presentation so women will be more popular. . . . Interest is declining. Some women compete in oversize shorts and long pants and appear baggy, almost like men."[30] In lieu of the significant backlash of the potential rule change, the BFW has decided to delay implementing the rule change officially. Although there appears to be hope that the BFW will scrap the sexist rule entirely, the badminton skirt/dress example provides further evidence of the sexist climate surrounding women Olympic athletes.[31]

Clearly, there continues to be a tendency to trivialize and control women's participation at the Olympic Games. My hope is that for future women Olympians, the only mention of gold, silver, and bronze will have to do with medals.

## Notes

On March 18, 2012, the FIVB announced modifications to the uniform rule for women's beach volleyball for the 2012 London Olympic Games. The modified rule permits shorts of a maximum length of three centimeters (1.18 inches) above the knee and sleeved or sleeveless tops. This new rule was implemented to make the game less exclusionary of those with customs or religious beliefs that prevented them from wearing the bikini-style uniforms. Despite the importance of the modified rule, I believe that the majority of women beach volleyball players will continue to wear the bikini-style uniform for the reasons addressed in this chapter (see www.fivb.org).

1. Anna Maranti, *Olympia and Olympic Games* (Athens: Toubis, 1999), 117.

2. Joy T. DeSensi, "Feminism in the Wake of Philosophy," *Journal of Philosophy of Sport* 11 (1992): 79–93.

3. Angela Schneider, "On the Definition of 'Woman' in the Sport Context," in

*Values in Sport,* ed. Torbjörn Tännsjö and Claudio Tamburrini (London: Taylor and Francis, 2000), 123–138.

4. Don Morrow and Kevin Wamsley, eds., *Sport in Canada: A History* (Toronto: Oxford University Press, 2004), 228.

5. Ibid, 229.

6. Ibid, 170.

7. See the Canadian Association for the Advancement of Women in Sport organization website, www.caaws.ca.

8. Sport is unfit to be nonsexual in the sense that the essential nature of sport is actually sexual, so we make a mistake in claiming that sport is unsexual.

9. Paul Davis, "Sexuality and Sexualization in Sport," in *Ethics and Sport,* ed. William Morgan, Klaus Meier, and Angela Schneider (Champaign IL: Human Kinetics, 2001), 285–292.

10. Ibid., 85.

11. Ibid., 286.

12. Ibid., 287.

13. Ibid., 289.

14. Ibid., 288–289.

15. See Martha Nussbaum, *Sex and Social Justice* (New York: Oxford University Press, 1999); Robert Baker, *Philosophy and Sex* (New York: Prometheus Books, 1994); Sandra Lee Bartky, *Femininity and Domination: Studies in the Phenomenology of Oppression* (New York: Routledge, 1990).

16. Brief mention should be made of male athletes and their potential sexualization. Though it is true that some male athletes can be sexualized, given the context of a sexist oppressive society, it is more difficult to sexualize and trivialize males' athletic performance than it is females'. It should also be noted that there are no rules within the Olympic program that explicitly encourage the sex appeal of male athletes, and male Olympians are also not restricted in the distances that they can jump, skate, ski, or fly.

17. Athens 2004 Olympic Games Beach Volleyball Specific Competition Regulations, www.fivb.org/EN, p. 42; and Stephanie Myles, "Less Is More on the Beach Volleyball Tour," *CanWest News* (Don Mills, Ontario), August 27, 2005.

18. Athens 2004 Olympic Games Beach Volleyball Specific Competition Regulations.

19. Myles, "Less Is More."

20. Mike Ulmer, "God Bless Bondi Beach," *Toronto Sun,* September 20, 2000, p. 9.

21. Mark Spector, "Athens 2004: Tradition Meets T & A," *National Post,* August 19, 2004.

22. Quoted in Sally Armstrong, "Olympia's Secret: You Know Those Skimpy Outfits that Olympic Beach Volleyball Players Wear? They're All Part of the Game," *Chatelaine,* September 2000.

23. Peter Ford, "The Great Olympic Beach Bash," *Christian Science Monitor,* August 23, 2004, www. csmonitor.com (accessed January 26, 2006).

24. Armstrong, "Olympia's Secret."

25. American Psychological Association, Task Force on the Sexualization of Girls, *Report of the APA Task Force on the Sexualization of Girls* (Washington, DC: American Psychological Association, 2007). Retrieved from www.apa.org/pi/wpo/ sexualization.html.

26. See online Sania Mirza blogsport: http://sania-mania.blogspot.com/2005 _10_09_sania-mania_archive.html (accessed May 5, 2009).

27. Christine Brooks, "Using Sex Appeal as a Sport Promotion Strategy," *Women in Sport and Physical Activity Journal* 10:1 (2001): 1–14.

28. Schneider, "On the Definition of 'Woman.'"

29. James Meikle, "Badminton Delays Skirt-Only Rule for Women," www . guardian.co.uk, May 29, 2011 (accessed July 21, 2011).

30. Ibid.

31. As this book was going to press, the Amateur International Boxing Association (AIBA) proposed that women boxers appear in skirts at the 2012 London Olympics. Officials argued that viewers were having difficulty differentiating between male and female boxers, especially on television. This is yet another example of the struggles women athletes face at the Olympics and the continuing ridiculous uniform rules for women Olympians.

**Part 6**

# POLITICAL POWER

*Charles Taliaferro and Michel Le Gall*

# THE ETHICS OF BOYCOTTING THE OLYMPICS

In the wake of the Soviet invasion of Afghanistan in December of 1979, the administration of President Jimmy Carter decided to boycott the Moscow summer games of 1980. That decision was hotly debated. Some athletes bemoaned the fact that their apolitical athletic interests were being subjected to political constraints. Politicians from both sides of the aisle supported Carter, while others criticized his apparent belief that the careers of these young men and women were expendable for reasons of state.

When should a nation or individual athletes boycott the Olympic Games? Consider some of the following reasons that might justify an Olympic boycott: the host nation is involved in clear cases of injustice either with respect to its own citizens and residents or peoples of other nations; the host nation will use the financial benefits of the games to fund future acts of injustice; there are compelling reasons to believe that the host nation will not be conducting fair competitions but systematically undermining the performance of others; the visiting athletes will be subject to overt acts of disrespect or humiliation; it is highly likely that the visiting athletes will be seriously harmed or killed; or even if serious harm is not probable, the athletes will not be adequately protected if there were an (improbable) threat to their persons.

With these questions as a framework, let us first consider some general facts about boycotts and then highlight what is most at stake in an Olympic boycott: the interest of the principal participants. Next, we argue that there must be a significant burden of proof on any nation or athlete that decides to boycott the Olympics.

## Some General Thoughts about Boycotts

In ancient Greece, probably the most well-known boycott was that portrayed in Aristophanes' comedy *Lysistrata*. On that occasion, the women of Greece sought to bring an end to war with a sex boycott. Art being neater than life, they succeed, and there is much celebrating and dancing at the end of the play. (Incidentally, *Lysistrata* is often revived in wartime, most recently in the United States after the invasion of Iraq.)

Although they may make for less humor, real-life boycotts have had considerable success. In modern history, one of the most compelling instances of the use of a boycott was Mahatma Gandhi's organized boycotting of British goods (as well as British educational and legal institutions). This boycott, combined with strikes and dramatic public displays of anti-imperial solidarity, eventually achieved India's independence from Great Britain in 1947. In American history, perhaps the three most famous boycotts were the 1765 colonial boycott of British goods; the Montgomery bus boycott that began on December 1, 1955, which secured Martin Luther King Jr.'s position as the leader of the civil rights movement; and the four-year boycott of grapes coordinated by the United Farm Workers Organizing Committee that, in 1970, succeeded in winning significant benefits for workers. The effective use of boycott was valorized by the charismatic labor activist César Chavez: "The consumer boycott is the only open door in the dark corridor of nothingness down which farm workers have had to walk for many years. It is a gate of hope through which they expect to find the sunlight of a better life for themselves and their families."[1]

We believe that the reasons behind the one fictional and the other "real world" boycotts were sound and the boycotts therefore justified. If a sex boycott could stop a war that perpetuated senseless violence, it would be worth trying (at least on a trial basis!). Aristophanes was the first person to put into dramatic form the proposal that we should make love, not war. Meanwhile, seeking independence from British imperial rule seemed to legitimize both the Indian and the colonial American boycotts, and boycotts to challenge racial segregation and the exploitation of labor seem completely warranted.

Apart from these historical examples of boycotts that were undertaken on behalf of minorities, native persons, colonialists, or wives of

warriors fed up with the manly pursuit of war, we are probably all familiar with the more typical cases of boycotts involving individual conscience. If someone is morally opposed to intensive animal confinement
and slaughter, we fully expect that person not to purchase meats that result from this process. It may be that such individual acts hardly amount
to what would normally be called a boycott. But movements often emerge
from an individual decision that in time and through concerted effort can
take on greater proportions and historical significance. As Robert Kennedy explained so well in his Day of Affirmation Address delivered in
Capetown, South Africa, on June 6, 1966, "Each time a man stands up
for an ideal, or acts to improve the lot of others, or strikes out against
injustice, he sends forth a tiny ripple of hope, and crossing each other
from a million different centers of energy and daring those ripples build
a current which can sweep down the mightiest walls of oppression and
resistance."[2]

Given the broad parameters of what constitutes a boycott, a few
points about the ethics of boycotting are in order here, and will serve as
a useful foundation before we consider the implications of boycotts for
Olympic athletes. First, boycotts in the real-world historical cases we
have referenced succeeded in mobilizing all those persons not previously
willing to contribute materially to what they regarded as morally or politically unacceptable. Philosophers sometimes draw a distinction between a material and a formal contribution to a cause. You materially
contribute to something when you directly and concretely assist in ad-
vancing its goal. So, if you were a resident of India prior to its independence from the British Empire and you purchased British products, it
may be said that you were concretely contributing to the well-being and
sustainability of the Empire. A formal contribution to a cause, by contrast, involves a case where you intentionally or symbolically signal your
approval or allegiance to something. So, when you salute a flag, for example, you do not materially contribute to the nation signified, but you
formally do so. (In that sense, *Lysistrata* might be construed as depicting
an instance of women refusing both materially and formally to contribute to their husbands' war efforts.)

Two other ethical points: the justification for a boycott often depends
upon the availability of alternatives and the stringency of values. Consider alternatives first: imagine someone is deeply opposed morally and

politically to the use of immigrant workers in harvesting oranges in California but has no objection to agricultural practices in Israel. This person has a choice between purchasing a bottle of orange juice from California or one from Israel. Other things being equal, we would expect him to choose the Israeli product. But now imagine that there is no alternative to the California orange juice, the person is a diabetic and needs something like orange juice to stabilize his insulin level, and the only resource available is the California orange juice. In this case we would not consider it hypocritical for the person to drink the California beverage. Now consider stringency: while the case of the orange juice seems (to us) clear, it could be that the values at stake do not ever permit participating or gaining from what you believe to be wrong. Arguably, during apartheid, persons of conscience felt they could not purchase any gold or diamonds from South Africa regardless of there being times when there was no comparable alternative. The evils of apartheid were graver than California labor practices.

## On to the Athletes and the Olympics!

One of the first things to appreciate as we turn to our central concern is that the Olympics involve, first and foremost, individual athletes and teams. Although there were no teams in the ancient Greek Olympics, and consequently individual victories did not always have political and patriotic implications, there is a sense in which athletes today may be thought of as representatives, ambassadors, or standard-bearers of their nations; but there is also the equally important point that the Olympics are an arena in which national identities and boundaries are not supposed to be a barrier to competition, although the fact that each team is limited in the size of its delegation may lead to almost arbitrary decisions as to who makes the team and who does not. The revived Olympics of the modern era are by nature and intent an *international* arena and forum for talent. True, with the revival of the Olympics in the late nineteenth century and the period between the world wars, the Olympics were an occasion for displaying national and imperial prestige, especially in the case of Great Britain, where sports are considered an essential component of a well-rounded education and upbringing; and less so in the case of France, where sports are considered less noble than intellectual activities. That said, both Great Britain and France viewed the Olympics as a forum in which to display and exalt the diversity and dimensions of their empires. As for the Olympics' role in antiquity, they were primarily thought of as providing a forum for individual competition. Athletes' home cities were identified, but the Games were not viewed primarily as a competition among those cities.

Given that the nature and the meaning of Olympic competition is not itself national, it follows then that the host country is actually a host, rather than the sole proprietor of the Olympics. There is a sense then that what takes place at the Olympics is not essentially Chinese, say, or American. That is so regardless of where the Olympics are hosted or whether Chinese or American athletes win the bulk of the medals. Attending the Olympics is not, ipso facto, a formal declaration that one endorses the policies of the state that hosts the Games.

Within this international framework, let us now consider the cost of a boycott. Attending and participating in the Olympics can be costly, and hosting is even more expensive: the 2004 Athens Olympics sucked $10–$12 billion (U.S. dollars) out of the Greek economy, at a moment when, as we now appreciate, Greece was less than able to afford it. The principal cost of a boycott, however, is counted in terms of the individual athletes themselves. We therefore set aside considerations that participation involves a material contribution to the host nation and focus on the athletes.

The cost of a boycott for athletes can be assessed according to a number of variables, including their age (are they at their prime for the given event?), their ability (has their skill level peaked?), and the opportunity cost (will a comparable chance ever present itself again?). Given these variables, a boycott, especially one that is declared on short notice (such as the U.S. boycott of the summer Olympics in Moscow following the Soviet invasion of Afghanistan in November 1979), can mean the unrecoverable loss of a good or, in some cases, the creation of a harm, and not the mere withdrawal of a benefit. That reality is clearly captured in the words of Luci Collins, a gymnast from Inglewood, California, who explained, "I truly did believe that if I had some of my best performances during those [1980] Olympic Games, which I was on track to do, there could have been a possible medal for me and some worldwide recognition past the gymnastics world. Missing out on that will always leave me with an empty space, because I never got the chance to fulfill that dream."[3]

It should be noted that the reasons we originally set forth for boycotting a given product or service do not readily apply to the issue of the Olympics. Boycotting the Games in an effort to end a war would not likely apply, at least in ancient times, since the ancient Greek Games were traditionally accompanied by the cessation of any violent conflict. As to whether boycotting might be important for reasons having to do with fighting racism in a particular society, one may argue that a racially oppressed minority that participates and performs well in the Olympics can actually further the cause of their group and bring it benefits. (More on this idea below.)

The real question is: What impact does *raison d'etat* (reason of state)—as in the U.S. boycott of the Moscow Summer Olympics—have on the athletes themselves? Is asking them to forgo the possible benefits and rewards of all their effort on behalf of themselves and their country not akin to ordering someone to make a great sacrifice, not unlike denying the diabetic orange juice? Or must athletes, to paraphrase the French philosopher Pascal, accept that "the state has its reasons that reason cannot understand"?

For an athlete who has devoted long hours before and after school or college for at least four or five years, there is no alternative but to compete. Indeed, there may be a moral obligation to do so—an obligation captured succinctly in the New Testament parable of the talents (Matthew 25:14–30 and Luke 19:12–27). In this parable, a wealthy man, before going on a journey, entrusts different amounts of talents (a "talent" here is a unit of money, roughly equivalent to $1,000 today) to three of his servants. Two of the servants invest the talents productively, but the third simply buries the talents he was given and does no investing at all. Of the three, he is found blameworthy when the wealthy chap returns. The moral of the parable is that you should not bury your talents. (In fact, the English word "talent," meaning skill, originally came into usage from early English translations of the Bible.) Based on this parable, one may rightly claim that there is a theological reason to compete (that is, to use your talents) when given the opportunity, especially when there is no pressing reason not to. In the context of the Olympic Games, a nation has alternative ways in which to demonstrate and mark its displeasure—ways that in fact can have greater economic, moral, and political weight than an Olympic boycott. The boycott of South Africa comes to mind, as do a variety of economic sanctions, especially if the nation expressing its outrage carries some economic and political clout on the global stage. This notion of the obligation to boycott is core to the very formulation of U.S. foreign policy as driven by moral intent, a reality that the late diplomat George Kennan repeatedly challenged: "Government is an agent, not a principal. Its primary obligation is to the interests of the national society it represents, not to the moral impulses that individual elements of that society may experience."[4]

Consequently, given the undue burden a boycott places on athletes, the lack of alternative courses of action open to the athletes, and the international character of the Olympics themselves, we contend that many of the boycotts of the past have not been justified morally.

The first boycott of the modern Olympics occurred in the 1956 Melbourne Games when seven countries refused to participate: Switzerland, Spain, and the Netherlands did not attend in protest of the U.S.S.R.'s invasion of Hungary; while Lebanon, Iraq, Egypt, and Cambodia did not attend because of Great Britain's—and by association the Commonwealth's—complicity in the Suez crisis. There is no evidence that these boycotts had any significant effect on Soviet foreign policy in Eastern Europe (in 1968, Soviet forces stormed Czechoslovakia) or any lasting effect on British foreign policy toward Gamal Abdul-Nasser. British Prime Minister Anthony Eden's successor continued to be suspicious of Nasser's intentions and saw him behind every anti-British or anti-Western sentiment through much of the 1960s. But the cost to the athletes was considerable. One case in point is the infamous water polo match played between the Hungarian and Soviet teams at the 1956 Melbourne Olympics. The game took place less than two months after the Soviet invasion of Hungary and ended in a victory for the Hungarian team (4–0), although one Hungarian player emerged from the pool with an eye bleeding profusely—the result of a punch delivered by a Soviet opponent.

The largest boycott in the history of the Olympics took place in 1980 on the occasion of the Moscow summer Olympics. Sixty-five nations refused to participate in protest of the Soviet invasion of Afghanistan. Again, there is no evidence that this affected the Soviet occupation. Indeed, if one is to believe the recent cinematic treatment of the war in the film *Charlie Wilson's War,* one individual in charge of U.S. secret appropriations had a far greater hand in the ultimate failure and withdrawal of Soviet forces than did any Olympic boycott.

One of the more compelling reasons for not boycotting the Olympics is to be found in the case of the 1936 Berlin Olympics and the good that was achieved by the forty-nine nations that participated. The bid to hold the Olympics in Berlin was settled by the International Olympic Commission in April 1931, when the Weimar Republic was still in existence and before the National Socialist German Workers Party and Adolf Hitler came to power. Hitler and his propaganda minister, Joseph Goebbels, quickly recognized the potential of the games as a monument to Aryan superiority, and to that end filmmaker Leni Riefenstahl was drafted to create a cinematic tribute to the Olympics and Aryan sporting abilities.

In the months leading up to the August 1936 games, voices in the United States were calling for the boycott of the Olympics. Avery Brundage, the longtime head of the U.S. Olympic Committee, argued that the U.S. teams should participate, since Jewish athletes were being permitted to participate. (Hitler had removed the signs "Juden Verboten" and similar slogans in anticipation of greeting an international crowd.) Brundage's arguments were not of the soundest construction: he argued that domestic U.S. opposition to the participation of the U.S. team was being led by a Communist-Jewish conspiracy.

Conversely, most African American spokesmen and media outlets supported the participation of black athletes in the Olympics on the grounds that it would be an opportunity to discredit Hitler's Aryan ideology. Jesse Owens made the point that participating was not tantamount to endorsing Hitler's regime, a point he made with a double-edged comment: "I wasn't invited to shake hands with Hitler, but I wasn't invited to the White House to shake hands with the president either."[5] They were correct. But that is not to say that Jesse Owens enjoyed unequivocal support even at home, where discrimination and segregation were the norm. In fact, a boycott by the United States might only have served later to advance the Nazi argument that the United States had, because of discrimination, already accepted certain premises of Nazi-Aryan ideology.

Jesse Owens went on to win four gold medals—out of a total of twenty-four U.S. gold medals—in the sprint and long jump events. And in contrast with official ideology, the German spectators were impressed by

Owens's performances and strength, as were a number of German athletes, notably Luz Long, who openly embraced Owens after a victory. Said Owens, "It took a lot of courage for him to befriend me in front of Hitler. . . . You can melt down all the medals and cups I have and they wouldn't be a plating on the 24-karat friendship I felt for Luz Long at that moment. Hitler must have gone crazy watching us embrace. The sad part of the story is I never saw Long again. He was killed in World War II."[6] The upshot was that Jesse Owens and the U.S. team had a far greater impact by participating in the Berlin Games than a boycott would have had.

## Reasons of State versus Reasons of Athletes

If we are correct in our reasoning above, there is a considerable burden on nations that impose a boycott on their athletes. There might be occasions when reasons of state prevent the financial backing of an Olympic team. Imagine that a nation has limited resources and must choose between fielding an Olympic team and feeding its people. In such a case, the nation may have to choose not to send athletes to compete. This, however, is different from boycotting. Boycotting is a political and also, depending on particular circumstances, a moral decision. But a decision by the African government of Togo not to participate in the winter Olympics is a purely cultural and economic one.

Let us now consider briefly some of the reasons why athletes themselves might decide to boycott the Olympics.

They may, for example, fear systematic unfair judgments in competitions, as was frequently the charge made against East German judges in figure skating competitions in the 1960s and 1970s. We contend that this is insufficient grounds for a boycott so long as there is some record or observation whereby others might see the unfairness. The behavior of East German figure skating judges became somewhat of an ongoing gag at every winter Olympics. U.S. figure skating coach Frank Carrol insisted that Linda Fratianne took silver instead of gold at the 1980 Winter Olympics in Lake Placid, New York, because of East-West connivance during the Cold War. He maintains that the results were rigged, with five German-speaking judges conspiring to hand the women's gold medal to Anett Poetzsch of the former East Germany and the men's gold to Robin Cousins of England.[7]

What if one were compelled to contravene one's individual conscience or religion, say by competing on the Sabbath? That is a matter of individual conscience and should not be cause for a boycott. Provisions and adjustments can be made. After all, the great Jewish baseball player, Sandy Koufax, never pitched on the Sabbath, and his team, the Los Angeles Dodgers, always found a way to accommodate his beliefs in their pitching rotation. And likewise Eric Liddell, who in the 1924 Paris Olympics won a gold medal for the 400 meter and a bronze medal for the 200 meter, refused to run on Sunday—in observance of his Christian faith.

What about a fear of humiliation? Although decorum and common sense might dictate that you refrain from participating in figure skating if you are, as they say, "an ankle skater," something can be said for courage over competence. The Jamaican bobsled team has shown that limited skill hardly constitutes an argument for nonparticipation, since the crowds often root for and respect the underdog and his or her decision to participate despite great odds.

What of a legitimate fear of bodily harm or a security threat? We propose that this is a genuine reason for athletes to boycott the Olympics. But again, this decision would have to be based on information supplied by state security agencies. And in that sense the individual judgment, although valid, would in fact have to be subordinated to information provided by a third party—not a direct assessment by the athlete. If the state, however, has good reason to believe that the athletes themselves will be subject to serious harm, then that is a good reason—indeed an obligation—to boycott. If the next winter Olympics were to be held in the mountains outside Kandahar, Afghanistan, for example, there would be ample reason to argue for—indeed insist on—a boycott for fear of the lives of a large group of Western athletes. Incidentally, this was the official reason offered by the Soviet Union and fourteen Eastern Bloc partners for their boycott of the Los Angeles Olympics in 1984—or at least they did so in protest against what they claimed were the anti-Soviet sentiments being fanned by the rhetoric of the U.S. government and its proclamation of the U.S.S.R. as "an evil empire." (The phrase was first used by President Ronald Reagan in a March 1983 speech in Florida.)

While we maintain that those anti-Soviet sentiments did not amount to a serious threat, and hence the grounds for boycotting those games were invalid, in principle the reasoning was sound. If Israel had suspected an attack against its athletes by Palestinian guerillas at the 1972 Munich games, it would have been justified in boycotting those games. Unfortunately, at the time, few intelligence organizations could have foreseen the ability of Palestinians to mount a major operation in a territory not directly adjacent to Israel.

In the final analysis, we maintain that Olympic boycotts have both philosophically limited grounds and historically limited effects. After all, the Games are for the athletes, and the host country is supposed to be neutral. This seems borne out even in extreme conditions. For example, Hitler played to that reality with a small gesture in 1936: he never shook the hand of any medal winner, not just Jesse Owens. As mentioned earlier, U.S. president Franklin Roosevelt did not shake Owens's hand, either. Maybe Roosevelt did not do so for racist reasons, or perhaps he was wise enough not to mix sport and politics, instead allowing Owens to bask in his moment of glory as a result of his own singular effort. We conclude that, in most cases, the threat and then the imposition of an Olympic boycott threatens and then robs athletes of such well-earned glory.

## Notes

1. Cesar Chavez, "Education of the Heart," United Farm Workers Official Website, 2006, http://www.ufw.org/_page.php?menu=research&inc=history/09.html (accessed March 2, 2011).

2. http://www.jfklibrary.org/Historical+Resources/Archives/Reference+Desk/Speeches/RFK/Day+of+Affirmation+Address+News+Release.htm.

3. "30 Years on, USOC Decision Still Stings," *Sport Perspectives*, April 7, 2010, http://www.sportsperspectives.com/archives/3027 (accessed March 2, 2011).

4. George F. Kennan, "Morality and Foreign Policy," *Foreign Affairs* 64 (Winter 1985–86), http://www.foreignaffairs.com/articles/40521/george-f-kennan/morality-and-foreign-policy (accessed March 2, 2011).

5. Jerry Schwartz, "Owens Pierced a Myth," *ESPN.com*, 2007, http://espn.go.com/sportscentury/features/00016393.html (accessed March 2, 2011).

6. Ibid.

7. Mark Hasty, "Evan Lysacek's Coach Thinks 1980 Olympics Were Rigged," *AOLnews*, January 21, 2010, http://olympics.fanhouse.com/2010/01/21/evan-lysaceks-coach-thinks-1980-olympics-were-rigged/ (accessed March 2, 2011).

*Alun R. Hardman and Hywel Iorwerth*

# SPORT, PATRIOTISM, AND THE OLYMPIC GAMES

The nation-swapping athlete has become an increasingly common, and enduring, phenomenon of Olympic history. The ancient Olympic Games were restricted to free Greeks; but later Romans, Egyptians, and other foreigners also competed. In addition, during the Hellenistic period, it was common for the best athletes to trade their talents to the highest-paying city-state. Greek politicians and rulers saw sport as "a successful means of legitimizing their position of power," particularly "if their worthiness to rule could not be constitutionally proved" (Hardy 1977, 6).

Since the end of the cold war, the phenomenon of nation swapping in sport has been on the rise. Most Britons remember South African–born 3000-meter runner Zola Budd, whose citizenship application was fast-tracked to allow her to compete for the United Kingdom in the 1984 Los Angeles Olympic Games. Jamaicans will be aware of three-time 200-meter World Champion Merlene Ottey, who was competing at the age of forty-nine for Slovenia. Another notable nationality transfer is the Kenyan-born 2005 World Champion of the 300-meter steeplechase, Stephen Cherono, who competes for Qatar. In track and field alone, the International Association of Athletic Federations (IAAF) lists over 500 transfers of nationality for athletes who have represented their countries at the junior level or above (Wikipedia 2010a).

IOC President Jacques Rogge has stated that IOC rules should discourage "countries or organizations wanting to buy athletes just for the money" (Mulhauser 2004). To that end, Rule 42 of the Olympic Charter limits athletes who have dual nationality, or have acquired a new nationality, from representing another country for three years after they last represented their former country. This three-year waiting period may be waived or decreased with the agreement of both national federations involved (International Olympic Committee 2007).

On one side of the debate, the argument is that the current legislation is too permissive and distorts the legitimate basis of international sporting competition. This view holds that international sport is predicated on competition between opponents who have deep-rooted enduring bonds, resemblances, and kinship connections with fellow nationals (Dixon 2000; Hoberman 1995; Morgan 1999, 2000). The present rules allow sportsmen and -women to become free agents who trade their talent, loyalty, and allegiance for the satisfaction of nationalistic goals of political leaders and sporting apparatchiks.

Those against Rule 42 argue that sportsmen and -women should be treated no differently than other migrants and that transfer of nationality regulations in sport acts as an unacceptable "restraint of trade." A number of liberal principles are given to support this economic argument. Paul Gomberg (2000, 2002), for example, suggests that a laissez-faire approach to international sporting representation aspires to equality among all peoples. He argues that promoting sporting universalism supersedes the iniquitous contingencies of nation-state obligations, which more often than not are the result of historical abuses of power on a grand and combative scale. This view holds that the free market of sporting talent helps erode the dangerous strands of excessive nationalism, which are often smoke screens for racist and ethnic bigotry (Hargreaves 1992; Gomberg 2002; Parry 2006).

Our argument in this chapter is that international sporting contests such as the Olympic Games ought to embody the moral ideals of "sincere internationalism," a viewpoint espoused by the founder of the modern Games, Pierre de Coubertin (Morgan 1995), which endorses the moral perspective of "reflective nationalism."[1] We believe that reflective nationals should develop an outlook that views the transfer of nationality for sporting purposes as morally problematic and something to be avoided. By contrast, the "cosmopolitan" is willing to transfer citizenship from one country to another in order to compete in international sport. We illustrate the normative differences between reflective nationals and cosmopolitans through a number of illustrative examples from track and field athletics. We conclude by suggesting a number of practical ways in which sincere internationalism can be enhanced by the IOC in order to inhibit transfers of nationality in sport.

## Sport, "Moderate Patriotism," and Coubertin's Ideal of International Sport

Those who argue for greater control on transfers of nationality in sport often base their argument on the idea that patriotism is a virtue undermined by greater migration of athletes. In his book *Patriotism, Morality, and Peace*, Stephen Nathanson (1993) argues for patriotism of a moderate kind. Philosophical support for his position can be traced to John Rawls's (1973) theory of justice as fairness and the subsequent significant and extended debate, which focused on the liberal and communitarian dimensions of Rawls's ideas. While an extended analysis of Rawls's influence on Nathanson's moderate patriotism is not undertaken here, our arguments reflect key considerations of Rawls's liberal philosophy.

Nathanson suggests that from a conceptual point of view it is possible to distinguish three possible types of patriotism. First, it may be expressed in the form of a *special* or *partial* concern for one's country. Second, there is *exclusive* concern, which entails both a concern for one's own country and negligence or indifference to the concerns of others. Finally, there is *aggressive* or *covetous* concern, which involves not only the pursuit of interests that benefit one's own country, but at the same time an attitude that seeks to either destroy or acquire for one's own country those interests that are of benefit to another country. Of these three possibilities, Nathanson argues that only the first, a special or partial concern for one's country, represents a morally acceptable point of view. This partial or special concern toward one's country is embedded in his concept of *moderate patriotism,* which holds that one can be virtuous in feeling loyalty to one's country "and be willing to promote its well-being, even if that can only be done at the cost of diminishing the well-being of other countries" (2002b, 88). The central feature of Nathanson's account is that it provides for a form of patriotism that prevents, on the one hand, the kind of moral neutrality that leads to an "indifference to one's country" and, on the other, to the kinds of "excessive patriotism" apparent in *exclusive* or *aggressive* versions of the ideal, which may result in inappropriate and disrespectful displays of chauvinism.

The preceding analysis suggests that moderate patriots aim to subject national allegiance in all things international, including sport, to certain constraints. Thus, for the moderate patriot, there ought to be limits on the wishes of acquisitive nations wanting to recruit foreign athletic talent as well as on the autonomy of the individual athlete wanting to pick and choose which country to represent. This means that as well as jumping legal hurdles to the transfer of nationality in sport, moderate patriotism establishes moral considerations as well.

Coubertin recognized the normative dimensions to nationalism and patriotism in developing his ideas and rationale for international sport (Morgan 1995). Coubertin too considered that the underpinning principles of liberalism, which otherwise might support freedom of association, should, in the context of international sport, be subject to the ideals of nationalism. Echoing Nathanson's ideas about moderate patriotism, Coubertin argued that the relationship between liberalism and nationalism could be best understood by the distinction he saw between what he termed "sincere internationalism" and "cosmopolitanism."

## Cosmopolitanism and International Sporting Representation

In developing his ideals of Olympism, Coubertin recognized that international sport would appeal to a cosmopolitan outlook and in doing so made a distinction between two types of cosmopolitanism—enlightened and nomadic. He suggested that enlightened cosmopolitanism promoted a form of objectivity and universalism that saw persons as individual agents who were independent of particular groups, practices, and institutions. Enlightened cosmopolitans consider membership of an egalitarian moral universe to be more important than social boundaries, and they seek to shake off their particular attachments in favor of some neutral vantage point (Polley 2004). Local and national notions, such as American, British, French, or Chinese, were to have no purchase.

To help illustrate Coubertin's account of enlightened cosmopolitanism, consider the narrative of Kenyan-born Qatari athlete Saif Saaeed Shaheen, previously named Stephen Cherono. Shaheen was born and brought up in Kenya and won gold for that country in the 3000-meter steeplechase at the 2002 Commonwealth Games. However, six weeks before the World Athletics Championship in Paris, he was granted Qatari citizenship and won the gold representing that country. His brother, Abraham, running for Kenya in the same race, walked off the track without congratulating him. He was barred from competing in the 2004 Athens Olympics because, despite Kenya's acquiescing to Qatar's requests, the IOC applied Rule 42 of the Olympic Charter in full, even though Shaheen had been able to compete in other sanctioned IAAF events. He repeated his World Championship victory in Helsinki in 2005 and is currently the 3000-meter steeplechase world record holder (Wikipedia 2010b).

Shaheen himself acknowledges that his move was motivated by the desire for long-term financial security at a time when he doubted his world class potential. He has indicated that the Qatari government agreed to pay him $1,000 a month for life (BBC Online 2007).[2] Though his official place of residency is listed as Doha, Qatar, and he claims he is happy to represent and run for Qatar, Shaheen has continued to train and live in Kenya with his Kenyan coach for extensive periods of the year, at which times he prefers to be called Stephen. He also has a residence in London (Skari 2003). Shaheen may appear to be an unattached "world citizen" because he abandoned his Kenyan citizenship and subsequently failed to engage meaningfully in becoming a Qatari patriot. His cosmopolitanism is further indicated by his flexible residency and international travel from one country to another. However, it is difficult to label him a truly enlightened cosmopolitan, primarily because he has failed to detach himself completely from his Kenyan way of life. In fact, his continued presence in the country, living and training very near to the place of his birth, suggest that beyond holding a Qatari passport and being an employee of the Qatari government, very little has changed in his nationalistic outlook. What we have here is an arrangement where one's legal citizenship status stands in stark contrast to ideals of moderate patriotism.

One might point out that even though Shaheen falls short of being an enlightened cosmopolitan, Qatar, with what appears to be a very liberal approach to citizenship, might advocate such ideals. Perhaps here we have a nation-state that promotes free-flowing citizenry based on minimal criteria—a country where the bonds of community are based on shared liberal ideals of freedom of individual choice rather than any rooted historical values. If this is the case, then Qatari athletes and current and prospective citizens should be able to come and go as they please and claim Qatari citizenship whenever they want.

However, there is evidence to suggest that we should be skeptical about the cosmopolitan credentials of nation-states like Qatar. The case of marathon runner Leonard Mucheru Maina, who, like Shaheen, was originally from Kenya, illustrates the point. Maina was recruited to represent the oil-rich state of Bahrain, gaining citizenship in 2003 and taking the name of Mushir Salem Jawher. In 2007, he competed and won a marathon race in Israel and was subsequently stripped of his Bahraini citizenship. Though Bahrain later reversed its decision, Maina reacquired Kenyan citizenship by the end of 2007 (Mynott 2005). His story suggests that not only is easy access to citizenship open to only a few (sporting) elites, but the limited number of nation-states who seek athletic talent may make restrictive demands on their new citizens' freedoms.

These particular examples are indicative of a broader global trend that suggests that greater international sports migration is not really about enlightened cosmopolitanism and the desire to live in a world devoid of national boundaries that no longer differentiates "us" from "them." Instead, migratory patterns indicate a range of nonmoral motivational outlooks and values that justify why athletes from one country move to represent another. The most stereotypical migratory patterns in track and field athletics over the last fifty years suggest the following:

- Most transfers are to North America (United States and Canada), Europe (France, the United Kingdom, Spain, Germany, Ireland), and Oceania (Australia).

- The fewest transfers are to Africa and Asia (Bahrain, Israel, Qatar are notable exceptions).

- The fewest transfers are from Western Europe and North America.

- Most transfers are between ex-colonial nations—mostly to a colonial power from a former colony (Morocco to France; Ukraine/Belarus/Uzbekistan to Russia; Cuba to Spain).

- Most transcontinental transfers (excluding ex-colonial nations) are from poorer countries to richer ones.

In short, the migratory patterns of the majority of track and field athletes, including Shaheen and Maina, are similar to general global migratory patterns. This indicates that sport is not immune from other social, economic, and political forces. In the main, nationality transfers in sport reinforce old geopolitical tensions such as those that resulted from nineteenth-century imperialism, post–World War II resettlement, post–cold-war realignments, and the emerging power of oil-rich nations. The patterns outlined above also emphasize that, for the most part, nationality transfers in sport are motivated principally by economics—talent-poor/economically rich nations fast-track and buy out the citizenship rights of athletes from talent-rich/economically poor nations in the pursuit of Olympic success. This, rather than any overriding ideal of enlightened cosmopolitanism, is closer to the truth. For Shaheen, defecting to Qatar secured the financial future of his family; therefore the act is done out of feelings of loyalty and attachment to that part of him that is Kenyan, rather than anything of him that is Qatari.

While the ideal of enlightened cosmopolitanism might represent a more indirect and hidden menace to sincere internationalism, the second form of cosmopolitanism—the nomadic kind—is more direct. Nomadic cosmopolitanism is represented by the modern-day trekker who has the freedom to travel around the globe in search of reward, adventure, and pleasure (Morgan 1995). Such nomads either do not engage in the foreign cultures at all or only engage in certain superficial aspects of these cultures. What demarcates the nomadic cosmopolitan athlete is the degree to which nationality transfers involve an equitable and freely negotiated economic quid pro quo. Whereas the dominant migratory sporting patterns noted previously reflect the desire of people living in relative poverty to improve their material conditions, the nomadic cosmopolitan athlete is largely unburdened by such pressures. Nomadic cosmopolitans already have a level of material wealth from a sporting career spent competing for their originating nation, or else are sufficiently independently wealthy for the economic implications of the transfer of nationality not to matter.

We get some sense of the nomadic cosmopolitan athlete from looking at the career of Jamaican-born Slovenian sprinter Merlene Ottey. Between 1980 and 2004, Ottey made the most Olympic appearances of any track and field athlete (seven), and also won the most World championship medals (fourteen, with three of them gold), of any female athlete. Following the 2000 Sydney Olympics, where she was accused of bullying her way into the team after failing to qualify in the national trials, Ottey, at the age of forty, moved to Slovenia to train with her Slovenian coach. In 2002 she was granted Slovenian citizenship and later competed for her new country in the Athens 2004 Olympics in the 100 meter. She narrowly missed qualifying for the 2008 Beijing Olympics at the age of forty-eight. At present Ottey continues to be involved in domestic athletics in Slovenia, running in meets in central Europe. During the winter she splits her time between family in California and warm-weather training in Florida. She rarely returns to her native Jamaica (Wilbon 2004).

Although it is not possible to truly know the motives behind Ottey's defection it is plausible that the external rewards are limited and she may have no burning desire to "become" Slovenian. It is also possible that Ottey's motives are not entirely selfish, and her move might improve the lives of other Slovenians. However, at present there is no evidence that she has invested significantly in Slovenian athletics in particular or Slovenian cultural life in general (Higham 2008).

According to Morgan (1995), Coubertin's dissatisfaction with nomadic cosmopolitans such as Ottey lies with their unwillingness or incapacity to engage in different cultures in any substantive way. Consequently Morgan does not believe that anything of worth will be learned from such encounters that could serve as the basis of meaningful conversations and relations between cultures. Thus nomadic cosmopolitanism is devoid of any normative or virtuous credentials that could serve the Olympic ideal of internationalism. From Coubertin's perspective, nomadic cosmopolitanism has to be rejected, because it concedes international representation to be a matter of unconstrained open choice—a perspective Coubertin found unacceptable.

## Sincere Internationalism and Olympic Sport

Coubertin's ideal of sincere internationalism stems from the view that persons first derive their understanding of right and wrong from the culture and communities of the nation in which they grow up. An individual's moral understanding therefore emerges from, and is dependent on, the values within a nation. He further attempted to show that this relationship was not only self-evident, but indeed normative, through his attempts to place nationalism within the boundaries of Olympism. Coubertin believed that only athletes and countries dedicated to sincere internationalism harbored the moral qualities he considered necessary to be involved in Olympic competition. Nathanson (2002a, 2002b) suggests that in addition to being nationally grounded, the morality of a nation is not simply a collection of particular judgments. Rather, in addition to specific judgments, it contains an open-ended set of general values, principles, ideals, and paradigms of proper behaviour. The morality that a person acquires from his or her nation will therefore, contain a large element of vagueness, ambiguity, and indeterminacy. There will be no rigid set of judgments which is simply the national morality. Hence, different notions of morality and of the requirements of loyalty may grow out of the same social soil and make possible the sort of flexibility of moral thought that permits individuals to contrast their nations' acts and policies with the requirements of morality as such. (2002a, 99)

For Nathanson, therefore, the essence of a national morality is to be understood as an ongoing dialectical process where moral perspectives are likely to contain inconsistent and competing elements that generate disagreement, debate, and argument between those who consider themselves members of that same nation. Furthermore, he supports the notion that if there is a universal national ideal it lies in the process of attempting to reconcile the competing demands of different interpretations of patriotism. Central to such a version of patriotism is a search for common values and understanding beyond the more local and immediate ties of family, friends, street, town, and city. In other words, a grounding premise of moderate patriotism is the notion that it demands a form of loyalty that strives against the arbitrariness and parochialism of much narrower forms of attachment.

Nathanson's view concedes that there may be times when competing demands between one's nation and one's narrower forms of attachment are in conflict to the extent that compromise and concessions will occur. A clear example of this is when individuals of different nationalities form bonds (marriage, civil partnerships, parenthood) with persons of different nationalities that may, depending on other circumstances, reshape existing loyalties or create new ones. Other circumstances might have a similar impact, such as migration for employment or educational purposes. Given the global movement of peoples it is irrational to think that one's formative patriotic attachments can never be subject to challenge and adaptation. In such circumstances, Nathanson argues that one's patriotic loyalties will bend, and in some cases break, where one's formative associations are short, weak, and fractured. So, for example, an orphan child fleeing a war-torn country of birth who then spends years moving from one country to another as a refugee might arrive into adulthood "apatriotic" because that person has had no opportunity to draw upon an enduring national moral discourse. However, and this is the important point, once permanence is achieved, such "apatriotic" individuals will seek out and engage in patriotically inspired moral discourses. And it is through such moral discourses that one's patriotic outlook might begin to emerge.

The same principle is true for individuals whose life circumstances change dramatically after they have already acquired a patriotic outlook. And while in this case there is likely to be ongoing tension between the individual's formative sense of patriotism and the expectations of his or her new country, moderate patriotism suggests that such discourse, dialogue, and contemplation should instantiate reflective nationalism.

Coubertin's sporting equivalent to Nathanson's moderate patriotism argues that athletes accept particularistic social attachments because they are not only essential in giving meaning to what they do in sport, but because it also serves as a foothold for intercultural dialogue, understanding, and cooperation (Chappelet and Bayle 2005). By advocating that international sporting competition should be a contest between "reflective nationals," we are not stating that individuals are forever bound by their particular context or tied forever to being a citizen of one nation. What is being argued is that unless we prioritize our particularistic social attachments and realize the normative relevance of national identity within universal movements such as the Olympics then we will not have a general concept to which each nation can sincerely commit in order to better acquaint ourselves with the diverse cultures of the world. If we are to continue to privilege power, money, and personal gain by advocating an overly flexible account of international sporting representation, then the whole virtuous potential of international sporting competition might be lost.

Reflective national athletes, therefore, are likely to be born and brought up in a particular country and show a sense of commitment and attachment to that country by representing it at the Olympic Games. For most Olympians the story often more or less ends here; and though moderate patriotism demands that the individual always reflect on the moral basis of his or her loyalty, the reflective process remains focused on the national morality of the person's country of birth. For those reflective national athletes whose personal attachments change significantly, possibly resulting in a move to another country, the importance of their previous culture remains, as it has influenced and shaped who they are. Reflective nationals are unlikely to drop all attachments to their country of birth; however, they will reflect on these attachments and attempt to seek similarities in their new culture—whether it be a respect for language, culture, or politics. Over time, these athletes might naturally develop a genuine relationship with the culture in which they now live and would show significant commitment to that culture. However, if the athlete is a true reflective national, the process of acquiring a new national identity will be a lengthy and vacillating one that would occur naturally over time.

Although the argument above suggests that it would be possible for reflective nationals to represent a country other than the one in which they were brought up, most reflective nationals would not consider defection. Thus, defection would be the exception, such as in cases where family history is complicated or where the individual (such as an orphaned refugee) has traveled extensively throughout life.[3]

Finding an example of a reflective nationalist who has defected is a difficult task (reaffirming that it is the exceptional case), but the middle-distance runner Wilson Kipketer might fit. Kipketer was born in Kenya but moved to Denmark when he was eighteen years old in order to study electronic engineering at the Copenhagen University. During his time at the university Kipketer ran for Denmark, and in 1995 he won his first of three World Championship gold medals. Kipketer was not allowed to run for Denmark in the 1996 Olympics as he had not yet gained full citizenship. However, seven years after his move to Denmark, Kipketer was granted Danish citizenship and subsequently won silver and bronze in the Olympic Games in 2000 and 2004, respectively. He married his Danish girlfriend in 2000 and continues to live in Denmark following his retirement from athletics in 2005.

Kipketer represents a different category from the one habited by athletes such as Saif Saeed Shaheen, Leonard Mucheru Maina, and Merlene Ottey, as Kipketer's behavior suggests that his motivation to represent Denmark goes beyond mere financial and personal gain, and is based on a genuine commitment to the country. Kipketer could not run for Denmark in the 1996 Olympic Games, but he still chose to wait for full Danish citizenship, which he received the following year. The fact that Kipketer married a Danish woman and continues to live in Denmark following his retirement suggests that he is a reflective national whose attachments have developed over time.

## Promoting Reflective Nationalism through Olympic Solidarity

The IOC strongly believes that more should be done to reduce the number of transfers of nationality for sporting purposes. In the main, the approaches adopted so far have attempted to establish tighter regulations that would make the costs to both individual athletes and adopting countries outweigh the benefits. Some have suggested that tighter regulations are the way forward and point to FIFA, soccer's governing body, where once players reach the age of eighteen they can play for only one country.

The problem here is that intense political negotiation would be required to ensure that all Olympic sports adopted and consistently applied the same rule. The diverse rules in place at the moment suggest that not all sport federations share the same view on this issue: some marginal sports (such as rugby and cricket) have much looser regulations that have, at times, allowed emerging nations to encourage sporting pilgrims (nomadic cosmopolitans) to transfer nationality as a means to accelerate the growth of the game in their country. For other sports, particularly those played on a global scale such as soccer, maintaining home-grown talent, particularly in the case of poorer nations, is likely to require more restrictive regulation.

Another approach might involve imposing further conditions beyond acquiring citizenship to make it more likely that only reflective nationals would undergo transfer of nationality. For athletes taking up residence in the United States, for example, an additional set of sports-specific requirements might be added to the U.S. Citizenship and Immigration Services (USCIS) test. However, as such requirements are likely to be administered and monitored by the very same national sports federations who try hard to ensure that new citizenship involves as little inconvenience as possible for the defecting athlete, it is unrealistic to think that such an idea would be embraced consistently and thoroughly, if at all, from one nation-state to the next. Nor is it feasible to place such a responsibility on the IOC to develop global agency designed to separate out sporting cosmopolitans from reflective nationals.

## Olympic Solidarity budget, 2009–2012

| Budget category | Budget amount |
|---|---|
| World programs | US$134,000,000 |
| Continental programs | US$122,000,000 |
| Olympic Games subsidies | US$42,000,000 |
| Administration/communication | US$13,000,000 |
| Total | US$311,000,000 |

*Source:* Olympic Solidarity 2010.

The inherent problem is that the world of elite sport is not universal in its distribution of wealth and power, and therefore rich countries and cultures (as long as they are not seen to be privileging foreign athletes to any greater degree than other migrants) will benefit more from the transnational migration of sporting talent (Grainger 2006; Maguire and Bale 1994; Magee and Sugden 2002). Both the current regulations and the economic principles driving elite-level sport encourage this process. Money and power rather than moderate patriotism are the greatest driving force behind the development of sporting loyalty, so the best option to remedy the situation lies in offsetting the material conditions that lead to transfers of nationality in sport in the first place.

The Olympic Solidarity movement provides one such mechanism for redistributing sporting wealth by sharing the revenue generated from the Olympic Games. With a budget of US$311 million for 2009–2012 (see the table "Olympic Solidarity budget"), funding is allocated to the various National Olympic Committees (NOCs) via the members of the Continental Olympic Association, who oversee the division of the projects within their continent.

Within these various funding streams monies are distributed to the various component parts that contribute to elite sports programs, such as the athletes themselves, infrastructure and capital funding for host nations, coach development, NOC management, and the promotion of Olympic values. The distribution of the US$122 million available for continental programs is shown in the second table, "Distribution of Olympic Solidarity funding for Continental programs."

The figures suggest that significant funds are available for revenue

## Distribution of Olympic Solidarity funding for Continental programs, 2009–2012

| Region | No. of NOCs | Funding allocated |
|---|---|---|
| Association of National Olympic Committees of Africa (ANOCA) | 53 | US$26,671,000 |
| Pan American Sports Organization (PASO—all Americas) | 42 | US$21,228,000 |
| Olympic Council of Asia (OCA) | 44 | US$22,257,000 |
| European Olympic Council (EOC) | 49 | US$25,089,000 |
| Oceania National Olympic Committee (ONOC) | 17 | US$14,198,000 |
| Association of National Olympic Committees (ANOC) | | US$12,557,000 |
| Total | | US$122,000,000 |

Source: Olympic Solidarity 2010.

Note: ANOC is made of 12 sovereign nations not affiliated with a continental program (e.g., Taiwan, Hong Kong, Palestine Authority, South Sudan).

redistribution, which may be conducted in a targeted way to improve the material condition of poorer countries, including sporting infrastructure in poorer nations. Specific programs might be developed to support sports and nations identified as being "at risk" of excessive nationality transfers. Such funding might likewise be withdrawn from countries that, over time, actively and systematically pursue foreign athletes. Such an approach might be preferable to the current imperfect agreements between exchanging nations, where it is often impossible to see whether the compensation for the loss of athletic talent is reinvested in full and where it is most needed in the poorer nation.

## Conclusion

In this chapter we have argued that the moderate patriot is unlikely to be persuaded that changing citizenship in order to pursue international sporting success is morally justified. The moderate patriot will instead be more concerned with how nationality transfers in sport preserve the goal of cultivating affection for one's country—of enhancing, rather than diminishing, "our" patriotic sense. Changes in citizenship undertaken for international sporting reasons at present do very little to further the development of such affection, particularly in cases where both the individual acquiring citizenship and the country providing citizenship view international sporting success as the only reason for the transfer of nationality.

We have argued that a cosmopolitan outlook on the Olympic Games would no longer represent a foothold for intercultural dialogue and understanding, but rather serve as an arena that might obscure the need for the recognition of difference (Morgan 1997). Instead we have suggested that moderate patriotism is better expressed through the outlook of reflective nationals, who believe that when transfers of nationality do take place they ought to involve affection for the new country. This means that such individuals should be immersed into their new national culture to allow for the "contamination" over time of their prior patriotic affections. For this to happen, they must encounter, experience, and evaluate the differences in culture made available through their acquired citizenship and, in that process, come to appreciate the goods and values made available to them in their new circumstances.

In addition, we have argued that the IOC can do more through the targeted use of Olympic Solidarity funding to more effectively address the material conditions of at-risk athletes in poorer nations. Such funding could also be withdrawn from nation-states who aggressively recruit foreign athletes. Measures like these, we conclude, retain the counter-hegemonic potential of the Olympic Games as a cultural arena where smaller and weaker nations can achieve due recognition as worthy conversational partners. It is only through upholding the moral credentials of moderate patriotism in sport that we can appreciate nations and communities beyond our particular contingencies.

## Notes

1. Our account of Coubertin on nationalism is based on Morgan's (1995) critical interpretation. His account is based on Pierre de Coubertin's paper "Does Cosmopolitan Life Lead to International Friendliness?" *American Monthly Review of Reviews* 4 (1898): 431.

2. In addition to the $1,000 a month for life, he was reported to have received up to $1 million in a one-off payment.

3. Reflective nationals are quite different from sporting refugees, who may also genuinely feel attached to their new culture while appreciation of their previous culture wanes. But even here it could be argued that the professed love sporting refugees now feel for their adopted nation has more to do with a sense of loss or betrayal they might feel toward their previous culture. In other words, the root cause of the change in allegiance stems from their social, political, or cultural persecution. Their revised belief is that their original nation no longer represents, or never did represent, the kinds of moral credentials that deserve patriotic association.

## References

BBC Online. 2007. "Kenya Refuses to Take Runner Back." *http://news.bbc.co.uk/1/hi/world/africa/6242323.stm* (accessed April 18, 2009).

Chappelet, J-L., and E. Bayle. 2005. *Strategic and Performance Management of Olympic Sport Organizations.* Champaign, IL: Human Kinetics.

Dixon, N. 2000. "A Justification of Moderate Patriotism in Sport." In *Values in Sport: Elitism, Nationalism, Gender Equality and the Scientific Manufacture of Winners,* ed. T. Tännsjö and C. Tamburrini. New York: Spon Press, 74–86.

Gomberg, P. 2000. "Patriotism in Sports and in War." In *Values in Sport: Elitism, Nationalism, Gender Equality and the Scientific Manufacture of Winners,* ed. T. Tännsjö and C. Tamburrini. New York, Spon Press, 87–98.

———. 2002. "Patriotism Is Like Racism." In *Patriotism,* ed. Igor Primoratz. New York: Humanity Books, 105–112.

Grainger, A. 2006. "From Immigrant to Overstayer: Samoan Identity, Rugby, and Cultural Politics of Race and Nation." *Journal of Sport and Social Issues* 30: 45–61.

Hardy, S. 1977. "Politicians, Promoters, and the Rise of Sport: The Case of Ancient Greece and Rome." *Canadian Journal of History of Sport and Physical Education* 8: 1–15.

Hargreaves, J. 1992. "Olympism and Nationalism: Some Preliminary Considerations." *International Review for the Sociology of Sport* 27: 119–134.

Higham, P. 2008. "Ottey Fails in Olympic Bid." *Sky Sports,* http://www.skysports.com/story/0,19528,14935_3853455,00.html (accessed April 18, 2009).

Hoberman, J. 1995. "Toward a Theory of Olympic Internationalism." *Journal of Sport History* 22: 1–37.

International Olympic Committee. 2007. *Olympic Charter.* Lausanne, Switzerland: International Olympic Committee.

Magee, J., and J. Sugden. 2002. "'The World at their Feet': Professional Football and International Labor Migration." *Journal of Sport and Social Issues* 26: 421–437.

Maguire, J., and J. Bale. 1994. "Sports Labour Migration in the Global Arena." In

*The Global Sports Arena: Athletic Talent Migration in an Interdependent World,* ed. J. Bale and J. Maguire. London: Frank Cass, 1–21.

Morgan, W. J. 1995. "Cosmopolitanism, Olympism, and Nationalism: A Critical Interpretation of Coubertin's Ideal of International Sporting Life." *Olympika: The International Journal of Olympic Studies* 4: 19–92.

———. 1997. "Sports and the Making of National Identities: A Moral View." *Journal of the Philosophy of Sport* 24: 1–20.

———. 1999. "Patriotic Sports and the Moral Making of Nations." *Journal of the Philosophy of Sport* 26: 50–67.

———. 2000. "Sport as the Moral Discourse of Nations." In *Values in Sport: Elitism, Nationalism, Gender Equality and the Scientific Manufacture of Winners,* ed. T. Tannsjo and C. Tamburrini. New York: Spon Press, 59–73.

Mulhauser, D. 2004. "On Your Marks, Set, Go Home! Why Can't Kenyan Stephen Cherono Race for Qatar in the Olympics?" *Legal Affairs,* http://www.legalaffairs .org/printerfriendly.msp?id=598 (accessed April 18, 2009).

Mynott, A. 2005. "Kenya Examines Track Star Defections." *BBC Online,* http:// news.bbc.co.uk/1/hi/world/africa/4566821.stm (accessed April 18, 2009).

Nathanson, S. 1993. *Patriotism, Morality, and Peace.* Lanham, MD: Rowman and Littlefield.

———. 2002a. "Is Patriotism Like Racism?" In *Patriotism,* ed. Igor Primoratz. New York: Humanity Books, 113–120.

———. 2002b. "In Defense of 'Moderate Patriotism.'" In *Patriotism,* ed. Igor Primoratz. New York: Humanity Books, 87–104.

Olympic Solidarity. 2010. "Where the Action Is: 2009–2012 Quadrennial Plan." http://www.olympic.org/Documents/PDF_files_0807/os_2009_2012_en.pdf (accessed April 11, 2010).

Parry, J. 2006. "Sport and Olympism: Universals and Multiculturalism." *Journal of the Philosophy of Sport* 33: 188–204.

Polley, M. 2004. "Sport and National Identity in Contemporary England." In *Sport and National Identity in the Post-War World,* ed. A. Smith and D. Porter. London: Routledge, 56–74.

Rawls, J. 1973. *A Theory of Justice.* Oxford: Oxford University Press.

Skari, T. 2003. "A Run for the Money." *Time,* http://www.time.com/time/magazine/ article/0,9171,480231,00.html (accessed April 20, 2009).

Wikipedia. 2010a. "List of Nationality Transfers in Sport." http://en.wikipedia.org/ wiki/List_of_nationality_transfers_in_sport (accessed April 18, 2009).

Wikipedia. 2010b. "Saif Saaeed Shaheen." http://en.wikipedia.org/wiki/Saif_Saaeed_ Shaheen (accessed April 11, 2010).

Wilbon, M. 2004. "Sprinter Ottey Doesn't Act Her Age." *Washington Post,* http:// www.washingtonpost.com/wp-dyn/articles/A20189-2004Aug20.html (accessed April 11, 2010).

*Matthew Sharpe*

# SHARING THE MOMENT
## On the Olympic Games as Spectacle

But you may say, there are some things disagreeable and troubling in life. And are there none in Olympia? Are you not scorched? Are you not pressed in a crowd? Are you not without comfortable means of bathing? Are you not wet when it rains? Have you not abundance of noise, clamour, and other disagreeable things? But I suppose that, setting all these things off against the magnificence of the spectacle, you bear and endure.
—Epictetus, *Discourses of Epictetus* I, first century CE

This chapter is largely on the Olympics and the philosophy of art. The topic might seem unlikely, compared with other contributions to this volume. It is easy enough to envisage philosophical reflections on the ethics of the Olympics, their political significance, or their history . . . but the philosophy of art? The philosophy of art or, as it is called in modern times, "aesthetics," is one of the more refined species of academic reflection. Yet the Olympics are a massive, mass-cultural event, as well as big business, big politics, and big money. Worlds divide the ivory tower and its professor's refined reflections on beauty from the gilded world of Olympic rings and IOC lobbyists.

To begin to see why the two concerns, the modern Olympic Games and the philosophy of aesthetics, nevertheless do speak to each other, let us begin with the most common lament about the Games today. This is that the Games are not what they were. Since 1980, when Juan Antonio

Samaranch—Franco's former minister of sport—took over the IOC, the Games have lost their amateur status, and their innocence.

## Let the Games Begin: From Big Money to High Aesthetics

The post-Samaranch, post-1980 Games are indeed the stuff of big money. The Athenian Games of 2004, in the home country of the ancient Olympics, cost an estimated US$14 billion, and the London Olympics of 2012 are due to cost at least £9.3 billion, according to present projections (that's £1,200 for every man, woman, and child in London). The four cities that fought to host the 2016 Summer Olympics—Chicago, Rio de Janeiro, Madrid, and Tokyo—had multibillion-dollar budgets for the Games. The projected $14.4 billion budget of Rio de Janeiro—the city that was awarded the Games—was the largest among the contenders. China's 2008 Games are presently being estimated to have cost that nation up to $40 billion. Costs for broadcasting rights (even adjusting for inflation) have also gone through the roof—from £80 paid to the IOC for the 1956 Melbourne Olympic Games broadcasting, to NBC's $3.5 billion deal with the IOC for broadcasting rights to all winter and summer Olympics between 2000 and 2008.

The IOC, for its part, has become an international byword for corruption and scandal. The costs and conduct of campaigns by cities to host this "proven" money spinner have also skyrocketed.[1] In their two books *The Lords of the Rings* and *The New Lords of the Rings*, Andrew Jennings and Vyv Simson have documented the sordid world of bribery and inducements to IOC officials—furs, jewelry, paintings, first-class travel and accommodation packages, college tuition fees, jobs for relatives, and cash payments. Such has become the stock-in-trade of the IOC's decisions concerning who will host the Games.[2] In Australia, the author's home country, the national public broadcaster ran a highly successful, biting television series called *The Games,* about the backroom swindles involved in winning and hosting what were touted as "the best Games ever" in 2000 (to cite Samaranch's words at their close).

So a question underlies all of this. Whatever the exact magnitude of their economic cost, what is certain is that the Olympic Games are a "product." They are a product that nations, companies, and corporations have shown themselves willing to throw millions and millions of dollars at. The literally million-dollar question then is: If the Games are such big business, what exactly is it that they are selling?

This seems easy enough to answer. There are admission tickets, first of all. Then there are the broadcast rights to beam the events all around the globe. Not to be scoffed at, in addition, is the advertising space the games and their venues afford. To purchase a space for a company logo on a sponsored medal stand by the time of the 2002 and 2004 winter and summer Olympics cost some $55 million, ten times the amount charged in 1984. The athletes may not directly win anything more than deathless fame and a medal in the Games. But everyone knows that such success guarantees them endorsements reaching into the millions, and instant celebrity. So, to repeat our question: What commodity is it, in the athletes and in the advertising space, that the business world agrees is so enticing?

To get closer to our answer, let's recall arguably the most remarkable scandal of the many scandals that shrouded the 2008 Beijing Summer Games, as thickly as the city's infamous smog.

Shortly after the astonishing opening ceremony (to which we will return), the *Beijing Times* revealed that the ceremony's amazing "footprint" fireworks sequence was computer generated and inserted into the official coverage to look like the real thing. The simulated images came complete with a "camera shake," as though the images were filmed from a helicopter. And the simulation—as if answering French theorist Jean Baudrillard's seemingly absurd claim that in the new media age we can no longer safely discern reality from simulacra—did not end there. The nine-year-old girl who appeared to emotively sing "Ode to the Motherland" that night was revealed to have lip-synced. The real singer was not considered pretty enough to display before the eyes of the world. Chinese officials also admitted to deploying cheer squads (legions of spectators wearing matching yellow shirts) to "create atmosphere" and hide the empty seats in the stadium.

And so we now come closer to an answer, via the opening and closing ceremonies: the Games are an aestheticized spectacle. The modern Games are a preeminent example, perhaps *the* preeminent example, of the type of phenomenon that Guy Debord's famous *Society of the Spectacle* aimed to describe. "In societies dominated by modern conditions of production, life is presented as an immense accumulation of spectacles," Debord proposes.[3] In this "immense accumulation" Debord famously sees the "ultimate fulfillment" of Marx's famed analysis of commodities (a thought to which we will return).[4] As a spectacle, indeed—"an affirmation of appearances and an identification of all human social life with appearances"[5]—the Olympic Games are probably peerless. They attract an almost unprecedentedly large global television audience, and for a reason.

There is something irresistible about the images of the Games: of tense young bodies in the extremes or grace of athletic motion, of athletes' strained expressions, of their concentration on the task, their joy and agony in victory and defeat, their embrace in mutual respect when the race is run. The media culture surrounding the Olympics has even developed its own peculiar term to describe what the Olympics is "all about": the games are about "moments," "Olympic moments," or "golden moments." A search for "Olympics" "moments" on Google presently (October 2009) yields 3.3 million hits. Many of these are newspaper polls asking viewers to list their most memorable moments, or reports by experts tasked with constructing lists of their own defining Olympic moments (for the record, the Times Online's top fifty is headed by Ben Johnson's faux 100-meter sprint victory in Seoul).[6] The 2000 Olympics in Sydney had the campaign slogan "Share the Moment" to invite global citizens to the millennial Games down under.

In what follows, I want to examine what might be involved in this phenomenon and rhetoric of the Olympic "moment," which seems so important to the product the Games have become. I ask what the power is in the Olympic "moment" and spectacle. For it is this power, however ethereal such "moments" might seem in our allegedly so-skeptical, so-materialistic age, that draws the money of the sponsors and the cities, and guarantees the continuing status of the Games as fabulous crown of the global, mediatic society of the spectacle.

In order to understand what could be involved in such "moments," the philosophy of aesthetics (our experience of beauty, sublimity, and art) can help. In the fourth century BCE Plato reported on what he termed an "ancient quarrel" between the philosophers and the poets or (loosely enough, for our purposes) artists. A great dramatist himself, Plato's concern was with the uncanny power of art, and the spectacle of the theatre in particular—an ancient predecessor to the modern sports stadium—to move people en masse, or to get them to "share the moment" in a way open to political manipulation. We can well imagine the author of the *Republic* nodding at Guy Debord's famous paraphrase of Marx, that "the spectacle is not a collection of images; it is a social relation between people that is mediated by images."[7] For herein lies the political value of aesthetic phenomena that so worried Plato—or so I will argue, by drawing on some more recent philosophy of art, and particularly modern aesthetics' great masterpiece, Immanuel Kant's *Critique of Judgment*. To anticipate, my claim is that Kant's understanding of aesthetic judgment as involving a pleasure in the beauty of what we experience—which we imaginatively suppose must be shared by all human beings simply as human beings—is oddly, uncannily evocative of the Olympic *ekecheiria* (truce): the famous call that the peoples of the world put aside political and other differences for the two weeks and three days when the Olympic Games take place. But let us proceed.[8]

## Art's *Ekecheiria:* Eagleton's Kant and the Ideologico-Aesthetic

Arguably one of the best accounts of the politics of art and peoples' enjoyment of it is *The Ideology of the Aesthetic* by Terry Eagleton, an English one-time Marxist and literary critic.[9] Eagleton looks at the increased cultural importance art and aesthetic experience has had in modern, secular societies, in contrast to premodern, religious societies. His explanation for this difference is political: "[o]nce the bourgeois has dismantled the central political apparatus of absolutism, in fantasy or in reality," Eagleton contends, "it finds itself bereft of any of the institutions which had previously organized social life as a whole" (22–23). Moreover, the middle classes' historical appeal to the values of liberty and equality, used with great political effect against "the brutal autocracies of feudalist absolutism" (8), gave legitimacy to ancient, democratic demands that the organization of power require the peoples' active consent or *servitude voluntaire*. As Eagleton put it, "with the growth of the early bourgeois society, the ratio between coercion and consent is undergoing gradual transformation; only a rule weighted towards the latter can effectively regulate individuals whose economic activity necessitates a high degree of autonomy" (23). It is in precisely this historical situation that philosophical aesthetics assumed such vital modern importance, according to Eagleton. On one hand, works of art, in this conjuncture—in their strange combination of creativity and lawfulness or order—stand as a kind of metaphor for the self-determining, free subject required by the capitalist-bourgeois society (23): "What is at stake here is nothing less than the production of an entirely new kind of subjectivity—one which, like the work of art itself, discovers the law in its own free identity, rather than in some oppressive external power. The liberated subject is the one who has appropriated the law as the very principle of its own autonomy, broken the forbidding tablets of the stone on which the law was originally written, in order to rewrite it on the heart of flesh" (42–43; cf. 207).

On the other hand, the way works of art can appeal to people's sense of creativity, as well as providing a distinct kind of pleasure (since we all enjoy looking at, watching, or hearing works of art) makes aesthetic experience look like a very good candidate to address something else. This is the problem of social and cultural integration in market societies, where individuals are encouraged to pursue their own, competing interests and ideas of the good.[10] The "invisible hand" of the market aside, reactionary critics and cultural conservatives have long called for returns to the family, nation, and god to minister to peoples' need for a sense of lived community, which complex modern societies do not allow. Art, Eagleton suggests in his *Ideology of the Aesthetic,* provides a kind of secular replacement and echo of what religion once was—and for that reason a potentially very powerful political tool for anyone who wishes to establish and mobilize popular support for political agendas.

The centerpiece of Eagleton's historical and political argument about the modern experience of art is his reading of the German idealist philosopher Immanuel Kant's great work *The Critique of Judgment.* "Surprisingly enough," Eagleton claims (and it is surprising, given how Kant is usually read), "Kantian aesthetics move us a little closer towards a materialist understanding of ideology" (95–96). The reason is that, according to Kant's understanding, what happens when we enjoy a work of art is that we briefly sense two kinds of harmony or participation otherwise lost to us as modern "bourgeois" individuals, competing with our fellows in markets, for economic wealth and for status:

*Our enjoyment of art yields us an affective, felt sense of harmony with the world of objects.* In Kant's aesthetics, Eagleton stresses, what is decisive is the way that the colors, sounds, shapes, stories of the beautiful artwork or natural scene are able (quite literally) to *affect* the subject. Art touches us, which is why we talk about aesthetic "taste." But how can some object(s) affect us so? Kant's claim is fascinating. The beautiful ordering and interaction of the different parts of the beautiful thing, he claims, set up a kind of echo with the internal ordering and interaction of our cognitive powers (according to his psychology: the senses, or "intuition"; imagination; understanding; and reason). The details of Kant's outdated "faculty-psychology" need not concern us here. What Eagleton highlights is how the sense of joy, even surprise or wonder, we get when we experience something (or someone) beautiful comes from the sense that, amidst the wholly impersonal nexus of indifferent nature, there are some objects that, "as though by some felicitous accident," seem "obediently commensurate with the mind's powers" (89). "Some of the pleasure of the aesthetic, then, arises from the quick sense of the world's delightful conformity to our faculties. . . . If the aesthetic yields us no knowledge . . . it proffers us something arguably deeper: the consciousness . . . that we are at home in the world because the world [as represented in the beautiful thing] is somehow mysteriously designed to suit our capacities" (85).[11]

*Our enjoyment of art yields an affective, felt harmony between us and other people.* Kant's second claim to a hidden sense of harmonious participation involved in aesthetic experience concerns our relation with other people. As Eagleton writes: "When, for Kant, we find ourselves concurring spontaneously on an aesthetic judgment, able to agree that a certain phenomenon is sublime or beautiful, we exercise a precious form of inter-subjectivity, establishing ourselves as a community of feeling subjects linked by a quick sense of our shared capacities" (75).

What is at issue here is the difference between when we say about something "It is beautiful" as against when we say things like "It is pleasant . . . pretty . . . I kind of like it . . . " When we make a claim about beauty, Kant says, it is as if we implicitly "demand" universal agreement. We are expressing something stronger than an individual preference, whether wrongly or rightly. *Everyone* should agree that this is beautiful, we feel. And the universality at stake in this implicit claim, as Eagleton emphasizes, involves *the subjects' feelings* as they confront a beautiful object. When we enjoy a work of art, our pleasant sense of its beauty invokes a kind of *sensus communis* (sense of community) in us, somehow carried in the force of the claim that the work is "beautiful."[12] In Eagleton's words: "The universal quality of taste (for Kant) cannot spring from the object, which is always contingent; or from any particular desire or interest of the subject, which are similarly parochial; so it must be a matter of the very cognitive structure of the subject itself, which is presumed to be invariable among all individuals. Part of what we enjoy in the aesthetic, then, is the knowledge that our very structural constitution as human subjects predisposes us to mutual harmony" (96).

It is exactly this "predisposition to mutual harmony" that Eagleton is interested in, given his political concerns in *The Ideology of the Aesthetic*. Invoking Marx's famous formulation of the logic of the commodity in *Capital* (which we earlier saw echoed by Debord's account of mass spectacles), we could indeed say that Eagleton's interest in Kant's analytic of beauty in *The Ideology of the Aesthetic* is animated by how Kant thinks that "a relation between people is operative beneath a relation between things" when people experience beauty (208–209). For Terry Eagleton, indeed, the appeal of the Kantian subject to a *sensus communis* in its aesthetic judgments ("This is beautiful!") opens up what he calls "the very paradigm of the ideological" (93–94), the "ideologico-aesthetic." For people's deepest ideological or political commitments, Eagleton notes, similarly condense attitudes about how the world is, and their strongest subjective passions:

> Just as it is illicit in Kant's view to decode the statement "x is beautiful" as "I like x," so it would clearly be inadequate to translate the [ideological] proposition "The Irish are inferior to the British" as "I don't like the Irish." If ideology were merely a question of subjective prejudice, it would no doubt be somewhat easier to uproot than it is. The rhetorical move which converts an emotive utterance to the grammatical form of the referential is an index of the fact that certain attitudes are at once "merely subjective" *and somehow necessary.* (95, my italics)

And it is this experienced necessity—and, behind it, a universality of feeling—that returns us to our Olympic pursuit. For what it points toward is what we might call ironically the aesthetic *ekecheiria*.

*Ekecheiria* (literally "the holding out of hands") was the term used in the ancient Greek world to describe the sacred truce in honor of Zeus struck between the Greek *poleis* (city-states) for one month on either side of the pan-Hellenic Games. During this time wars were suspended, armies were prohibited from entering Elis or threatening the Games, and legal disputes and the carrying out of death penalties were forbidden.

*Ekecheiria* has been revived in the modern Games. According to the statement by U.N. Secretary General Ban Ki-Moon on the eve of the Beijing Games, the Olympic truce "calls for a worldwide cessation of all hostilities for the duration of the Games."[13] In other words, we are dealing with a "state of exception" of a kind that has recently been very much at the center of theoretical and political attention: an exceptional period wherein the ordinary conflicts and conduct of political life are suspended. The paradox that Eagleton picks up on, and that we now take up, is how this suspension of normal political life, with its delimited truce, can and has been used politically. The Olympic *ekecheiria* is itself a political thing all on its own, what Italian thinker Giorgio Agamben might call an "inclusive exclusion" from ordinary political life.[14] The Olympic spectacle, which this *ekecheiria* leaves the world free to consume, we would add, has the potent capacity to aesthetically intimate to people their common humanity the *ekecheiria* temporarily promises. It is as though in aesthetic experience (and, we would add, in the Olympic "moments"), as Eagleton writes:

> [P]rior to any determinate dialogue or debate, we are always already in agreement, *fashioned to concur*. . . . Once any determinate concept is removed from our grasp, we are left delighting in nothing but a universal solidarity beyond any vulgar utility. Such solidarity is a kind of *sensus communis;* which Kant opposes . . . to that fragmentary, unreflective collection of prejudices and opinions which is *doxa* or common sense. Such *doxa* is what Kant himself, had he used the word, might have called ideology; but *sensus communis* is ideology purified, ideology raised to the second power, idealized beyond all mere sectarian prejudice or customary reflex to resemble the ghostly shape of rationality itself. (96, my italics)

It is to such "ideology raised to the second power" that we now turn, to understand the Games' power as spectacle.

## A Festival of Beauty, a Festival of the People

Today's extravagant opening and closing ceremonies are only the most elaborate and technologically advanced examples of how the Olympics are a great spectacle for the world to consume. Probably the most famous (or infamous) example of the Olympic spectacle was the Berlin 1936 Games, in the Germany of Adolf Hitler and the National Socialist (Nazi) Party.

Much has been written on the Nazis' remarkable use of art and spectacle to motivate political loyalty, and ultimately their political crimes. The *locus classicus* is "The Work of Art in the Age of Mechanical Reproduction" by Walter Benjamin. *"Fiat ars—pereat mundus* [let art triumph, even if the world perishes], says fascism": so the final paragraph of Benjamin's "Epilogue," on the fascist aestheticization of politics and violence, begins. Hitler himself was of course a disappointed artist, and like his propaganda chief Joseph Goebbels had an innate sense of the political power of art and spectacle. Throughout his reign, he cultivated friendships with leading German artists. Arguably the most famous of these, Leni Riefenstahl, produced a masterpiece of fascist propaganda, *The Triumph of the Will.* It is almost certainly with this film in mind that Benjamin added the final footnote to "The Work of Art . . ." in 1935, the year of the film's appearance:

> Mass reproduction [of art in films, musical recordings, etc.] is aided especially by the reproduction of masses. In big parades and monster rallies, in sports events, and in war, all of which are nowadays captured by camera and sound process, the masses are brought face to face with themselves. The process, whose significance need not be stressed, is intimately connected with the development of techniques of reproduction and photography. Mass movements are usually discerned more clearly by a camera than by the naked eye. A bird's eye view best captures gatherings of hundreds of thousands.[15]

The opportunity that the IOC's 1931 awarding of the Games to Germany offered, to display the new Germany to the world, did not escape the Nazi propaganda machine. Indeed, and as troubling as this may be to acknowledge, many of the features that we now associate with the modern Games were inaugurated by the Nazis' Berlin Games. Today you can visit the site in Greece where the Olympic torch is lit, beginning the relay to the host city. But the torch relay is not an ancient inheritance. The first Olympic torch relay took place in 1936. It is a Nazi interpolation into the Olympic movement. Nazi propaganda seized upon the metaphoric connection between the route from Olympia to Berlin and the historical connection between the Nazis' rejuvenated Germany and classical ideals.

The abiding document to the Nazis' manipulation of the 1936 Games as an aesthetic spectacle is Leni Riefenstahl's *Olympia,* which was awarded the prize at the Venice international film festival, and another unquestioned masterpiece.[16] *Olympia* was the first "documentary" film about the modern Games. But, like *Triumph of the Will,* it is much more than a documentary. Tellingly, its two parts are entitled "Festival of the People" and "Festival of Beauty." Equally tellingly, the film's opening eight-minute sequence begins with a series of slowly moving shots surveying the Athenian Acropolis, accompanied by Herbert Windt Walter Gronostay's music. Five and a half minutes into the film, we witness the transformation of an ancient statue of a discus thrower into a living Aryan male nude, who casts the discus into the distance, then hurls a javelin, before pensively lighting the Olympic flame, his silhouette sheathed in flame.[17]

In German idealist Georg Wilhelm Hegel's philosophy of art, the Greeks' "religion of art" represented a kind of apogee of what Hegel termed "the sensuous appearance of the Idea": the consummation of the realm of beauty. According to Hegel, "Nothing can be more beautiful."[18] In the noble self-sufficiency of classical sculpture, Hegel saw the clearest expression of the universal human aspiration for freedom and belonging in the world.[19] It is something of this sense of wondrous reverie in the natural grace of human bodies that Riefenstahl captures in the famous diving sequence in *Olympia.* Here the most advanced modern techniques of juxtaposed camera angles, slow motion, and "smash cuts" (between different sequences) combine to create the uncanny sense of the divers hovering weightlessly, swanlike, above the water.[20]

So to question the role of art in the Olympic phenomenon is necessarily to reflect upon the key role the Nazis had in using the Games politically to consolidate their regime. As the American foreign correspondent William Shirer in Berlin recorded in his diary on August 16, 1936: "I'm afraid the Nazis have succeeded with their propaganda. First, the Nazis have run the Games on a lavish scale never before experienced, and this has appealed to the athletes. Second, the Nazis have put up a very good front for the general visitors, especially the big businessmen."[21]

Many of the filming techniques that Riefenstahl's *Olympia* pioneered have formed the basis for all subsequent televisual Olympic (and general sports) coverage, from the slow-motion shots to running cameras along rails beside the action.

Our point here is not to denigrate the Olympic spectacle as a whole or to propose that we should puritanically shun art per se, because both may be put to all kinds of political uses, from the noblest to the most barbaric. In the words of French thinker Jacques Rancière in his book *The Politics of Aesthetics:* "there are no criteria" when it comes to deciding how art may be used politically: it has the power to move people simply, whether for good or evil.[22] On one hand, there will always be a case for reminding audiences glued to their screens that the Olympic *ekecheiria* is a passing thing—often honored in the breach—and that the cosmopolitan world order it aesthetically intimates remains, sadly, a fiction. We should also remain aware of how, for their own benefit, private interests "buy into" or feed off the Olympic moments and the cosmopolitan *ésprit* they invoke. On the other hand, we should not forget that, however cynical its political and economic manipulations, those who instrumentally use the Games can only do so by trading on the transpolitical, global *sensus communis* the Olympic spirit names: a sense of common humanity that can also be appealed to in opposing the intended and unintended ills visited upon peoples by the globalization of capitalist social relations and economic institutions. It is salutary to remember that Hitler himself was initially *against* the Nazis hosting the Games precisely because he associated the Olympic Games with modern cosmopolitanism, and only relented when Goebbels changed his mind.

Of course, the way the Games are packaged for the media will change, as have the aesthetics of the Olympic spectacle. Although we cannot pursue this here, it seems, for one thing, that alongside the neoclassical images of athletes in action, the cameras focus most these days on moments when the athletes break down, in the highest moments of anguish, triumph, and passion. It is as if, aping Hegel's history of art, the paradigm of the Olympics-as-spectacle has shifted from the classical to what Hegel calls a "romantic" aesthetic paradigm. Today's heroes of godlike grace and movement are also mortals with real emotions and an inner life just like our own—and this is what the cameras want to capture for us. What remains constant is the unquestioned power of the aesthetic and of the spectacle to capture audiences and to invoke a lived *sensus communis,* which politicians have always seen and appreciated. It is such a truly Olympian aesthetic power, to make us "share the moment" through images and the spectacle, that the Olympic Games will continue to draw on, beneath all the money and corruption, and both for worse and for better.

## Notes

1. The mayor of Montreal famously said when that city was preparing to host the 1976 Games that the Olympics "can no more have a deficit than a man can have a baby," although economists do not agree. Sadly, the Athenian Games of 2004 at least seem to have proved the mayor of Montreal false.

2. See Vyv Simson and Andrew Jennings, *The Lords of the Rings: Power, Money and Drugs in the Modern Olympics* (London: Simon and Shuster, 1992); and Andrew Jennings, *The New Lords of the Rings: Olympic Corruption and How to Buy Gold Medals* (London: Pocket Books, 1996).

3. Guy Debord, *The Society of the Spectacle* (1967). Complete text available at http://www.marxists.org/reference/archive/debord/society.htm (accessed October 2009), subsection 1.

4. Ibid., subsection 36.

5. Ibid., subsection 10.

6. See www.timesonline.co.uk/tol.sport/olympics/article4316031.ece (accessed October 2009).

7. Debord, *Society of the Spectacle,* subsection 4.

8. A longer, differently framed version of the following argument appears in Matthew Sharpe, "The Aesthetics of Ideology, or 'The Critique of Ideological Judgment' in Eagleton and Zizek," *Political Theory* 34:1 (2006): 95–120.

9. Terry Eagleton, *The Ideology of the Aesthetic* (London: Blackwell, 2000), 3. All parenthetical page references in this section of the text are to this volume. Citations to Kant are made through Eagleton's reading, which I believe is substantially accurate, if directed to Eagleton's ends.

10. In an argument drawn from Lukacs and the Frankfurt School Marxists, the claim is that modern subjectivity and social life tend to be divided between a series of oppositions: public versus private, the state versus the market, the citizen versus the bourgeois/proletariat, production versus consumption, leisure versus work. Aesthetic experience, Eagleton claims, attracts because it intimates a more reconciled individual experience, and a social whole.

11. Or Eagleton again: "It is as though the aesthetic (in Kant) represents some residual feeling left over from an earlier social order, where a sense of transcendental meaning and harmony, and of the centrality of the human subject, were still active" (88).

12. In effect, Kant's position is that the statement "X is beautiful" expresses a counterfactual claim with something like the form "Every human being, were he to perceive the object under some particular non-aesthetic conditions of observation would be in a state of disinterested pleasure triggered by his recognition of 'free' conformity."

13. See Paul J. Hayes, "Kremlin crushes truce of the Games," *The Australian,* August 15 2008, http://www.theaustralian.news.com.au/story/0,25197,24182332–7583,00.html (accessed October 2009).

14. Cf. Giorgio Agamben, *State of Exception,* trans. Kevin Attell (Chicago: University of Chicago Press, 2005).

15. Walter Benjamin, "The Work of Art in the Age of Mechanical Reproduction," in *Illuminations* (New York: Schocken Books, 1968), 240.

16. See "The Complete List—All-*Time* 100 Movies," http://www.time.com/time/2005/100movies/the_complete_list.html (accessed October 2009).

17. This sequence is available in the public domain at http://www.youtube.com/watch?v=x6–0Cz73wwQ&feature=fvw (accessed October 2009).

18. Hegel quoted in Stephen Houlgate, *Freedom, Truth and History: An Introduction to Hegel's Philosophy* (London: Routledge, 1991), 213, 233.

19. Ibid., 221.

20. This sequence is available in the public domain at http://www.youtube.com/watch?v=KwmYFz01MxA (accessed October 2009).

21. Shirer quoted in "The Nazi Olympics, Berlin 1936," at the United States Holocaust Memorial Museum website, http://www.ushmm.org/museum/exhibit/online/olympics/detail.php?content=sports&lang=en (accessed October 2009).

22. Jacques Rancière, *The Politics of Aesthetics* (London: Continuum, 2006), 61.

# CONTRIBUTORS

MICHAEL W. AUSTIN is professor of philosophy at Eastern Kentucky University, where he works primarily in ethics, philosophy of religion, and philosophy of sport. His published books include *Conceptions of Parenthood* (Ashgate, 2007), *Running and Philosophy* (Wiley-Blackwell, 2007), *Football and Philosophy* (University Press of Kentucky, 2008), and *Being Good: Christian Virtues for Everyday Life* (Eerdmans, 2012). He is a passionate and mediocre cyclist, runner, and soccer player. He blogs about ethical issues in daily life at Ethics for Everyone: http://www.psychologytoday.com/blog/ethics-everyone

RAYMOND ANGELO BELLIOTTI is SUNY Distinguished Teaching Professor of Philosophy at State University of New York at Fredonia. He first failed in his efforts to replace Phil Rizzuto as shortstop of the New York Yankees. After stints at blue-collar work convinced him that he was too lazy for hard labor, he turned to philosophy. He is the author of twelve books on topics including jurisprudence, sexual ethics, ethnic identity, Nietzsche, happiness, the meaning of life, Machiavelli, the philosophy of baseball, Roman philosophy, Dante, and posthumous harm.

PAUL A. CANTOR is Clifton Waller Barrett Professor of English at the University of Virginia. His books include *Shakespeare's Rome: Republic and Empire* (Cornell, 1976), *Creature and Creator: Myth-making in English Romanticism* (Cambridge, 1984), *Shakespeare: Hamlet* (Cambridge, 1989, 2004), *Gilligan Unbound: Pop Culture in the Age of Globalization*

(Rowman & Littlefield, 2001), and *Literature and the Economics of Liberty: Spontaneous Order in Culture* (Mises Institute, 2009, coedited with Stephen Cox). He has dim memories of being on the Harvard varsity fencing team in the 1960s and compiling a perfect record of 0–8 in two years of intercollegiate competition.

JEFFREY P. FRY is associate professor in the Department of Philosophy and Religious Studies at Ball State University. He serves on the editorial boards of the *Journal of the Philosophy of Sport* and *Sport, Ethics and Philosophy*, and he formerly directed the Center for Sport, Ethics & Culture at Ball State. His recent publications include "Making a Comeback" in *Sport, Ethics and Philosophy* and "On the Supposed Duty to Try One's Hardest in Sport" in *Philosophy in the Contemporary World*. He is currently interested in the intersection of sport, ethics, and neuroscience.

ALUN R. HARDMAN has his PhD from Pennsylvania State University and is a senior lecturer in the Socio-Cultural Aspects of Sport at Cardiff Metropolitan University. His research interests include sport philosophy and ethics in sport. He is coeditor (with Carwyn Jones) of *The Ethics of Sports Coaching* (Routledge) and has published in the *Journal of the Philosophy of Sport* and *Sport, Ethics, and Philosophy*.

MILAN HOSTA is a director at Spolint Institute of Sport Development (www.spolint.org), where he leads the innovative Playness Culture approach to enhance physical activity internationally, and supports the Sportikus fair play initiative as a tool for promoting Olympic values. He is a part-time assistant professor at University of Primorska, lecturing in sport ethics, Olympism, and inclusive kinesiology. His book *Ethics in Sport: A Manifesto for the Twenty-First Century* (2007) presented a philosophical discussion of sport in Slovenia. Among his variety of sport interests, breathing exercises are currently his priority.

PETER HUFNAGEL is dean of the faculty of the Miller School of Albemarle. He has published on John Milton in *Forum for World Literature Studies* and on H. G. Wells in *Studies in the Novel* (reprinted in the Norton Critical Edition of *The Time Machine*). As a cyclist at the University of Virginia, he won both the ACC Cycling Road Race Championship and the ACC Team Time Trial Championship. More recently, he won the Charlottesville Olympic Distance Triathlon three years in a row. His wife, Andrea Dvorak, is a world-class professional cyclist and has been named to the U.S. Cycling 2012 Olympic Long Team in women's road cycling and is thus in contention to make the U.S. Team for the 2012 London Olympics.

JESÚS ILUNDÁIN-AGURRUZA is associate professor of philosophy at Linfield College in Oregon. His primary areas of research and teaching are philosophy of sport, value theory (aesthetics, ethics), Asian philosophy (Daoism; Zen Buddhism), philosophy of literature, and consciousness studies. He has coedited *Cycling—Philosophy for Everyone,* and has published chapters both in English and Spanish in books on risk sports, hunting, sailing, martial arts, and soccer, in addition to articles and reviews for *Sport, Ethics, and Philosophy* and *Proteus.* Originally from Pamplona, Spain, he no longer plays with the bulls. Before the cycling bug bit him (he is a category 2 bicycle racer whose best days are probably behind him), he was competitive in swimming, tennis, and track and field. Because for him thoughts flow best when moving around, he is currently exploring other active endeavors as sources of excitement and novel reflective perspectives. More about him can be found at http://www.atisbos.com.

HYWEL IORWERTH was recently awarded his PhD from the Cardiff Metropolitan University for his thesis on ethical issues surrounding sport and national identity. He is a lecturer in the Socio-Cultural Aspects of Sport at Cardiff Metropolitan University. His work has been published in the *International Journal of Olympic Studies* and will be featured in a special Olympic edition of *Sports, Ethics, and Philosophy.*

KUTTE JÖNSSON is associate professor of sport philosophy and sport ethics at Malmö University, Sweden. He is the author of three books, among them two on sport ethics (all of them in Swedish). He has also published in journals such as *Sport, Ethics, and Philosophy* and *Sport in Society.* Apart from his academic work, he is involved in the ongoing debate on sport, gender issues, and ethics. During the Olympics in 2008, he was engaged by Swedish television to comment on philosophical and ethical issues in relation to the Games.

STEPHEN KERSHNAR is professor of philosophy at the State University of New York at Fredonia and is also an attorney. His research focuses on applied ethics and political philosophy. He has written on such diverse topics as affirmative action, abortion, punishment, pornography, God, interrogational torture, the most valuable player in professional sports, hell, discrimination against women, and Batman. He has written five books: *Desert, Retribution, and Torture* (2001), *Justice for the Past* (2004), *Sex, Discrimination, and Violence: Surprising and Unpopular Results in Applied Ethics* (2009), *Desert and Virtue: A Theory of Intrinsic Value* (2010), and *For Torture: A Rights-Based Defense.*

MICHEL LE GALL holds a PhD in Near Eastern studies from Princeton University. A former associate professor of history at St. Olaf College, he is now a corporate speechwriter in New York City who specializes in topics related to professional services and globalization. His hobbies include photography, writing, and occasionally editing the books of his friends.

JOSEPH D. LEWANDOWSKI is a philosopher, writer, and avid pugilist. The author of *Interpreting Culture: Rethinking Method and Truth in Social Theory* and coeditor of *Trust and Transitions: Social Capital in a Changing World* and *Urban Social Capital: Civil Society and City Life,* his essays have appeared in *Theory, Culture & Society, Journal of the Philosophy of Sport, European Journal of Social Theory, Journal of Poverty, Public Reason,* and elsewhere. He currently serves as dean of the Honors College and professor of philosophy at the University of Central Missouri. He has trained at a local Kansas City boxing gym and has published extensively on boxing and urban culture. His current project is entitled *The Epistemology of Cool: Essays on Boxing and Ghetto Life.*

PELLOM McDANIELS III is assistant professor of history and American studies, specializing in African American history, biography, sports, and masculinities studies at the University of Missouri–Kansas City. McDaniels has published essays in *Baseball and Philosophy* (Open Court, 2006), *All-Stars and Movie Stars: Sports in Film History* (University Press of Kentucky, 2008), and *What's Up With the Brothas* (Men's Studies Press, 2010). Currently he is researching and writing a biography on the life and career of the nineteenth-century jockey Isaac Burns Murphy. He blogs about sports, manhood, and African American masculinity at http://meditations-msmm.blogspot.com.

DOUGLAS W. McLAUGHLIN is an assistant professor of kinesiology at California State University, Northridge. His research interests are directed toward the philosophy of kinesiology, ethics, and sport, and Olympic studies. His enthusiasm for playing Ultimate still trumps the frustrations related to his diminishing skills. His Olympic dream is that Ultimate will one day be included in the Olympic program.

SCOTT F. PARKER'S books include the memoir *Running After Prefontaine,* the poetry collection *Revisited: Notes on Bob Dylan,* and *Coffee—Philosophy for Everyone: Grounds for Debate,* which he coedited with Mike Austin. His writing has also appeared in *Philosophy Now, Running Times,* and *Rain Taxi Review of Books,* among other publications. One of his proudest athletic moments was finishing the Seoul Marathon in Jamsil Olympic Stadium, where his childhood idol Carl Lewis had raced in 1988.

HEATHER L. REID is professor and chair of philosophy at Morningside College in Sioux City, Iowa. A competitive cyclist in her youth, she won a national intercollegiate championship and qualified for the final Olympic trials in 1984 and 1988. As a scholar, she has published numerous books and articles in ancient philosophy, philosophy of sport, and Olympic studies. She has also been invited to lecture on these topics in Beijing, Rome, London, and at the International Olympic Academy in Olympia, Greece. She serves on the boards of the *Journal of the Philosophy of Sport* and *Sport, Ethics, and Philosophy,* and is coeditor of the Ethics and Sport book series, which includes her most recent monograph, *Athletics and Philosophy in the Ancient World: Contests of Virtue.* She remains an active cyclist, leading regular tours through Italy, where she is also developing a study abroad program that uses sport as a medium for intercultural communication.

REGAN REITSMA is associate professor of philosophy and director of the Center for Ethics and Public Life at King's College in Wilkes-Barre,

Pennsylvania. He works primarily in ethics and moral decision-making, especially on topics such as tolerance, forgiveness, cheating, the moral right to personal beliefs, and philosophical questions raised by sports.

MATTHEW SHARPE teaches philosophy and psychoanalytic studies at Deakin University. He is the coauthor of *The Times Will Suit Them: Postmodern Conservatism in Australia* (Allen & Unwin, 2008), of *Zizek and Politics* (Edinburgh, 2010), and of various articles on philosophy, politics, critical theory, and psychoanalysis. His 2012 interests include classical philosophy and the work of Pierre Hadot, and he is presently attempting to better his distance running and the lived practice of Stoicism.

CHARLES TALIAFERRO, professor of philosophy at St. Olaf College and visiting scholar at Bethel University (2011–2012), is the author or editor of eighteen books, most recently *The Image in Mind,* coauthored with Jil Evans (Continuum), and *Turning Images,* coedited with Jil Evans (Oxford University Press). While he has been a competitive runner, the closest he got to being an Olympian was jogging around (fully clothed, but unsupervised) the original site of the Olympic Games during a recent trip to Greece.

CESAR R. TORRES is associate professor in the Department of Kinesiology, Sport Studies, and Physical Education at The College at Brockport, State University of New York. His most recent book is *Gol de Media Cancha: Conversaciones para disfrutar el deporte plenamente* (Miño y Dávila, 2011). He is a past president of the International Association for the Philosophy of Sport and has published extensively on the philosophy and history of sport.

CHARLENE WEAVING is associate professor of human kinetics at St. Francis Xavier University, where she teaches undergraduate courses in gender and sport, history, and philosophy and Modern Olympic Games. With Paul Davis, she coedited *Philosophical Perspectives on Gender in Sport and Physical Activity* (Routledge, 2010). She is the secretary-treasurer of the International Association for the Philosophy of Sport (IAPS) and enjoys hiking and skiing with her puppies, one of whom is named Bilodeau after the first Canadian Olympian to win gold on home soil.

# INDEX

# The Philosophy of Popular Culture

The books published in the Philosophy of Popular Culture series will illuminate and explore philosophical themes and ideas that occur in popular culture. The goal of this series is to demonstrate how philosophical inquiry has been reinvigorated by increased scholarly interest in the intersection of popular culture and philosophy, as well as to explore through philosophical analysis beloved modes of entertainment, such as movies, TV shows, and music. Philosophical concepts will be made accessible to the general reader through examples in popular culture. This series seeks to publish both established and emerging scholars who will engage a major area of popular culture for philosophical interpretation and examine the philosophical underpinnings of its themes. Eschewing ephemeral trends of philosophical and cultural theory, authors will establish and elaborate on connections between traditional philosophical ideas from important thinkers and the ever-expanding world of popular culture.

### Series Editor
Mark T. Conard, Marymount Manhattan College, NY

### Books in the Series
*The Philosophy of Stanley Kubrick*, edited by Jerold J. Abrams
*Football and Philosophy*, edited by Michael W. Austin
*Tennis and Philosophy*, edited by David Baggett
*The Philosophy of Film Noir*, edited by Mark T. Conard
*The Philosophy of Martin Scorsese*, edited by Mark T. Conard
*The Philosophy of Neo-Noir*, edited by Mark T. Conard
*The Philosophy of Spike Lee*, edited by Mark T. Conard
*The Philosophy of the Coen Brothers*, edited by Mark T. Conard
*The Philosophy of David Lynch*, edited by William J. Devlin and Shai Biderman
*The Philosophy of the Beats*, edited by Sharin N. Elkholy
*The Philosophy of Horror*, edited by Thomas Fahy
*The Philosophy of* The X-Files, edited by Dean A. Kowalski
*Steven Spielberg and Philosophy*, edited by Dean A. Kowalski
*The Philosophy of Joss Whedon*, edited by Dean A. Kowalski and S. Evan Kreider
*The Philosophy of Charlie Kaufman*, edited by David LaRocca
*The Philosophy of the Western*, edited by Jennifer L. McMahon and B. Steve Csaki

CPSIA information can be obtained at www.ICGtesting.com
Printed in the USA
BVOW021554140612

R4594700001B/R45947PG292175BVX1B/1/P